BBC

ARABIC
Phrase book

Nagi El-Bay and Victoria Floyer-Acland

Series Editor: Carol Stanley

NTC *Publishing Group*
Lincolnwood, Illinois

Other language titles in this series:

Czech
French
German
Greek
Italian
Japanese
Mandarin
Polish
Portuguese
Russian
Spanish
Thai
Turkish

This edition first published in 1995 by NTC Publishing Group
A division of NTC/Contemporary Publishing Group, Inc.
4255 West Touhy Avenue
Lincolnwood (Chicago), Illinois 60712-1975 U.S.A.
Published in cooperation with BBC Worldwide Limited. "BBC"
and the BBC logotype are trademarks of the British
Broadcasting Corporation, and are used under license.
Printed in Canada
International Standard Book Number: 0-8442-9223-0

03 04 TCP 14 13 12 11 10 9 8 7 6

Contents

HOW TO USE THIS BOOK

Communicating in a foreign language doesn't have to be difficult – you can convey a lot with just a few words (plus a few gestures and a bit of mime). Just remember: keep it simple. Don't try to come out with long, grammatically perfect sentences when one or two words will get your meaning across.

Arabic can seem rather more difficult than some other languages because it uses a different alphabet. Don't worry about it: you can still learn to communicate effectively by following the pronunciation guide given in this book, and then you can work on the written language later if you want to. Where you need to understand written words, you will find them in the 'You may see' sections of each chapter, the Menu reader, or in General signs and notices.

Inside the back cover of this book is a list of All-purpose phrases. Some will help you to make contact – greetings, 'please' and 'thank you', 'yes' and 'no'. Some are to get people to help you understand what they're saying to you. And some are questions like 'Do you have . . .?' and 'Where is . . .?', to which you can add words from the Dictionary at the back of the book.

The book is divided into sections for different situations, such as Road travel, Shopping, Health and so on. In each section you'll find
- Useful tips and information
- Words and phrases that you'll see on signs or in print
- Phrases you are likely to want to say
- Things that people may say to you

Many of the phrases can be adapted by simply using a word from the Dictionary. For instance, take the question *maTaar be*ᵃ*eed* – Is the airport far away? If you want if the museum is far away, just substitute the word for museum, *il matHaf* for *il maTaar* to give *il matHaf be^aeed*.

The pronunciation guide used for the phrases is based on English sounds and is explained in Pronunciation (page 14).

If you want some guidance on how the Arabic language works, see Basic grammar (page 158).

There's a handy reference section (starts on page 168) which contains a list of days and months, countries and nationalities, place names, general signs and notices, conversion tables, national holidays, useful addresses and numbers.

There is a 3,500-word English–Arabic Dictionary, where words are given with both the Arabic script (so you can show it to someone you're talking to) and a simple pronunciation guide.

A concise list of numbers is printed inside the front cover for easy reference (there's also a chapter on Numbers, page 188). At the end of the book is an Emergencies section (which we hope you won't have to use).

Wherever possible, work out in advance what you want to say – if you're going shopping, for instance, write out a shopping list using the Arabic pronunciation guides. If you're buying travel tickets, work out how to say where you want to go, how many tickets you want, single or return etc.

Practise saying things out loud – the cassette that goes with this book will help you to get used to the sounds of Arabic.

Above all – don't be shy! It'll be appreciated if you try to say a few words, even if it's only 'good morning' and 'goodbye' (or the appropriate responses if someone else greets you). In fact, these are the sorts of phrases that are worth memorising as you'll hear them and need to use them all the time.

There are two kinds of Arabic: literary (classical) and spoken.

Classical Arabic is used in writing throughout the Arab world and also on more formal occasions – for speeches, sermons, news broadcasts and so on. Colloquial Arabic is used in everyday speech and varies from country to country within the Arab world.

We have chosen colloquial northern Egyptian Arabic as the basis for this book, because it is the most widely used and understood in the Arab world. Practically everyone in the region is exposed to colloquial Egyptian Arabic, especially through films, cassettes of popular songs and television soap operas. This form of the language is generally held to be the most prestigious spoken variety and whichever country you visit you will find that people can understand and adapt to Egyptian Arabic.

Generally speaking, we have given the classical Arabic forms of words in the 'You may see' sections, since this is the standard written form.

The background information in this book applies generally throughout the Arab world, although obviously there are variations depending on the country you are visiting. Some countries in the region are more relaxed than others on cultural and religious forms of behaviour, the position of women in society, alcohol and so on; it is always wise to speak to the relevant tourist office or embassy before travelling to find out the exact situation in each country.

If you'd like to learn more about Arabic, BBC Books also publishes *Get by in Arabic*. BBC phrase books are also available for the following languages: French, German, Greek, Italian, Portuguese, Spanish and Turkish.

The authors would welcome any suggestions or comments about this book, but in the meantime, have a good trip – رحله سعيده (*reHla sa*^a*eeda*).

RELIGION AND CULTURE

More than 20 different states make up the Arab world, and they cover a vast geographical area stretching from Morocco on the Atlantic Ocean in the west to Kuwait on the Persian Gulf in the east, and from Syria on the Mediterranean in the north to Oman on the Indian Ocean in the south.

Islam, Christianity and Judaism all started in the area and close links exist between them. Today Islam is the predominant faith, practised by some 100 million Arabs. Muslims, however, acknowledge and respect the teachings of the Torah and the Bible as well as the Islamic holy book the Koran.

The essential element linking all three religions is that there is one God, who is believed to be behind every action, word or thought. Agnosticism or atheism are extremely rare phenomena and derogatory remarks about any aspect of the three religions are not viewed kindly. God is constantly referred to in daily conversations as you'll see in the Arabic phrases referred to in this book. Often Muslims will preface things like eating, drinking, driving, or making a speech with *bismilla*, 'In the name of God', and end by saying *il Hamdoo lilla*, 'Thanks be to God'.

Public behaviour

Arabs greet their friends, relatives and guests with handshakes, embraces and kisses on both cheeks – as long as they're of the same sex, or are immediate family. It's not acceptable to do so otherwise, even for husbands and wives. (Expansive displays of affection between Westerners of opposite sexes will certainly be disapproved of, and stared at.)

Openness and frankness are characteristic of the Arab world. There's little distinction between what's considered personal and what isn't and you'll find that people share much of their lives with each other. This means, for example, that it's quite acceptable to join in anyone's conversation in public to air your personal views.

The Arabic language encourages already frank people to say exactly what they mean. For example, there's no polite way to say 'There appears to be a mistake on this bill'; instead you'd say: 'This bill is wrong' or 'You've made a mistake'.

In some parts of the Arab world – particularly rural or bedouin communities – you'll find that some older cultural traditions and behaviour still prevail. It may cause offence if you use the left hand to eat, give or receive things; others consider it rude to sit with the soles of your shoes pointing at another person.

Tipping

Tipping is a feature of life in the Arab world, and you may find yourself giving tips several times a day – so be sure to carry plenty of loose change. Large numbers of people engaged (officially and unofficially) in providing public services rely on tips (*bae'sheesh*) for their wages. For example, when you arrive at the airport you'll find several people ready to find you a taxi.

Punctuality and appointments

Time is quite flexible in many parts of the Arab world. *bokra* ('tomorrow') often means 'in the near future', while *insha alla* ('if God wills') is more l likely to mean 'in the fullness of time'.

It's not a personal insult if people turn up late for appointments

– and don't be surprised if a business meeting intended for two individuals becomes an extended gathering to which other unexpected people have been invited.

Clothing

It's advisable to wear formal clothing to meetings, conferences and dinners. On these occasions it's considered lacking in respect for your hosts to dress too casually, and people are less likely to take you seriously.

During the daytime people will wear a variety of clothes depending on their social class, status, job, religious belief, or whether they're in mourning. Both men and women are expected to cover their bodies, arms and legs with comfortable, loose clothing. In some countries women also cover their heads, and the severity with which standards of dress are imposed on women in particular vary considerably.

Generally speaking, other than on beaches and at swimming pools and sports centres it's offensive not to be reasonably well covered. In most Arab countries it's acceptable for women to wear short sleeves as long as garments are not too tight or revealing, and the knees are covered. However, in Saudi Arabia and most Gulf States it is offensive for a woman to appear in public without being entirely covered with loose dark clothing covering her head, face, body and ankles. Western women should take advice on their wardrobe before travelling.

Women

There are two sets of standards controlling social life in most Arab countries: one for men and one for women. Women are brought up to believe that their whole life must be primarily dedicated to bringing up a family. A strict code of practice

concerning their dress and public behaviour protects and ensures the continuation of that role. Women who wear short, tight and revealing clothes cause offence by challenging the social norm, and effectively present themselves as 'sex objects'. They're stared at by men and laughed at by women.

As a visitor, it's worth showing respect for local sensibilities regarding dress, otherwise you'll find yourself receiving a lot of unwelcome attention and even harassment – varying from repeated invitations out for a meal or a drink to more demanding, physical attentions, or even offers of marriage! This is usually as far as it gets since actual physical violence against foreign women is very rare.

If you are harassed, you can start by loudly telling your admirer to leave you alone. If this doesn't work, it's acceptable to seek the assistance of another female – usually you'll receive sympathy and help (even if *she* doesn't approve of your dress).

If you do experience physical violence then ask a woman to take you to a female doctor or nurse. If you wish to contact the police then do so with the assistance of your female friend.

If you're travelling on your own, wear unrevealing clothes, avoid eye contact with men you don't know and ignore personal comments. It also helps to wear a wedding ring and tell everyone that you're married with children even if you aren't, but be prepared to explain why you aren't with your family.

Hygiene hint

If you're visiting remote areas, be sure to take with you any toiletries you might need, including a basic first aid kit, tampons or sanitary towels and antiseptic toilet seat wipes.

Mosques

Mosques, like churches, are places of worship. Most of the ones that you'll want to visit will be of some historical as well as religious value. Lists of interesting mosques should be available at the relevant tourist information office. They will also supply information about access to, and conduct in, mosques by tourists, and especially women. Alternatively, you may find it at the entrance to the mosque. If not, simply copy what other people do. (See Sightseeing, page 127.)

Ramadan

Muslims become Muslims by declaring their faith in one God. Their faith is demonstrated in a variety of ways, including fasting for 30 consecutive days during the holy month of Ramadan. During this period they abstain from food, drink, cigarettes and all bodily pleasures from sunrise to sunset. This, it is believed, releases the soul and stimulates meditation, contemplation and unity with other Muslims.

Ramadan is a time for people to visit each other, to eat and pray together. Shops close early during this month, and in terms of business, Ramadan is a slack period in the Arab world. People are often tired during the day and busy praying and feasting with family and friends in the evening.

During Ramadan most public eating houses will be closed during daylight hours. Some nightclubs which might normally serve alcohol will stop doing so. Christians living in Muslim countries, though not celebrating Ramadan, tend not to eat and drink in public during the daytime out of respect for their Muslim neighbours.

If you arrive in the Arab world during Ramadan make sure you book your breakfast and lunch at one of the 5-star hotels, or

find out the names of restaurants which are open during the day. Dinner should not be a problem, since all public eating houses will start re-opening around 6.00–7.00 p.m. in winter, and 8.00–9.00 p.m. in summer.

Ramadan is an exciting time to be out and about during the evening: streets are brightly decorated, shops are open late, and restaurants are crowded with big family parties celebrating into the early hours.

PRONUNCIATION

You don't need perfect pronunciation to be able to communicate – it's enough to get the sounds approximately right. If you want to hear real (Egyptian) Arab voices and practise trying to sound like them, then listen to the cassette.

Arabic pronunciation is quite regular – you can usually tell how a word is pronounced from the way it's written, once you know what each letter (or group of letters) represents. Most of the phrases in this book have been given in a transliterated form, following a system based on English sounds as described below. Hardly any of the Arabic sounds presents any difficulties.

Stress

In speech, some Arabic words are stressed, while others are not. As a general rule, the last but one syllable in a word is stressed, but this is not always the case. For example, the word *sawra* carries equal stress on both syllables.

In this book, a stressed syllable is shown in the pronunciation guide by bold type: *gowzi*, *molokhaya*. Where no bold type is used, the stress is equal on all syllables.

NB: Stress may change according to the word's ending, and its position in the sentence. It also varies from one country to another.

The following is a guide to the written symbols used and the sounds they represent.

Vowels

		Approx. English equivalent	Shown in book as	Example	
اَ		a as in 'hat' (short)	a	gamal	جمل
	or	a as in 'car' (long)	aa	Taar	طار
	or	ae as in 'aeroplane'	ae	kitaeb	كتاب
و		o as in 'doll'	o	foll	فل
	or	o as in 'know'	ow	yowm	يوم
	or	oo as in 'boot'	oo	noor	نور
ى		i as in 'hit'	i	min	من
	or	ee as in 'keen'	ee	meen	مين

Other compound vowel sounds used are:

أى		ai as in 'aisle'	ai	raiyiH	رايح
	or	ay as in 'day'	ay	fayn	فين
أو		ow as in 'now'	aw	gaw	جو
		e as in 'egg'	e	hena	هنا
		e-oo	ew	bitewga[a]	بتوجع

In short words such as *fi* (at, in), *wi* (and) or *li* (to, for), the *i* often disappears when another vowel precedes or follows:

il walad wil bint (the boy and the girl)
fil qahira (in Cairo)

Consonants

Some letters are pronounced differently in colloquial Egyptian from classical Arabic. For example, 'th' is not used for the letter ث in colloquial Egyptian Arabic; instead, it is usually pronounced as a 't' or 's'. The same is true of the letter ذ which is pronounced 'z' as in 'zoo' in classical Arabic, but in colloquial Egyptian Arabic comes out as 'd'.

'Thick' consonants

The capital letters *S*, *T*, *D* and *Z* are used in this book to represent 'heavy' or 'thick' versions of *s*, *t*, *d* and *z*. They're pronounced with the tip of the tongue touching the roof of the mouth against the front teeth, and the rest of the tongue fairly relaxed.

The sound represented by the capital *H* is another 'thick' letter, pronounced with the back of the tongue almost touching the back of the mouth, producing a 'strangled' *h* sound.

There is no easy equivalent to any of these in English – but don't worry, it's not that difficult to give a fair approximation of the sounds with a bit of practice, and you'll have no problem being understood.

Arabic		Approx. English equivalent	Shown in book as	Example	
ء		glottal stop, as in cockney 'bu'er' or 'Sco'land'	'	ma'aaes	مقاس
ب		b in 'bay'	b	baeb	باب
ت		t in 'tea'	t	taeb	تاب
ث		th in 'think'	th	thawra	ثوره
	or	s in 'see'	s	sawra	
ا	or	t in 'tea'	t	ta*a*lab	تعلب
ج		g in 'gap'	g	gamal	جمل
ج	or	j in 'Jim'	j	jadeed	جديد

ح		'thick' h, as if you're breathing on glass or silver before polishing	*H*	*Haarb*	حرب
خ		ch in Scottish 'loch'	*kh*	*khabaT*	خبط
د		d in 'dog'	*d*	*dorg*	درج
ذ	or	z in 'zoo' d in 'dog'	*z* *d*	*zahab* *dahab*	ذهب
ر		r in 'rabbit', rolled like the Scottish r	*r*	*ragil*	راجل
ز		z in 'zoo'	*z*	*zatoon*	زيتون
س		s in 'sign'	*s*	*sabbat*	سبت
ش		sh in 'shore'	*sh*	*shams*	شمس
ص		'thick' s	*S*	*maSaSa*	مصاصه
ض		'thick' d	*D*	*min faDlak*	من فضلك
ط		'thick' t	*T*	*baTeekha*	بطيخه
ظ		'thick' z	*Z*	*manZar*	منظر
ع		almost silent, a sound between a glottal stop and French 'r' (like a very brief gargle)	*ª*	*ªarabi*	عربى
غ		a cross between Scottish 'ch' and French 'r'	*gh*	*ghaeli*	غالى
ف		f in 'food'	*f*	*fannaen*	فنان

ق	not found in English, similar to k but produced further back in the throat	*q*	*qahira*	قاهره
ك	k in 'kettle'	*k*	*kalb*	كلب
ل	l in 'like'	*l*	*lazeez*	لذيذ
م	m in 'meat'	*m*	*midaen*	ميدان
ن	n in 'nice'	*n*	*naedi*	نادى
ه	h in 'here'	*h*	*haram*	هرم
و	w in 'window'	*w*	*waedi*	وادى
ى	y in 'yes'	*y*	*yaman*	يمن

Note

The sound **v** appears in some words borrowed from other languages, e.g. *video*, pronounced *vidyo*. It is written as ڤ.

The letter ج (geem) is pronounced as a hard **g** (as in 'get') in Egypt, while in most other countries it is soft, more like an English **j**, in which case it is written as چ.

The article ال is normally pronounced *il*, but when it's followed by a word beginning with one of the sounds *t, d, r, z, s, sh, S, D, T, Z, l* or *n*, the *l* sound is often lost, e.g. 'medicine' may be pronounced *adawa* (not *al dawa*), and 'trip' *(il reHla)* becomes *ireHla*.

Where the pronunciation shows double consonants, these must both be pronounced, to give a long sound, e.g. *fannaen* is pronounced *fan-naen*; *Salla* is pronounced *Sal-la*.

If a word ends in a thick consonant and the following word also begins with a consonant, a 'helping' vowel is placed between the two to avoid the difficulty of pronouncing them together, e.g. *noS i keeloo*.

THE ARABIC ALPHABET

The Arabic alphabet has 28 characters. A character has different forms depending on whether it's used by itself or comes at the beginning, middle or end of a word.

Isolated	Initial	Middle	Final	Name pronounced	Shown as
أ	أ	ـا	ـا	*alif*	a, ae, aa
ب	بـ	ـبـ	ـب	*ba'*	b
ت	تـ	ـتـ	ـت	*ta'*	t
ث	ثـ	ـثـ	ـث	*thae'*	th, t
ج	جـ	ـجـ	ـج	*geem* or	g
ج	جـ	ـجـ	ـج	*jeem*	j
ح	حـ	ـحـ	ـح	*Haa'*	H
خ	خـ	ـخـ	ـخ	*khaa'*	kh
د	د	ـد	ـد	*dael*	d
ذ	ذ	ـذ	ـذ	*zael*	z, d
ر	ر	ـر	ـر	*re*	r
ز	ز	ـز	ـز	*zayn*	z
س	سـ	ـسـ	ـس	*seen*	s
ش	شـ	ـشـ	ـش	*sheen*	sh
ص	صـ	ـصـ	ـص	*SaaD*	S
ض	ضـ	ـضـ	ـض	*DaaD*	D
ط	ط	ـطـ	ـط	*Ta*	T
ظ	ظ	ـظـ	ـظ	*Zaa*	Z
ع	عـ	ـعـ	ـع	*ªayn*	a

غ	غ	ـغـ	غ	ghayn	gh
ف	ف	ـفـ	ف	fa'	f
ق	ق	ـقـ	ق	qaaf	q
ك	ک	ـكـ	ك	kaf	k
ل	ل	ـلـ	لـ	laem	l
م	مـ	ـمـ	م	meem	m
ن	ن	ـنـ	ن	noon	n
ه	ه	ـهـ	ه	ha'	h
و	و	ـو	و	waaw	w
ى	ي	ـيـ	ى	ya'	y

In the Arabic script there are three vowel signs:
َ (a), و (w), ِ (i). These are written either above or below the letter to which they belong, e.g.

*a*arab   عرب   *a*arabi عربى
Saboon صابُون   bint بنت

Arabic text is written horizontally, from right to left. There are no capital letters. Punctuation is the same as in English, but written back to front, e.g. ، ؟

Arabic composite numerals, on the other hand, are written from left to right, as in English, e.g. 1993 = ١٩٩٣ ; 25 piastres = ٢٥ قرش .

GENERAL CONVERSATION

● Formulaic greetings are an essential part of conversation, and there's a special phrase for every time of day and different occasion. References to God are made frequently in daily life, reflecting the strongly held belief that everyone and everything belongs to God (see Religion and culture, page 8). Gratitude and thanks to God are particularly often expressed in the context of greetings and introductions.

● In Arabic, the form of words used can vary, according to whether you're speaking to a man or a woman, or to a group of people (see Basic grammar, page 158). Generally, in this book we've given the forms for speaking to a man and a woman for most phrases (although people will seldom take offence if you use the wrong one). With greetings, however, it's a good idea to learn the different forms.

Different forms are labelled as follows:
(m) if you're male
(f) if you're female
(to m) if you're talking to a man
(to f) if you're talking to a woman
(to group) if you're talking to a group.

● People address each other by their first names, preceded by *sayed* (Mr), *sayeda* (Madam) or *aenisa* (Miss). Respect for learning or rank is shown by replacing one of these three with the appropriate title, such as 'Doctor' *(doktowr* or *doktowra)*.

● If you're greeting someone, *assalaamoo ᵃalaykom* is used when you're visiting, while *ahlan wa sahlan* is used when you're receiving visitors. A big smile always helps to support what you're saying.

● In the morning you say *SabaH il kheer*; the correct reply to this is *SabaH innoor*.

In the evening, the greeting is *misa' il kheer*, to which you reply by repeating the phrase, or by saying *misa' innoor*.

● People will frequently shake hands with you, for example when you arrive at someone's house, when you leave and each time you meet – even if it's later on the same day.

● Arab people use a lot of body language. Physical contact is often an intrinsic part of the greeting amongst intimate friends. Women kiss other women on both cheeks; men do the same amongst themselves. You'll find that Arab people generally come closer when talking to you than is customary in Western societies, and are more ready to embrace members of the same sex. Physical contact with a member of the opposite sex, however – unless they're a blood relative – is not customary (see Religion and culture, page 8).

Greetings

Hello
ahlan wa sahlan

Good morning
SabaH il kheer

Good evening
misa' il kheer

Good night
tiSbaH ªala kheer (to m)
tiSbaHi ªala kheer (to f)
tiSbaHoo ªala kheer
   (to group)

Goodbye
maªassalaema

Hello, how are things?
ahlan kayf ilHal

How are you?
izzayak (to m)
izzayik (to f)
izzayokom (to group)

Fine, thanks
kwayyis il Hamdoo lilla (m)
kwayissa il Hamdoo lilla (f)

And how are you? *(said in reply)*
winta izzayak (to m)
winti izzayik (to f)
wintom izzayokom (to group)

You may hear

assalaam ªalaykom
Peace be on you
REPLY: *ªalaykom assalaam*

ahlan wa sahlan
Welcome
REPLY: *ahlan ahlan*

SabaH il kheer
Good morning
REPLY: *SabaH innoor*

misa' il kheer
Good evening
REPLY: *misa' innoor*

tiSbaH/tiSbaHi ªala kheer
Good night
REPLY: *tiSbaH ªala kheer* (to m)
tiSbaHi ªala kheer (to f)

maªassalaema
Goodbye
REPLY: *alla yessalemak* (to m)
alla yessalemik (to f)

ahlan kayf ilHal
Hello, how are things?

izzayak/izzayik
How are you?

Introductions

My name is . . .
ismi . . .

This is Mr Brown
isayid brawn

This is Mrs Clark
isayida klark

This is Miss Smith
il aenisa smith

This is my husband
gowzi

This is my wife
miraati

This is my son
ibni

This is my daughter
binti

Pleased to meet you
forSa saªeeda

Talking about yourself and your family

(*see* Countries and nationalities, *page 174*)

I am English
ana ingleezi (m)/
ingleezaya (f)

I am Scottish
ana iskotlandi (m)/
iskotlandaya (f)

I am Irish
ana ayrlandi (m)/
ayrlandaya (f)

I am from Wales
ana min waylz

We live in Newcastle
iHna ªaysheen fi nyookasel

I am a student
ana Taalib (m)/*Taaliba* (f)

I am a nurse
ana momarriD (m)/
momarriDa (f)

I work in/for . . .
ana bashtaghal fi . . .

I work in a bank
ana bashtaghal fi bank

I work for a computer firm
*ana bashtaghal fi shirkit
kombyootar*

I work in an office
ana bashtaghal fi maktaeb

I work in a factory
ana bashtaghal fi maSnaª

I am unemployed
ana ªaaTil

I am single
ana ªaezib (m)/*ana mish
metgawiza* (f)

I am married
ana metgawiz (m)/
metgawiza (f)

I am separated
ana monfaSil (m)/
monfaSila (f)

I am divorced
ana meTaala' (m)/
meTaala'a (f)

I am a widower
ana armal

I am a widow
ana armala

I have a son
ªandi walad

I have a daughter
ªandi bint

I have three children
andi talat aTfaal

I speak a little Arabic
batkalim ªarabi baseeT

I don't have any children
maªandeesh aTfaal

My husband is . . .
gowzi . . .

I have one brother
ªandi akh

My wife is . . .
miraati . . .

I have three sisters
ªandi talat tekhwaet banaet

My husband is a policeman
gowzi fil bolees

I'm on holiday here
ana hena fi 'agaeza

My wife is an accountant
miraati moHassba

I'm here on business
ana hena fi ma'mooraya

My husband works in . . .
gowzi biyishtaghal fi . . .

I'm here with my husband
ana hena maªa gowzi

My wife works in . . .
miraati bitishtaghal fi . . .

I'm here with my wife
ana hena maªa miraati

My son is five years old
ibni ªomro khamas sineen

I'm here with my family
ana hena maªa ahli

My daughter is eight years old
binti ªomraha taman sineen

You may hear

inta/inti min ay balaed
Where are you from?

bitedris/bitedresi ay
What are you studying?

ismak ay/ismik ay
What's your name?

metgawiz/metgawiza
Are you married?

bitishtaghal/bitishtaghali ay
What work do you do?

ªandak/ªandik aTfaal
Do you have children?

aandak/ aandik ikhwaet
Do you have brothers and
  sisters?

aomrohom kaem sana
How old are they?

aando/ aandaha kaem sana
How old is he/she?

aomrak/ aomrik kaem sana
How old are you?

da gowzik/SaHbik
Is this your husband/
  boyfriend?

di miratak/SaHbitak
Is this your wife/girlfriend?

howa laTeef 'awi
He is very nice

haya laTeefa 'awi
She is very nice

raiyiH/raiyHa fayn
Where are you going?

aayesh/ aaysha fayn
Where are you staying?

*aayesh/ aaysha fayn fi
  briTanya*
Where do you live in
  Britain?

Talking about their country and yours

(*see* Countries and nationalities, *page 174*)

I like Egypt very much
baHib maSr 'awi

Syria is very beautiful
sorya Helwa 'awi

It's the first time I've been
  to Saudi Arabia
*di awil marra azoor
  iso aodaya*

I come to Oman often
basaefer aoman kiteer

Do you live here?
inta aayesh hena (to m)
inti aaysha hena (to f)

Have you ever been to . . .?
aomrak roHt (to m)/
  aomrik roHti (to f) . . .

. . . England/Scotland/
  Ireland/Wales?
. . . *ingilterra/skotlanda/
  ayrlanda/waylz?*

Did you like it?
aagabetak/ aagabetik

You may hear

ªagabetak/ªagabetik maSr
Do you like Egypt?

*di awil marra tezoor/
tezoori lebnaen*
Is this your first time in
Lebanon?

'aªid/'aªda hena 'ad ay
How long are you here for?

ay ra'ayak/ra'ayik fi . . .
What do you think of . . .?

ay ra'ayak/ra'ayik fi maSr
What do you think of
Egypt?

*bititkalim/bititkalimi
ªarabi kwayyis*
Your Arabic is very good

Likes and dislikes

I like . . .
baHib . . .

I like football
baHib korit il qaddam

I like swimming
baHib il ªowm

I like strawberries
baHib il firawla

I don't like . . .
mabaHibish il . . .

I don't like beer
mabaHibish il beera

I don't like theatre
mabaHibish il masraH

Do you like . . .?
*teHib (to m)/
teHibi (to f) . . .*

Do you like olives?
teHib/teHibi zatoon

Invitations and replies

Would you like . . .?
teHib (to m)/*teHibi* (to f) . . .

Yes please
aywa min faDlak (to m)/
min faDlik (to f)

Would you like a drink?
teHib tishrab/teHibi
tishrabi ay

No, thank you
la'a shokran

Would you like something
to eat?
teHib taekool/teHibi
taekli ay

Please leave me alone
law samaHt sebni fi Haeli

Are you going out tonight?
Hatokhrog (m)/
Hatokhrogi (f) *ilayla*

Would you like to come
with us?
*teHib/teHibi teegi ma*a*ana*

What time shall we meet?
net'aebil imta

Would you like to go
dancing?
teHib tor'os/teHibi tor'osi

Where shall we meet?
net'aebil fayn

Would you like to go and eat?
teHib/teHibi naekool barra

Good wishes and exclamations

Congratulations!
mabrook
REPLY: *alla yibaerik feek*
(to m)
alla yibaerik feeki (to f)
alla yibaerik feekom
(to group)

Happy Christmas!
*a*eed milaed sa*a*eed*

Happy New Year!
kolisana winta Tayeb (to m)
kolisana winti Tayeba (to f)
kolisana wentom Tayeben
(to group)
REPLY: *winta Tayeb* (to m)
winta Tayeba (to f)
wentom Tayeben (to group)

Happy Birthday!
*a*eed milaed sa*a*eed*

Happy Biram! *(see page 183)*
ᵃeed saᵃeed

Blessed Ramadan!
ramadaan kareem
REPLY: *alla akram*

Good luck!
Haz saᵃeed

Have a good journey!
reHla saᵃeeda

Enjoy yourself/yourselves!
*atamanna 'an t'aDi/t'aDoo
wa'at saᵃeed*

Bless you! *(including after sneeze)*
baarak fikom

Enjoy your meal!
bilhana wishefa

Cheers!
fi SeHetak (to m)
fi SeHetik (to f)
fi SeHetkom (to group)

What a pity!
khoSara

If only!
law

It's no problem
baseeTa

Talking about the weather

The weather's fine
il gaw laTeef

The weather's bad
il gaw weHish

It's very hot
il gaw Haar

It's very cold
il gaw baerid

It's a wonderful day
yowm saᵃeed

I don't like the heat
mabaHibish il Har

I don't like the cold
mabaHibish il bard

Phew, it's hot!
il donya Har

It's very windy!
il reeH shadeed

What's the weather like today?
il gaw ay inaharda

Do you think it will rain?
teftekir (to m)/*teftekri* (to f)
HatnaTar

ARRIVING IN AN ARAB COUNTRY

● You will probably not need to say anything in Arabic unless you are asked the purpose of your visit, or have something to declare at Customs. If you need to say what you have to declare (rather than just showing it), look up the words in the Dictionary.

● You'll need a valid passport and visa to visit any Arab country. You should also have up-to-date vaccination certificates. Check with each country's authorities a few weeks before travelling for the latest information on vaccinations needed; in some cases you won't be allowed to enter the country without the necessary immunisation papers.

● On arrival in some Arab countries you'll be asked how much money you are bringing into the country. For currency and other restrictions (e.g. alcohol), enquire at the relevant tourist office or embassy before departure; as a general rule, you cannot take alcohol into any of the Gulf States.

● When visiting some countries in the area, a valid visa to visit Israel before or after your stay in that country could cause a delay in the immigration or customs procedure. This doesn't apply to Egypt, which has diplomatic relations with Israel.

You may see

الجمرك	Customs
الجوازات	Passport control
الصالة الحمراء	Red hall (goods to declare)

الصالة الخضراء	Green hall (nothing to declare)
جوازات أخرى	Other passports
مرحباً	Welcome

You may want to say

I am here on holiday
ana hena fi 'agaeza

I am here on business
ana hena fi ma'mooraya

It's a joint passport
gawaez saffar moshtarak

I have something to declare
ma^aaya Hagaet tetgamrak

I have this
ma^aaya da

I have two bottles of perfume
ma^aaya izaztayn barfaen

I have two cartons of cigarettes
ma^aaya khartoshtayn sagayyer

I have a receipt (for this)
ma^aaya waSl

Do I have to pay duty on this?
^aalayha Dareeba

You may hear

basborak/basborik min faDlak/faDlik
Your passport, please

'awra'ak/'awra'ik
Your documents

sabab izayaara
What is the purpose of your visit?

inta/inti hena fi shoghl walla 'agaeza
Are you here on business or holiday?

Hato'^aod/Hato'^aodi 'ad ay
How long are you going to stay here?

*iftaH/iftaHi ishanTa di
min faDlak/faDlik*
Please open this bag/
suitcase

*iftaH/iftaHi ishanTa
min faDlak/faDlik*
Please open the car boot

*ᵃayzeen nefatesh il
ᵃarabaya*
We have to search the car

maᵃak/maᵃaki Haga tanya
Do you have any other
luggage?

*maᵃak/maᵃaki mashroobaet
koHoolaya*
Do you have any alcohol
with you?

di ᵃalayha Dareeba
There is duty to pay on this

taᵃala/taᵃali maᵃaya
Come with me

*istanna/istanni hena
min faDlak/faDlik*
Wait here, please

maᵃak/maᵃaki . . .
Have you got . . .?

*maᵃak/maᵃaki sharayiT
vidyo*
Have you got any video
tapes?

vidyo
A video recorder

kamerit vidyo
A video camera

sagageed Seenee
Chinese rugs

ta'm Seenee
A set of china

dahab
Any gold

*maᵃak/maᵃaki fatoora/
fawateer*
Have you got the receipt(s)?

DIRECTIONS

● When you need to ask the way somewhere, the easiest thing is just to name the place you're looking for and add 'please', e.g. *il maTaar min faDlak/faDlik* ('The airport, please?'). Or you can start with 'where is . . .?': *fayn maHatit il otobees min faDlak/faDlik* ('Where is the bus stop, please?'); *fayn il matHaf il islaemi min faDlak/faDlik* ('Where is the Islamic museum, please?').

● If you're looking for a particular address, have it written down in Arabic as well as in its transliteration. In Arabic-speaking countries, addresses are written down with the house number first, followed by the street name and then the apartment numbers, district and town or city name.

7 Pyramid Street	*Sabªa shareª il haram*	٧ شارع الهرم
Apartment 24	*shaªa arbaªa wi ªishreen*	شقه ٢٤
Giza	*il geeza*	الجيزه
Cairo	*il qahira*	القاهره

● When you're being given directions, listen out for the important bits (such as whether to turn left or right), and try to repeat each bit to make sure you've understood it correctly. If you can't understand something, ask the person to say it again more slowly, *taeni min faDlak/faDlik* ('Again, please'), and *bishwaysh min faDlak/faDlik* ('Slowly, please').

You may see

المحطة الرئيسية	Main station
جامع	Mosque
حارة	Alley
خاص	Private
سوق	Market-place, bazaar

شارع	Street
عبورالمشاه	Pedestrian crossing
قصر	Palace
قلعه	Castle, fortress
كاتدرائيه	Cathedral
كنيسه	Church
متحف	Museum
مترو والأنفاق	Underground railway
محطة اتوبيس	Bus stop
محطه	Station, stop
محطة ترومای	Tram stop
محكمه	(Law) court
معرض	Art gallery, exhibition
ممنوع الدخول	Entrance prohibited
ميدان	Square

You may want to say

Excuse me
law samaHt (to m)
law samaHti (to f)

Pardon?
ba'd iznak (to m)
ba'd iznik (to f)

Can you repeat that, please?
taeni min faDlak/faDlik

More slowly, please
*bishwaysh min faDlak/
faDlik*

Where are we?
iHna fayn

Where does this road/street
lead to?
ishare' da birooH lifayn

Can you show me on the
map?
*momkin tewareenee 'alal
khareeTa*

The station, please?
*il maHaTa min faDlak/
faDlik*

The town centre, please?
*wesT il balaed min faDlak/
faDlik*

The road to Rabat?
iTaree' lil rabaaT

I want to get to . . .
°awez (m)/*°awza* (f)
'aroH . . .

We want to get to . . .
°awzeen neroH . . .

I want to get to the airport
°awez (m)/*°awza* (f) *aroH
il maTaar*

We want to get to Aleppo
°awzeen neroH li Halab

We want to visit the
Pyramids
°awzeen nezoor il ahraam

I want to get to this address
*(if you've got it written
down)*
*°awez/°awza aroH lil
°enwaen da*

Where is/are . . .?
fayn . . .

Where is the tourist office?
fayn maktaeb il siyaHa

Where is the Post Office?
fayn maktaeb il bosTa

Where is the bank?
fayn il bank

Where is the nearest
restaurant?
fayn a'rab maT°am

Where is this office?
fayn il maktaeb da

Where are the toilets?
fayn itowalit

Is it far?
be°eed

Is the airport far away?
il maTaar be°eed

How far is it?
masaefit 'ad ay

How long does it take (on
foot/by bus)?
*Hawaeli 'ad ay (mashi/bil
otobees)*

Can I go by bus?
momkin aroH bil otobees

Can I get there on foot?
momkin aroH mashi

Can I get there by car?
momkin aroH bil °arabaya

Is there . . .?
fi . . .

Is there a chemist here?
fi agzakhaena hena

You may hear

mish hena
It's not here

iHna hena
We are here

hena
Here

hinaek
There

roH . . .
Go . . .

roH hinaek
Go over there

soo' . . .
Drive . . .

min hena
This way, Along here

min hinaek
That way, Along there

teHawid yemeen
Turn right

teHawid shimael
Turn left

ªala Tool
Straight on

awil shareª ªalal yemeen
The first street/turning on
  the right

taeni shareª ªalashimael
The second street/turning
  on the left

fi aekhir ishareª
At the end/bottom of the
  street

ªadi il midaen
Cross the square

ªala inaSya
On the corner

taHt
Down, Downstairs

fo'
Up, Upstairs

wara
Behind there

taHt inakhla
Under the palm tree

ªala ikobri
Over the bridge

'abl ishaarit il moroor
Before the traffic lights

baªd igameª
After/Past the mosque

oddaem il madrasa
Opposite the school

lighayit inahr
As far as the river

oddaem il bank
In front of the bank

wara il matHaf
Behind the museum

orayyib min il maTaar
Near/Close to the airport

fil midaen
It's in the square

fi . . .
At/Into/In . . .

fitiga wesT il balaed
Towards the town centre

ªadi ikobri
Cross the bridge

khod yemeenak/shimaelak
Take a right/left turn

talit shareª ªala (il yemeen)
Take the third exit (on the right)

Hawid ªand ishaarit il moroor
Turn off at the traffic lights

fi door itaelit
It's on the third floor

il baeb il awil/il taeni
The first/second door

(mish) beªeed
It's (not) far away

orayyib
Very/quite close

khamas da'aye' min hena
It's five minutes away

ªishreen keeloo min hena
It's twenty kilometres away

Hatakhod/Hatakhdi il otobees/il 'aTr
You will (have to) catch the bus/train

ROAD TRAVEL

● It is unlikely that you will want to take your car to the Arab world, but if you do, consult motoring organisations for advice. You will need a valid international driving licence, insurance and registration documents.

● If you hire a vehicle, make sure you do so through one of the big international hire firms. They have offices at airports and large 5-star hotels, which are usually staffed by people who speak English. Ensure that you have fully comprehensive insurance which is valid in the country you're visiting. Motor insurance is not compulsory for drivers in many Arab countries, and 'local insurance' is unlikely to do you any good if you actually have an accident.

● Women are not permitted to drive in Saudi Arabia, Libya or the Gulf States.

● Seatbelts and crash helmets are not compulsory, but are advisable.

● You drive on the right in all Middle Eastern countries. Vehicles already on roundabouts have priority over those about to join them.

● Speed limits in Arab countries usually vary up to 100 km per hour for small vehicles and 70 km per hour for trucks and lorries on intercity routes. Main roads, dual carriageways and flyovers will probably have a 60 km per hour limit. In towns the limit is 30 km per hour, but city traffic is usually so congested (for example, in Cairo or Damascus) that no speed limits are necessary! Radars are in place throughout Egypt to check speeding vehicles.

For speed limits and additional information on driving in the country you plan to visit, consult relevant motoring organisations or tourist information centres.

● Some of the best and fastest three-lane motorway networks are found in Saudi Arabia and the Gulf States. There are good motorways in several Arab countries but even some of the main roads can be very rough. On some routes, you may have to pay a small toll (*Dareeba*).

● When there's a road accident, the parties concerned usually sort it out between themselves before continuing with their journies. However, as a foreigner it would be advisable to wait until a traffic policeman arrives. If someone is seriously injured, or the police are called for another reason, they will probably assess the situation and issue an on-the-spot fine, perhaps taking a driver's licence away for a few days as well.

● Petrol (*banzeen*) comes in two grades – 2-star and 4-star or 'super'. Unleaded petrol is not yet available. Diesel (*deezil*) can be found all over the Arab world.

● Parking is not easy in the big capitals. Car parks may be found in main squares, and in Cairo, at least, there are cheap multi-storey car-parks. You may have to tip the car park attendant, whichever country you are in.

● Garages for breakdowns are available, but it may not always be possible to telephone for help. You may have to go and fetch a mechanic yourself. If you break down in the desert, stay with your vehicle until help arrives, and always make sure that you have a plentiful supply of water if you plan a desert journey.

● Beware of inadvertently crossing national borders while driving in the desert; it is often impossible to tell where they actually lie.

You may see

اتجاه واحد	One-way street
استعمل النورالأمامى	Use headlights
اسعاف أولى	First-aid post
اشغال طرق	Road works
إفسح الطريق	Give way
إفسح للسيار	Give way to vehicles from the left
إفسح لليمين	Give way to vehicles from the right
الزم اليمين	Keep right
انتبه	Caution
اوتوستراد	Motorway
بنزين	Petrol
تحويله	Diversion
جرك	Customs
حدودالسرعه	Speed limit
خطر	Danger
خروج	Exit
دخول	Entry
ديزل	Diesel
سوبر	Super (4-star)
سيارات للأيجار	Cars for hire
ضريبه	Toll
طريق دائرى	Ring road
الطريق الزراعى	Agricultural highway
الطريق الصحراوى	Desert highway
طريق غير ممهد	Uneven road surface
طريق للدراجات	Bicycle path

40

طريق مسدود	Cul-de-sac, no through road
طريق مغلق	Road closed
عاده	Standard (2-star)
عبور خطر	Dangerous crossroad
عبور سكة حديد	Level crossing
عبور مشاه	Pedestrian crossing
قف	Stop
قنطرة	Viaduct
محطة خدمه	Service/petrol station
مدرسة	School
مشاه	Pedestrians
مغلق	Closed
مفتوح	Open
ممنوع ألأنتظار	Parking prohibited
ممنوع التجاوز	No overtaking
ممنوع الدخول	No entry
ممنوع للسيارات اللورى	Closed to heavy goods vehicles
منحنى خطر	Dangerous bend
منطقه اثرية	Archaeological site
موقف انتظار السيارات	Car park
ميكانيكى	Repair shop
نهاية الأوتوستراد	End of highway
هدئ السرعه	Dead slow
وسط البلد	Town/City centre

41

You may want to say

Where is there a petrol station?	4-star
fayn maHaTit il banzeen	*soobar*

2-star
ada

Diesel
deezil

20 litres of 4-star, please
'ishreen litr soobar min faDlak/faDlik

5 pounds' worth of diesel
bi khamsa ginay deezil

Fill it up with 4-star/2-star
fool tank soobar/'ada

A can of oil/petrol
'elbit zayt/banzeen

Water, please
maiya min faDlak/faDlik

Air, please
hawa min faDlak/faDlik

Can you change the tyre?
momkin teghaiyyar il kawetch

Can you clean the windscreen?
momkin tinaDaf il izaez

Where is the air?
fayn Trombit il hawa

Where is the car wash?
fayn maw'af ghaseel il saiyaraat

How much is it?
bikaem

Parking

Where can I park?
arkin fayn

Can I park here?
momkin arkin hena

How long can I park here?
momkin arkin hena 'ad ay

How much is it per hour?
bikaem issa'a

Hiring a car

(*see* Days, months, dates, *page 168*)

I want to hire a car
'ayiz (m)/*'ayza* (f) *a'agar 'arabaya*

A small car, please
'arabaya Soghayara min faDlak/faDlik

A medium-sized car
arabaya meTawaseTa

A large car
arabaya kibeera

An automatic car
arabaya otomatik

A car with a driver
arabaya bisawae'

For three days
limodit talat tiyaem

For a week
limodit izboo

For two weeks
*limodit izboo*ayn*

From . . . to . . .
min . . . li . . .

From Monday to Friday
*min yowm il itnayn li yowm il gom*a*

From 5th December to 12th December
min khamsa disambir li itnashar disambir

How much is it?
bikaem

Per day
fil yowm

Per week
fil izboo

Per kilometre
fil keeloo

Is mileage (kilometrage) included?
hal il iygaar yeshmal il masaefa

Is petrol included?
hal il iygaar yeshmal il banzeen

Is insurance included?
hal il iygaar yeshmal il ta'meen

Comprehensive insurance cover
ta'meen shaemil

My husband is driving too
gowzi kamaen Haysoo'

My wife is driving too
miraati kamaen Hatsoo'

Do you take credit cards?
bitakhod karnay i'timaen

Do you take travellers' cheques?
bitakhod shikaet siyaHaya

Can I leave the car in Tunis?
*momkin aseeb il *arabaya fi toonis*

Can I leave the car at the airport?
momkin aseeb il ªarabaya fil maTaar

How do the controls work?
bitishtaghal izay

Breakdowns and repairs

(*see* Car and bicycle parts, *page 46*)

My car has broken down
ªarabiti bayZa

Is there a mechanic around here?
fi mikaneekee orayyib

Can you telephone a mechanic?
momkin teTiSil (to m)/ *teTiSli* (to f) *bil mikaneekee*

Can you send a mechanic?
momkin tebªat (to m)/ *tebªati* (to f) *mikaneekee*

Can you tow the car to the nearest mechanic?
momkin tigor il ªarabaya li a'rab mikaneekee

Do you do repairs?
bitSalaH ªarabayaet

I don't know what's wrong
mish ªarif (m)/ *ªarfa* (f) *lay mish bitishtaghal*

I think . . .
met-haya'lee . . .

It's the clutch
il dibriyaj

It's the radiator
il radyater

It's the brakes
il faramil

The car won't start
mish ªayza te'oom

The battery is flat
il baTarayya naemit

The engine is overheating
il maTowr biyeskhan

It's losing water/oil
na'Sa maiya/zayt

I have a puncture
fi khorm fil kawetch

The . . . doesn't work
il . . . mish biyeshtaghal

44

I need a . . .
ayiz (m)/*ayza* (f) . . .

Can you repair it (today)?
momkin tiSalaHa (inaharda)

When will it be ready?
HatikhlaS imta

How much will it cost?
Hatitkalif kaem

You may hear

Petrol

teHib/teHibi
What would you like?

'ad ay
How much do you want?

*il moftaeH min faDlak/
    faDlik*
The key, please

Parking

mamnoo *il inti'Zaar hena*
You can't park here

*bi . . . fil sa*a*
It's . . . an hour

*matedfa*sh*
You don't pay

bibalaesh
It's free

fi maw'af saiyaraat hinaek
There's a car park over there

Hiring a car

teHib/teHibi *arabaya
    now* *ay*
What kind of car do you
    want?

limodit 'ad ay
For how long?

limodit kaem yowm
For how many days?

meen ellee Haysoo'
Who is driving?

meen kamaen Haysoo'
Is anyone else driving?

itaman . . .
The price is . . .

fil yowm
Per day

fil izboo^a
Per week

rokhSetak/rokhSetik min faDlak/faDlik
Your driving licence, please

^enwaenak/^enwaenik ay
What is your address?

il mafateeH ahay
Here are the keys

ragga^a il ^arabaya fool tank min faDlak/faDlik
Please return the car with a full tank

ragga^a il ^arabaya issa^a setta
Return the car before six o'clock

Breakdowns and repairs

mish bitishtaghal lay
What's wrong with it?

ma^aandeesh qeta^a gheyar
I don't have the parts

laezim aTlob qeta^a gheyar
I will have to order the parts

Ha tekhalas yowm italaet
It will be ready next Tuesday

Ha titkalif tamaneen ginay
It will cost eighty pounds

Car and bicycle parts

Accelerator	*dawaesit* (f) *il banzeen*	دواسة البنزين
Air filter	*filtar* (m) *il hawa*	فلترالهواء
Alternator	*monaZim* (m) *il kahraba*	منظم الكهرباء
Battery	*baTarayya* (f)	بطاريه

English	Transliteration	Arabic
Bonnet	*kabboot* (m)	كابوت
Boot	*shanTa* (f)	شنطه
Brakes (front/ rear)	*faramil (amamaya/ khalfaya)* (pl)	فرامل (اماميه/ خلفيه)
Brake cable	*selk* (m) il *faramil*	سلك الفرامل
Brake fluid	*zayt* (m) il *faramil*	زيت الفرامل
Brake hose	*kharToom* (m) il *faramil*	خرطوم الفرامل
Disc brakes	*teel* (m) il *faramil*	تيل الفرامل
Carburettor	*karborayTar* (m)	كاربوريتر
Chain	*ganzeer* (m)	جنزير
Choke	*shafaaT* (m) il *banzeen*	شفاط البنزين
Clutch	*dibriyaj* (m)	دبرياج
Cooling system	*gihaez* (m) il *tabreed*	جهاز التبريد
Distributor	*il mowazi^a* (m)	الموزع
Electrical system	*gihaez* (m) il *kahraba*	جهاز الكهرباء
Engine	*il maTowr* (m)	الموتور
Exhaust pipe	*shakmaen* (m)	الشاكمان
Fanbelt	*sayr* (m) il *marwaHa*	سير المروحه
Frame (*bicycle*)	*il bodi* (m)	البودى
Front fork	*il dera^a* (m)	الدراع

English	Transliteration	Arabic
Fuel gauge	*mo'ashir* (m) *il banzeen*	مؤشر البنزين
Fuel pump	*Tromba* (f)	الطرمبه
Fuses	*fyowzaet* (pl)	الفيوزات
Gear lever	*fetays* (m)	فتيس
Gears	*teroos* (pl)	تروس
Gearbox	*ªelbit* (f) *il teroos*	علبة التروس
Handbrake	*farmalit* (f) *il yad*	فرملة اليد
Handlebars	*gadown* (m)	جدون
Headlights	*il noor il ªalee* (m)	النور العالي
Heater	*il dafaya* (f)	الدفايه
Horn	*il kalaks* (m)	الكلكس
Ignition	*il kontakt* (m)	الكونتاكت
Ignition key	*moftaeH* (m) *il kontakt*	مفتاح الكونتاكت
Indicators	*isharaet* (pl)	اشارات
Inner tube	*il 'alb* (m) *il gowani*	القلب الجواني
Lights (front/ rear)	*il noor (amami/ khalfi)* (m)	النور (امامي/ خلفي)
Lock	*il terbaes* (m)	الترباس
Oil filter	*filtar izayt* (m)	فلتر الزيت
Oil gauge	*mo'ashir izayt* (m)	مؤشر الزيت
Pedal	*badael* (m)	بدال
Points	*bowjeehaet* (pl)	بوجيهات
Pump	*Tromba* (f)	طرمبه
Radiator	*radyater* (m)	راديتر

Radiator hose (top/bottom)	*kharToom* (m) il *radyater* (*ªelwee/asfal*)	خرطوم الرادياتر (علوى/ اسفل)
Reversing light	*noor il marsh aryer* (m)	نورالمارش ارير
Rotor arm	*dawaar* (m) il *moHarik*	دوارالمحرك
Saddle	*korsi* (m)	كرسى
Silencer	*shakmaen* (m)	شاكمان
Spare wheel	*ªagala* (f) *istebn*	عجله استبن
Spark plugs	*bowjeehaet* (pl)	بوجيهات
Speedometer	*ªadaed isorªa* (m)	عدادالسرعه
Spokes	*silk* (m) il *ªagala*	سلك العجله
Starter motor	il *marsh* (m)	المارش
Steering, steering wheel	*idireksyon* (m)	الدريكسيون
Transmission	*na'l* (m) *isorªaet*	نقل السرعات
Automatic transmission	*na'l* (m) *tomateekee*	نقل اوتوماتيك
Tyre (front/rear)	*kawetch (amami/ khalfi)* (m)	كاوتش (امامى/ خلفى)
Wheel rim	*iTaSa* (f)	الطاسه
Window	*ishibaek* (m)	الشباك
Windscreen	il *barbareez* (m)	البربريز
Windscreen washer	*maiyit* (f) il *masaHaet*	مايةالمساحات
Windscreen wiper	*masaHaet* (pl) il *barbareez*	مساحات البربريز

TAXIS

● Travelling by taxi is usually an easy and convenient way to get about, particularly if you're in a hurry or reluctant to be squashed into a crowded city bus. However it's important to haggle and agree fares in advance or you may find it expensive!

● You can hail taxis in the street, or find them at a taxi rank. It's always best to use registered taxis. In Bahrain, they're easily spotted by their orange side wings; in Cairo, they're black with white side wings.

● Some taxis have meters, but – even if you find a driver who is willing to use his – it's still a good idea to ask what the fare will be. More usual practice is to haggle over the fare, much as you would in a market stall; start at rock bottom and don't be afraid to stand your ground! It's better to agree a price before getting into a taxi and write it down to save disagreements later.

● For urban taxis with meters, there should be a fixed starting charge. There may be extra charges at night, on weekends and public holidays. Extras for luggage, airport pick-ups etc. may not be shown on the meter.

● A tip of 10% or so is usual.

● Sharing a taxi is a routine practice, so don't be afraid to hail one that's already got a passenger – and don't be surprised if the taxi you're in stops for someone else. If you get into a taxi that's already got a passenger, first make sure you agree how much your fare should be. In Jordan and Egypt, sharing a taxi is a popular way of travelling and many taxis make regular daily runs along set routes both in towns and throughout the country.

● Write clearly, in capital Roman letters, the address of your destination. If it's at all complicated or off the tourist track, try to have it written in Arabic as well.

You may want to say

(see also Directions, page 33)

Is there a taxi rank around
here?
*fi maw'af taksi orayyib min
hena*

I need a taxi
ªayiz (m)/*ªayza* (f) *taksi*

Can you call me a taxi,
please?
*momkin tenadeelee taksi
min faDlak/faDlik*

Now
delwa'ti

Can you book me a taxi for
tomorrow at nine o'clock?
momkin teHgiz (to m)/
teHgizi (to f) *li taksi
lebokra issaªa tesªa*

To go to the airport
lil maTaar

The airport, please
*il maTaar min faDlak/
faDlik*

The train station
maHaTit issekal Hadeed

The bus station
maHaTit il otobees

The Hotel Alexandria,
please
*hotayl il iskinderayya
min faDlak/faDlik*

To this address, please
*il ªenwaen da
min faDlak/faDlik*

Is it far?
beªeed

How much will it cost?
tamaen ireHla 'ad ay

I am in a hurry
ana mistaªgil (m)/
ana mistaªgila (f)

Stop here, please
*wa'af hena min faDlak/
faDlik*

Can you wait, please?
*momkin testanaeni
min faDlak/faDlik*

How much is it?
Hissaebak/Hissaebik kaem

That is too much
kiteer 'awi

51

I will give you . . .
Hadilak/Hadilik . . .

I will give you ten dinars
*Hadilak/Hadilik ªashra
dananeer*

There is a mistake
il Hissaeb mish mazboot

On the meter it's 50 riyals
*il ªaddad biy'ool
khamseen riyal*

You said the journey would
cost only five pounds
*inta 'olt/inti 'olti ireHla
Hatitkalif khamsa ginay
bas*

You said that the fee
included the luggage
*inta 'olt/inti 'olti il'ogra
teshmal il shonaaT*

Keep the change
khalli il ba'ee

Can you give me a receipt?
momkin teddeenee waSl

For five pounds
bi khamsa ginay

52

You may hear

*Hawaeli ªashra keeloo min
hena*
It's about ten kilometres
away

taman ireHla Hawaeli . . .
It will cost about . . .

talaeta ginay
It's three pounds

AIR TRAVEL

● There are regular flights between the major cities throughout the Arab world.

● At airports and airline offices, you'll generally find someone who speaks English, but be prepared to say a few things in Arabic.

● Signs at major airports will be in French and/or English and Arabic.

● Generally, children under 16 pay 50% of the adult fare in the Arab world.

● International car hire firms have offices at major airports where you can arrange to hire or pick up cars.

You may see

ادفع	Push
إجزب	Pull
استعلامات	Information
الجمرك	Customs
الرجاء ربط الأحزمة	Fasten seatbelts please
الرحلات الداخليه	Domestic departures
الرحلات الدوليه	International departures
الصالة الحمراء	Goods to declare (Red hall)
الصالة الخضراء	Nothing to declare (Green hall)
اوتوبيس (وسط البلد)	Buses (to the town/city centre)
بوابة	Gate

تأخير	Delay
تاكسى	Taxis
تواليت	Toilets
جوازات أخرى	Other passports
خروج	Exit
دخول	Entrance
رقابة الجوازات	Passport control
سيارات للأيجار	Car hire
صالة الأمتعة	Luggage reclaim hall
صالة السفر	Departure (lounge)
مكتب تحويل العملة	Bureau de change
ممنوع التدخين	No smoking
وصول	Arrivals

You may want to say

(see also Numbers, inside front cover; Days, months, dates, page 168; and Time, page 172)

Is there a flight (from Cairo) to Khartoum?
fi Taiyaara (min ilqahira) lil kharToom

Today
inaharda

This morning
inaharda iSobH

This afternoon
inaharda baªd iDohr

Tomorrow (morning/ afternoon)
bokra (iSobH/baªd iDohr)

Do you have a timetable of flights to Tunis?
ªandak (to m)/ªandik (to f) gadwal mawaªeed il reHlaet ila Toonis

What time is . . .?
. . . issaªa kaem

What time is the first flight to Marrakesh?
awil reHla li marakesh issa^aa kaem

The next flight
il reHla illi ba^ad keda

The last flight
il reHla il 'akheera

What time does it arrive (in Tripoli)?
yewSal (Tarablos) issa^aa kaem

A ticket to Bahrain, please
tazkara lil baHrayn min faDlak/faDlik

Two tickets to Cairo
tazkartayn lil qahira

Single
tazkara raiyiH

Return
raiyiH gay

First class/Economy class
daraga 'oola/daraga tanya

For the eleven o'clock flight
reHlit issa^aa Hidashar

I want to cancel my reservation
^aawez (m)/^aawza (f) alghee il Hagz

I want to change my reservation
^aawez/^aawza aghaiyyar il Hagz

What is the number of my flight?
raqam il reHla 'ay

What time must I be at the airport?
awSal il maTaar issa^aa kaem

Which gate/hall is it?
anhi madkhal/Saala

Is there a delay?
fi ta'kheer

Where is the luggage from the flight from London?
fayn il shonaaT illi weSlit min landan

My luggage is not here
mish la'ee shonaaTi

Is there a bus to the centre of town?
fi otobees biyewaSal li wesT il balaed

55

You may hear

*teHib to'ªod/teHibi
to'ªodi ganb il shibaek*
Would you like a seat by
the window?

*teHib to'ªod/teHibi
to'ªodi ganb il mamar*
Would you like a seat on
the aisle?

bitdakhan/bitdakhani
Do you smoke?

*il Taiyaara Hat'oom
issaªa . . .*
The flight will be called/
board at . . . *(time)*

bawaeba raqam sabªa
Gate number seven

*tazkartak min faDlak/
tazkartik min faDlik*
Your ticket, please

*gawaez isaffar/basbor
min faDlak/faDlik*
Your travel documents/
passport, please

*kart il rekoob min faDlak/
faDlik*
Your boarding card, please

*iwSifli ishonaaT bitaªtak/
bitaªtik*
What does your luggage
look like?

*tazkarit ishonaaT min
faDlak/faDlik*
The reclaim tag, please

reHla
Flight

il neda' il akheer
Final call

ta'kheer
Delay

bawaeba
Gate

TRAVELLING BY TRAIN

● Railways in the Arab world are generally state-owned. The extent of the rail network and standards of comfort on trains vary from country to country. It is worth checking the rail service with the appropriate tourist office before you travel.

In some countries trains run 24 hours a day, and there are inter-city express trains.

● Passenger seating is usually in three categories: *daraga 'oola* (first class), *daraga tanya* (second class) and *daraga talta* (third class). The third class, with its cramped, uncomfortable wooden seats and friendly atmosphere, still exists but is being phased out in many countries. First class compartments and carriages are usually air-conditioned, have dining facilities and washrooms, and can be attractively furnished as well as being well-equipped.

● Long-distance trains have two classes of sleeper: 'tourist' (*siyaHee*) and 'ordinary' (*ªada*), which costs half as much. They must be booked in advance, from railway stations or travel agents.

● Discounted tickets may be available for children, students and senior citizens. Students should carry an International Student Card with them. For information on any other offers that may be available to overseas visitors, contact the relevant tourist office well in advance of travel.

● You can take bicycles or animals on trains in most Arab countries, but you should book well in advance.

● Main central stations are often well equipped with washing facilities, toilets, eating places, lost property offices and Tourist Information Centres. As a rule there are no left luggage facilities on stations.

• Beware of theft on trains, particularly on well-travelled tourist routes. When travelling, take all the usual precautions with your valuables.

You may see

استعلامات	Information
بوفيه	Buffet
تاكسى	Taxis
تذاكر	Tickets
تواليت	Toilets
جداول السفر	Train timetables
جرس انذار	Alarm
حجرة الأنتظار	Waiting room
حجز	Reservations
درجة اولى	First class
درجة ثانية	Second class
درجة ثالثه	Third class
درجة سياحية	Tourist class
خروج	Exit
رجال	Gentlemen
رحلة	Trip
رصيف	Platform
سفر	Departures
عربة الأكل	Dining car
عربة البضاعة	Luggage van
عربة النوم	Sleeping car
محطة السكه الحديد	Railway station
مدخل	Entrance

مدير المحطة	Station master
ممنوع الدخول	No access
مكتب الحجز	Booking office
مكتب المفقودات	Lost property office
نساء	Ladies
وصول	Arrivals

You may want to say

Information

Is there a train to Fez?
fi 'aTr li faes

Do you have a timetable of
trains to Luxor?
fi gadwal saffar li lo'Sor

What time . . . ?
. . . issaªa kaem

What time is the train to
Idfoo?
'aTr idfoo issaªa kaem

What time is the first train
to Aleppo?
awil 'aTr Halab issaªa kaem

The next train
il 'aTr illi baªd keda

The last train
akheer 'aTr

What time does it arrive (at
Amman)?
yewSal (ªamaen) issaªa kaem

What time does the train
from Port Said arrive?
*'aTr borsaªeed biyewSal
issaªa kaem*

The train to Khartoum,
please
*'aTr il kharToom
min faDlak/faDlik*

Which platform?
raSeef nemra kaem

Does this train go to
Riyadh?
il 'aTr da biyroH irriyaaD

Is this a direct route?
il khaT da mobaeshir

Where do I change trains?
aghaiyyar il 'aTr fayn

59

Tickets

(*see* Time, *page 172*; Numbers, *inside front cover*)

One/Two tickets to Luxor, please
tazkara/tazkartayn li lo'Sor min faDlak/faDlik

Single
tazkara raiyiH

Return
raiyiH gay

For one adult/two adults
tazkara ªada/tazkartayn ªada

And one child/two children
wi Tefl/wi Teflayn

First class/Second class
daraga 'oola/daraga tanya

For the ten o'clock train to Cairo
'aTr issaªa ªashra lil qahira

For the express to Alexandria
sareeª lil iskinderayya

I want to reserve a seat
ªayiz (m)/ªayza (f) aHgiz korsi

I want to reserve two seats to Amman
ªayiz/ªayza aHgiz korsiyayn li ªamaen

I want to reserve a sleeper
ªayiz/ªayza aHgiz fi ªarabayit inowm

How much is it?
bikaem

On the train

I have reserved a seat
ana Hagazt korsi

I have reserved a sleeper
ana Hagazt fi ªarabayit inowm

Is this seat taken?
il korsi da faaDi

Excuse me
ªan iznak (to m)/ªan iznik (to f)

Where is the dining-car?
fayn ªarabayit il 'akl

Where is the sleeping-car?
fayn ªarabayit inowm

Where is the buffet?
fayn il boffay

May I open the window?
momkin aftaH ishibaek

May I smoke?
momkin adakhan

Where are we?
iHna fayn

Have we arrived at Amman?
woSelna ªamaen

How long does the train
  stop here?
il 'aTr Ha yow'af hena 'ad ay

Can you tell me when we
  get to Aswan?
*momkin te'olli lama
  newSal aswan*

You may hear

Information

biy'oom issaªa ªashra wi noS
It leaves at 10.30

*biyewSal issaªa arbaªa ila
  ªashra*
It arrives at ten to four

*laezim teghaiyyar/
  teghaiyyari fi TanTa*
You have to change trains
  at Tanta

raSeef raqam arbaªa
It's platform number four

Tickets

(*see* Time, *page 172*; Numbers, *inside front cover*)

*ªayiz tisafir/ªayza tisafri
  imta*
When do you want to
  travel?

raiyiH walla raiyiH gay
Single or return?

bitdakhan/bitdakhani
Do you smoke?

ªayiz tergaª/ªayza tergaªi imta
When do you want to return?

bi ªishreen ginay
(It's) 20 pounds

il 'aTr da daraga 'oola bas
That train is first class only

BUSES AND COACHES

● As well as town and city bus services, there are many buses between towns and villages throughout the Arab world. Inter-city buses and coaches are also available. Bus travel is cheap and popular and wherever you travel, you can be sure that they will be crowded with passengers.

● There are seldom any timetables, especially in rural districts: you just have to sit and wait, or ask someone when the bus is due.

● Bus fares are usually paid to a conductor. Coach fares are paid for either at the main coach station or to a conductor on the coach. You can buy bus passes in Egypt and Morocco, which allow unlimited travel at discounted prices, normally for one week or one month periods.

You may see

أخرج من الباب الأوسط	Alight by the centre door
ادخل من الباب الأمامى	Enter by the front door
اشترى تذكره السفر قبل	Buy your ticket before
ركوب الأتوبيس	boarding the coach
خروج	Exit
دخول	Entrance
لاتتحدث مع السائق	Do not talk to the driver
محطة اوتوبيس	Bus stop

You may want to say

(*for sightseeing bus tours, see* Sightseeing, *page 127*)

Where is the bus stop/
station?
fayn maHatit il otobees

Is there a bus to the
Pyramids?
fi otobees lil haram

What number is the bus to
the station?
*il otobees illi biyroH il
maHaTa nemra kaem*

How often do they run?
biyeegee kol 'ad ay

What time is . . .?
. . . issa^aa kaem

What time is the coach to
Alexandria?
*otobees iskinderayya
issa^aa kaem*

What time is the first bus to
Maadi?
*awil otobees lil ma^aadi
issa^aa kaem*

The next bus
il otobees illi ba^ado

The last bus
akheer otobees

What time does it arrive?
biyewSal issa^aa kaem

Where can I buy a ticket?
ashteri tazkara min ayn

Where does the bus to the
town centre leave from?
*otobees noSil balaed
biy'oom minayn*

Does the bus to the airport
leave from here?
*otobees il maTaar biy'oom
min hena*

Does this bus go to
Ar Raml Square?
*il otobees da biyroH
midaen iraml*

Can you tell me where to
get off?
momkin te'olli anzil fayn

Is this the stop for the
Mohamed Ali Mosque?
*di maHaTit game^a
mahamad ^aali*

The next stop, please
*il maHaTa il gaya
min faDlak/faDlik*

63

Open the door, please!
*iftaH/iftaHi il baeb
min faDlak/faDlik*

Excuse me, may I get by?
*ᵃan iznak/iznik momkin
'ᵃadi*

One ticket to Cairo, please
*tazkara lil qahira
min faDlak/faDlik*

Two single tickets to Rabat
tazkartayn raiyiH lil rabaaT

A return to Amman
ᵃamaen raiyiH gay

How much is it?
bikaem

You may hear

*otobees wesT il balaed min
il maHaTa di*
The bus to the centre leaves
from that stop there

*otobees sabaᵃa wi khamseen
biyroH il maHaTa*
The 57 goes to the station

maᵃak/maᵃaki tazakir
Have you got tickets?

biy'oom kol ᵃashar da'ayi'
It goes every ten minutes

*biy'oom issaᵃa itnashar wi
noS*
It leaves at 12.30

biyewSal issaᵃa itnayn
It arrives at 2.00

raiyiH walla raiyiH gay
Single or return?

Hatenzil/Hatenzili hena
Are you getting off here?

il maHaTa illi gaya
It's the next stop

fatitak/fatitik il maHaTa
You've missed the stop

64

UNDERGROUND TRAVEL

● Cairo has an underground system, of which the first stretch of line opened in 1987. Called *metro il anfa'*, it is both very clean and very safe, and relatively easy to use. It has a single line, and most of the stops are actually above ground – which can make it a good and relaxing way of seeing something of the city. The trains run at five-minute intervals. Station names are written in both Arabic and Roman script.

● Tickets – which cost very little – are bought at manned ticket offices, rather than from machines, so you will need to have a few words of Arabic ready. You can buy cheap season tickets, and children pay half price.

You may see

تذاكر	Tickets
خروج	Exit
دخول	Entrance
مترو الأنفاق	Underground (metro)
ممنوع التدخين	No smoking

You may want to say

Do you have a map of the underground?
fi khareeTa li metro il anfa'

One/Two, please
*waHid/itnayn
min faDlak/faDlik*

Which platform is it for Helwan?
anhi raSeef li Hilwaen

Which stop is it for the Pyramids?
anhi maHaTa lil ahraam

Where are we?
iHna fayn

Is this the stop for the
railway station?
*da maw'af maHaTit il
sekkal Hadeed*

Does this train go to
Tahreer Square?
*il metro da biyroH midaen
itaHreer*

You may hear

il maHaTa illi gaya
It's the next stop

il maHaTa illi fatit
It was the last stop

fatitak/fatitik il maHaTa
You've missed the stop

BOATS AND FERRIES

● Egypt is renowned for its river cruises. There are long- and short-distance cruises by boat and steamer on the river Nile, which stretches for over 1,000 kilometres from the Nile Delta in the north to Aswan and Abu Simbel Temple in the south. The trip up the Nile from Cairo to Aswan is not to be missed if you have the time. It lasts approximately three days.

● You can also find boat trips from Latakia, Alexandria, Algiers, Port Said and all along the north African coast on the Mediterranean, and from Suez and Ismalia on the Red Sea. Mediterranean cruisers also go all the way to Cyprus, Greece, Venice, Naples, Genoa and Marseilles from all the major north African ports.

● There are ferries around Port Said and Port Tewfik and between various towns on the Nile.

You may see

اطواق نجاه	Lifebelts
رحلات حول الخليج	Trips around the bay
رحلات فى النيل	Trips on the Nile
فيلوكه	Felucca
مراكب	Boats
مرسى	Pier
معديه	Ferry
ميناء	Port, harbour
كباين	Cabins

You may want to say

(see Time, *page 172*)

Is there a boat to Tripoli today?
fi markib li Tarablos inaharda

Is there a ferry to Aswan?
*fi ma*ᵃ*adaya li aswan*

Are there any boat trips?
fi reHlaet nahraya (on river)/*baHaraya* (by sea)

What time . . .?
*. . . issa*ᵃ*a kaem*

What time is the boat to Casablanca?
*markib idaar ilbayDa issa*ᵃ*a kaem*

What time is the first boat?
*il markib il awalanaya issa*ᵃ*a kaem*

The next boat
il markib illi gaya

The last boat
il markib il akhranaya

What time does it arrive?
*HatewSal issa*ᵃ*a kaem*

What time does it return?
*Haterga*ᵃ *issa*ᵃ*a kaem*

How long is the crossing?
*bit*ᵃ*adi fi 'ad ay*

Where is the ferry for Port Tewfik?
*fayn ma*ᵃ*adayit bortawfee'*

Where does the boat for Algiers leave from?
il markib illi raiyHa algazae'ir Hat'oom minayn

Where can I buy tickets?
ashteri itazakir minayn

Is the sea rough today?
il baHr hayig inaharda

Tickets

Four tickets to Suez, please
*arba*ᵃ *tazakir lisoways min faDlak/faDlik*

Two adults and two children
itnayn ᵃ*ada wi itnayn aTfaal*

Single
tazkara raiyiH

Return
raiyiH gay

I want to book tickets for
   a cruise to Luxor
ayiz (m)/*ayza* (f)
   *aHgiz tazakir li reHla
   inahraya li lo'Sor*

I want to book a cabin
*ayiz/ *ayza aHgiz kabeena*

For one person
nafar waHid

For two people
nafarayn

For a family
*lil *ayla*

How much is it?
bikaem

On board

I have reserved a cabin
ana Hagazt kabeena

I have reserved two berths
ana Hagazt sereerayn

Where are the cabins?
fayn il kabayin

Where is cabin number 20?
*fayn kabeena nemra
   ishreen

Can we go out on deck?
*momkin no'af *ala saT-H
   il markib*

You may hear

*fi markib yowm il itnayn
   wil khamees*
There are boats on
   Mondays and Thursdays

*il ma*adaya illi raiyHa
   komombo Hat'oom
   issa*a tes*a*
The ferry to Komombo
   leaves at nine o'clock

Haterga issa*a arba*a wi
   noS*
It returns at half past four

*markib asyoot Hat'oom
   min marsa raqam itnayn*
The boat to Asiut leaves
   from pier number two

il baHr haedee
The sea is calm

il baHr hayig
The sea is rough

AT THE TOURIST OFFICE

● There are tourist information offices all over Cairo, Alexandria, Luxor and Aswan. Look for the name 'Misr Travel': the organisation has branches in most 5-star and 4-star hotels. They will be able to supply leaflets about sights worth seeing, and will also book hotel rooms and transport.

In Arabic, Misr Travel is مصرللسياحه *(miSr lilsiyaHa)*.

● In Jordan, Syria and the Gulf States tourist information is available from Ministry of Tourism desks in 5-star and 4-star hotels, the airport and some tourist sites.

● Tourist offices in Morocco are located in the centre of towns and offer free city maps indicating the main tourist sites.

You may see

إدارة الأستعلامات	Department of Information
استعلامات	Information
خرائط	Maps
دليل	Guides
رحلات بمرشد	Guided Tours
قسم الحجز	Reservations
مصرللسياحه	Misr Travel
وزاره السياحه	Ministry of Tourism

You may want to say

(see Directions, *page 33*; Sightseeing, *page 127*; Time, *page 172*)

Where is the tourist office?
fayn maktaeb isiyaHa

Do you have . . .?
andak (to m)/
  andik (to f) . . .

Do you have a plan of the town?
andak/andik khareeTa lil balaed

Do you have a map of the area?
andak/andik khareeTa lil mante'a

Do you have a list of hotels and restaurants?
andak/andik lista lil hotilaet wil maTa'im

Do you have a list of campsites?
andak/andik lista li mo'askaraat ishabaeb

Can you recommend a cheap hotel?
momkin tikhtar (to m)/
  tikhtari (to f) *li hotayl rekheeS*

Can you recommend a restaurant?
momkin tikhtar/tikhtari li maT'am

Can you book a hotel for me?
momkin teHgiz (to m)/
  teHgizi (to f) *li hotayl*

Can you find a room for me?
momkin teHgiz/teHgizi li 'owda

I want a room overlooking the Nile
ayiz/ayza 'owda alal neel

With a bathroom
bi Hammaem

A single room
'owda bisereer mofrad

A twin-bedded room
'owda bisereerayn

A double room
'owda mozdawaga

Where can I change sterling/travellers' cheques/dollars?
aghaiyyar isterleenee/ shikaet siyaHaya/ dolaraat fayn

71

Where can I hire a bicycle?
*'a'agar *agala fayn*

Have you got information about . . .?
*andak/*andik ma*loomaet *an . . .*

Have you got information about the Roman ruins?
*andak/*andik ma*loomaet *an il athaar il romanaya*

Have you got information in English?
*andak/*andik ma*loomaet bilingleezi*

What is there to see here?
fi ay hena

Do you have any leaflets?
*andak/*andik manshooraat*

Where is the archaeological museum?
fayn matHaf il athaar

Can I show me on the map?
*momkin tewareenee *alal khareeTa*

When is the National Theatre open?
*il masraH il qawmi biyeftaH issa*a kaem*

Are there any excursions?
fi reHlaet

You may hear

*momkin asa*dak/asa*dik*
Can I help you?

inta ingleezi/inti ingleezaya
Are you English?

almaeni/almanaya
German?

inta/inti min ay balaed
Where are you from?

*a*id/a*da hena 'ad ay*
How long are you going to be here?

naezil/naezla fayn
Where are you staying?

*ayiz/*ayza hotayl daraga kaem*
What grade of hotel do you want?

khamas negoom/arba negoom*
5-star/4-star

ᵃayiz/ᵃayza 'owda fi bansyown
Would you like a room in a private house?

teHib/teHibi 'owda bi Hammaem
Would you like a room with a bathroom?

teHib/teHibi 'owda ᵃalal neel
Would you like a room overlooking the Nile?

fi maSr il 'adeema
It's in the old part of Cairo

ACCOMMODATION

● There is a wide range of accommodation throughout the Arab world. In Egypt, hotels are not officially graded, unless they belong to international chains such as Hilton, Sheraton, Meridian etc., in which case they will be 4- or 5-star; standards of other hotels vary enormously.

Jordan and Syria boast a wide range of accommodation, from deluxe hotels to small inn-type *pensions*. There are also tourist 'rest houses' near major tourist attractions and on main highways; these are mainly owned by the Ministry of Tourism.

Saudi Arabia and all the Gulf States have mainly large, deluxe hotels, with prices to match.

Morocco and Tunisia, on the other hand, have hotels across the range, the majority graded according to the European star system. The prices of all but 5-star hotels are fixed by the government. Lists of hotels and campsites are provided free of charge at national tourist offices.

● You may find 'bed only' hotels (*fondoq*), and for those who wish to experience life with a local family, there are many *pension* (*bansyown*) rooms available. Tourist offices may help.

● You may also rent a flat or an apartment. Rents vary enormously, depending particularly on location. Where possible rent apartments that are known to you through recommendation, rather than at random. You will probably find an opportunity here to practise your haggling skills!

● There are very few youth hostels in Arab countries; those that do exist are mainly in Cairo, Alexandria, Marrakesh, Rabat and Damascus. They are very cheap.

● When you book in anywhere you will be asked for your

passport which the proprietor has to show to the police before it can be returned to you. As a general rule, however, always keep your passport, money and valuables on you.

● Campsites aren't widespread in the Arab world, but you do find them in the more popular tourist areas, especially in Morocco. They are almost invariably near beaches or rivers, and facilities are usually very basic.

Information requested on a registration card

First name	الأسم الأول
Family name	اسم العائلة
Address	العنوان
Nationality	الجنسية
Occupation	الوظيفة
Date of birth	تاريخ الميلاد
Place of birth	محل الميلاد
Passport number	رقم جوازالسفر
Issued at	صدر من
Arrived from	وصل من
Further destination	مسافر إلى
Date	التاريخ
Signature	التوقيع

You may see

أستراحة	Rest house
استقبال	Reception
أطلب خدمة	Call for service
إقامة كاملة	Full board

الدور الأرضى	Ground floor
الدور الأول	First floor
الدور الثانى	Second floor
بنسيون	Pension
بيت شباب	Youth hostel
بيت ضيافه	Guest house
تواليت	Toilets
جراج	Garage
حجرة الأكل	Dining-room
حجرات للأيجار	Rooms for rent
حمام	Bathroom
خروج (طوارئ)	(Emergency) exit
دش	Showers
روم سرفيس	Room service
زبالة	Rubbish
سراير	Beds
صالون	Lounge
غسيل	Laundry
فندق	Bed only hotel
كهرباء	Electricity
كومبليه	Full up
للأيجار	To let
لوكاندة	Hotel
مصعد	Lift
معسكر	Campsite
مياه صالحه للشرب	Drinking water
نصف إقامه	Half board
هوتيل	Hotel
هوتيل لوكس (خمس نجوم)	Luxury hotel (five stars)

You may want to say

Booking in and out

I've reserved a room
Hagazt 'owda

I've reserved two rooms
Hagazt 'owdtayn

My name is . . .
ismi . . .

Do you have a room?
^aandak (to m)/
^aandik (to f) *'owda*

A single room
'owda bisereer mofrad

A twin-bedded room
'owda bisereerayn

A double room
'owda mozdawaga

For one night
layla waHda

For two nights
layltayn

With bath/shower
bi Hammaem/dosh

How much is it?
bikaem

Per night
filayla

Per week
fil izboo^a

Is there a reduction for
children?
fi takhfeeD lil aTfaal

Is breakfast included?
il fiTaar maDmoon

A room at the back, please
*'owda fil khalf
min faDlak/faDlik*

A room overlooking the
sea, please
*'owda ^aalal baHr
min faDlak/faDlik*

Can I see the room?
momkin ashoof il 'owda

It's too expensive
ghaeli 'awi

Do you have anything
cheaper?
*^aandak/^aandik Haga
arkhaS*

Do you have anything
bigger?
*^aandak/^aandik Haga
akbar*

77

Do you have anything
    smaller?
*andak/*andik Haga aSghar*

I'd like to stay another night
*kamaen layla min faDlak/
    faDlik*

I am leaving tomorrow
    morning
ana mashi bokra iSobH

The bill, please
il fatoora min faDlak/faDlik

Do you take credit cards?
momkin adfa bi karnay
    i'timaen*

Do you take travellers'
    cheques?
momkin adfa bi shikaet
    siyaHaya*

Can you recommend a
    hotel in Jeddah?
momkin tikhtar (to m)/
    tikhtari (to f) *li hotayl fi
    gadda*

Can you phone them to
    make a booking, please?
momkin teHgiz (to m)/
    teHgizi (to f) *li bil tilifown*

In hotels

(see Problems and complaints, *page 151*; Time, *page 172*)

Where can I park?
arkin fayn

Do you have a cot for the
    baby?
andokom sereer Tefl

Do you have facilities for
    the disabled?
*andokom khadamaet lil
    mo*awiqeen*

Is there room service?
fi qesm li room servis

Can I have breakfast in the
    room?
momkin afTar fil 'owda

What time is breakfast?
*il fiTaar issa*a kaem*

What time is dinner?
*il *asha issa*a kaem*

What time does the hotel
    close?
*il hotayl bi ye'fil issa*a
    kaem*

I'll be back very late
ana Harga mit'akhar*

(Key) number 42, please
*(moftaeH) nemra itneen wi arb*ᵃ*een min faDlak/faDlik*

Are there any messages for me?
fi rasayel ᵃ*ashani*

Where is the bathroom?
fayn il Hammaem

Where is the dining-room?
fayn otil akl

Can I leave this in the safe?
momkin aseeb da fil khazna

Can you give me my things from the safe?
momkin akhod Hagti min il khazna

Can you wake me at eight o'clock?
*momkin tiSaHeenee issa*ᵃ*a tamanya*

Can you order me a taxi?
momkin toTlob (to m)/ toTlobi (to f) li taksi

For tomorrow at nine o'clock
*issa*ᵃ*a tes*ᵃ*a iSobH*

Can you clean this jacket for me?
momkin tinaDafli (to m)/ tinaDafeelee (to f) il jaketta di

Can you book me a babysitter?
momkin teHgiz/teHgizi li galeesit aTfaal

Can you put it on the bill?
momkin tiHoT (to m)/ tiHoTi (to f) da ᵃ*ala il fatoora*

Room number 21
'owda nemra waHid wi ᵃ*ishreen*

I need another pillow
ana ᵃ*ayiz (m)/* ᵃ*ayza (f) kamaen makhadda*

I need a towel
ana ᵃ*ayiz/* ᵃ*ayza fooTa*

Camping

Is there a campsite around here?
fi mo ᵃ*askar hena*

Where can I put the tent?
aHoT il khayma fayn

Where are the showers?
fayn il dosh

Is there an extra charge for the showers?
fi ogra ziyaeda lil dosh

Where are the toilets?
fayn il towalit

Is there a laundry-room?
fi 'owda lil ghaseel

Where are the dustbins?
fayn SafayiH izibaela

Is the water drinkable?
il maiya di SalHa lil shorb

Self-catering accommodation

(*see* Directions, *page 33*; Problems and complaints, *page 151*)

I have rented a villa
ana 'agart vila

Where is the stopcock?
fayn il maHbas

It's called Sun Villa
ismaha vilit ishams

Where is the fusebox?
fayn Sandoo' il fayash

I have rented an apartment
ana 'agart sha'a

How does the cooker work?
il botagaez biyeshtaghal izay

We're in number 11
iHna fi raqam Hidashar

How does the water-heater
work?
il sakhaen biyeshtaghal izay

My name is . . .
ismi . . .

What is the address?
ay il ªenwaen

Is there air conditioning?
fi takyeef

How do I get there?
aroH izay

Is there a spare gas bottle?
*fi amboobit botagaez
iDafaya*

Can you give me the key,
please?
*momkin teddeenee il
moftaeH min faDlak/
faDlik*

Are there any more
blankets?
fi baTateen ziyaeda

What day do they come to
clean?
biyenaDafoo imta

Where is . . .?
fayn . . .

Where do I put the rubbish?
aHoT izibaela fayn

Where can I contact you?
aTeSil beek fayn

When do they collect the rubbish?
biyakhdoo izibaela imta

Are there any shops round here?
fi maHalaet hena

You may hear

momkin asaᵃdak/asaᵃdik
Can I help you?

ismak/ismik ay
What's your name, please?

kaem layla
For how many nights?

kaem nafar
For how many people?

bi Hammaem walla min ghayr Hammaem
With bath or without bath?

aesif/asfa iHna komblay
I'm sorry, we're full

basborak/basborik min faDlak/faDlik
Your passport, please

momkin temDi hena min faDlak/faDlik
Can you sign here, please

il shaghaela biteegee kol yowm
The maid comes every day

momkin aegi yowm il gomᵃa
I can come on Friday

biyeegoo yowm baᵃd yowm
They come every other day

biyelemmo izibaela kol yowm
They collect the rubbish every day

81

TELEPHONES

● Local calls can be made from public telephones, which are usually found in district post offices, larger shops and in main squares. Some kiosks also allow you to make local calls. You may be able to make long-distance and international calls from your hotel if you are staying in one of the large international chains; otherwise, go to the central telephone office.

● To call abroad you usually dial 00, followed by the country code; for the UK it's 44. Follow this with the city code minus the 0, and then the number you want. For example, to call central London from Egypt, dial 00 44 71, then the number.

● Phone cards are available in some countries; they can be purchased from Post Offices or central telephone offices.

● You start a telephone conversation by greeting your respondent and sending your best wishes to all his/her family. You'll receive similar greetings, to which your response should always be accompanied by *il Hamdoo lilla*, 'thanks be to God'. (See Greetings, page 22.)

You may see

اسعاف	Ambulance
تليفون	Telephone
بوليس	Police
مصلحة التليفونات	Telephone company
مكالمات دوليه	International calls
مكالمات محلية	Local calls
مطافئى	Fire brigade

You may want to say

Is there a telephone?
fi tilifown

Where is the telephone?
fayn itilifown

Can I make a phone call, please?
momkin atkalim fi tilifown min faDlak/faDlik

Do you have change for the telephone?
ªandak (to m)/*ªandik* (to f) *fakka li tilifown*

Do you have a phone card, please?
ªandak/ªandik biTaªa lil tilifown min faDlak/faDlik

Do you have the Cairo telephone directory?
ªandak/ªandik daleel tilifownaet il qahira

I want to call England
ªayiz (m)/*ªayza* (f) *akalim ingilterra*

Hello
allow

Mr Osman, please
ilostaz ªosman min faDlak/faDlik

Extension number 121, please
tawSeela raqam maya waHid wi ªishreen

It's Mrs Howard (speaking)
ana madam howard

It's Stephen (speaking)
ana stefaen

My name is . . .
ismi . . .

When will he/she be back?
Hayergaª/Haterga ª issa ªa kaem

I'll call later
Hakalimak baªdayn (to m)/ *Hakalimik baªdayn* (to f)

Can I leave a message for him/her?
momkin aseeblo/aseeblaha risaela

Please tell him/her that (*your name*) called
o'llo/o'llaha . . . itkalim min faDlak/faDlik

I am in the Hotel Alexandria
ana fi hotayl iskinderayya

My telephone number is . . .
nemrit tilifowni . . .

83

Can he/she call me?
momkin yekalimni/
tekalimni

Can you repeat that, please?
taeni min faDlak/faDlik

Slowly
bishwaysh

We were cut off
il khaT it'aTa[a]

How much is the call?
bikaem il mokalma

You may hear

alow
Hello?

aywa
Yes?/Speaking

meen biyetkalim/bitetkalim
Who's calling?

sanya waHda min faDlak/
faDlik
One moment, please

istanna/istanni min faDlak/
faDlik
Please wait

HawaSalak/HawaSalik
I'm putting you through

il khaT mashghool
The line's engaged

teHib tintaZir/teHibi
tintaZiri
Do you want to hold on?

mafeesh rad
There's no answer

mish mawgood/mawgooda
He/She is not in

innemra ghalaT
You've got the wrong
number

EATING AND DRINKING

● Eating is a major element of social life in the Arab world. It is a means of welcoming friends and relatives, and even of showing off. People are very hospitable and generous even when they can't afford it (and expect reciprocal generosity at a later date).

● Lunch is eaten around two to three o'clock and is usually the main meal of the day. Meat, vegetables, rice and fruit are served. When entertaining, many different dishes are usually offered – and you'll find that, if you're invited to someone's home, you're expected to eat large quantities of everything. Great pride is taken in home-cooked food.

● Is is usual in Arab countries for a variety of appetizers to be served before the main meal. Called *mezza*, they are small plates of hors d'œuvres of all kinds: meats, vegetables, pickles, fish and so on.

● Whether you're eating in a private house or in anywhere but the smartest of restaurants, all the dishes available will be served at once; you just help yourself periodically to whatever you want from the dishes in the middle of the table.

● There are many different types of public eating places throughout the Arab world. Some of these are restaurants that specialize in particular kinds of food, such as charcoal-grilled lamb, fish and seafood, or pigeon. *kafiterya* are snack bars that sell sweets and desserts, and/or fresh fruit drinks, such as sugar cane and mango drinks.

● Some eating places open all day, and some open for lunch and then from 6.00 p.m. till late in the evening.

● The most popular foods for a sit-down or take-away snack are *fool* and *falafel*.

CHANGING MONEY

● The Egyptian unit of currency is the pound, which is made up of 100 piastres. Syria has the lira, also made up of 100 piastres. Jordan, Bahrain, Kuwait have the dinar; Saudi Arabia, Qatar and Oman the riyal; and Morocco and the United Arab Emirates the dirham. (Each country's currency has a different rate of exchange, although the names are the same.)

● Generally speaking, when you arrive anywhere in the Arab world, except the Gulf States, you will have to declare all currency – local or foreign – that you bring in with you, and you should keep all exchange and purchase receipts in case these are checked when you leave to make sure the amounts correspond. Some countries limit or forbid the import or export of the local currency.

● Banking hours vary throughout the region, but banks are usually open between 9.00 a.m. and 1.30 p.m., Saturday to Thursday. However some bank branches remain open until 8.00 p.m., and have an afternoon break between 2.00 p.m. and 4.00 p.m.

It is advisable to check bank opening hours before departure, to avoid being caught out without any money (although big international hotels will often exchange cash or travellers' cheques for you). Banking hours may vary during Ramadan.

● In some countries changing money in banks can be a lengthy, frustrating and even confusing process. You may find it quicker and easier to change money at hotel or travel offices' exchange counters, where possible.

● Dollars are preferred to sterling throughout the Arab world, but you should not experience any problems in using either –

CHANGING MONEY

● The Egyptian unit of currency is the pound, which is made up of 100 piastres. Syria has the lira, also made up of 100 piastres. Jordan, Bahrain, Kuwait have the dinar; Saudi Arabia, Qatar and Oman the riyal; and Morocco and the United Arab Emirates the dirham. (Each country's currency has a different rate of exchange, although the names are the same.)

● Generally speaking, when you arrive anywhere in the Arab world, except the Gulf States, you will have to declare all currency – local or foreign – that you bring in with you, and you should keep all exchange and purchase receipts in case these are checked when you leave to make sure the amounts correspond. Some countries limit or forbid the import or export of the local currency.

● Banking hours vary throughout the region, but banks are usually open between 9.00 a.m. and 1.30 p.m., Saturday to Thursday. However some bank branches remain open until 8.00 p.m., and have an afternoon break between 2.00 p.m. and 4.00 p.m.

It is advisable to check bank opening hours before departure, to avoid being caught out without any money (although big international hotels will often exchange cash or travellers' cheques for you). Banking hours may vary during Ramadan.

● In some countries changing money in banks can be a lengthy, frustrating and even confusing process. You may find it quicker and easier to change money at hotel or travel offices' exchange counters, where possible.

● Dollars are preferred to sterling throughout the Arab world, but you should not experience any problems in using either –

in the form of cash or travellers' cheques. It's often handy to have a small dollar or sterling note in reserve in case you get caught out without any local currency; you may find a shopkeeper who is happy to change it for you at more or less the going rate.

● You can get money with credit cards from some banks and exchange centres, but cash dispensers are not widely used. Large international hotels should accept payment by credit card.

● Apart from banks, there are now official money-changing centres (*maktaeb taHweel ⁿomla*) in Egypt, so don't make any back-street deals on money – this is illegal, and you would probably lose out on the exchange rate in any case.

You may see

بنك	Bank
بيع عملات أجنبيه	Foreign currency sales
خروج	Exit
دخول	Entrance
فاتح	Open
شراء عملات أجنبيه	Foreign currency purchases
شيكات سياحيه	Travellers' cheques
مغلق	Closed
مكتب تحويل عمله	Exchange, Bureau de change
مواعيد العمل	Opening hours

You may want to say

(see Numbers, *inside front cover*)

I'd like to change some
pounds sterling
ayiz (m)/*ayza* (f)
aghaiyyar isterleenee

I'd like to change some
travellers' cheques
*ayiz/*ayza aghaiyyar*
shikaet siyaHaya

I'd like to get some money
with this credit card
*ayiz/*ayza aTalla* filoos*
ala karnay il i'timaen

What's the exchange rate
today?
nesbit il taghyeer 'ad ay
inaharda

Can you give me some
change, please?
momkin tedeenee fakka
min faDlak/faDlik

Can you give me five
twenty-dinar notes?
momkin tedeenee khamas
war'aet bi ishreen dinar*

I'm at the Palace Hotel
ana fi hotayl balas

I'm staying with friends
*ana 'a*id ma*a aS-Haab*

The address is . . .
il enwaen . . .*

You may hear

basborak/basborik
min faDlak/faDlik
Your passport, please

*ayiz tighaiyyar/*ayza*
tighaiyyari 'ad ay
How much do you want to
change?

*enwaenak/*enwaenik*
min faDlak/faDlik
Your address, please?

ism il hotayl min faDlak/
faDlik
The name of your hotel,
please?

imDi hena min faDlak/
faDlik
Sign here, please

roH shibaek iSarf min
faDlak/faDlik
Please go to the cashier

EATING AND DRINKING

● Eating is a major element of social life in the Arab world. It is a means of welcoming friends and relatives, and even of showing off. People are very hospitable and generous even when they can't afford it (and expect reciprocal generosity at a later date).

● Lunch is eaten around two to three o'clock and is usually the main meal of the day. Meat, vegetables, rice and fruit are served. When entertaining, many different dishes are usually offered – and you'll find that, if you're invited to someone's home, you're expected to eat large quantities of everything. Great pride is taken in home-cooked food.

● Is is usual in Arab countries for a variety of appetizers to be served before the main meal. Called *mezza*, they are small plates of hors d'œuvres of all kinds: meats, vegetables, pickles, fish and so on.

● Whether you're eating in a private house or in anywhere but the smartest of restaurants, all the dishes available will be served at once; you just help yourself periodically to whatever you want from the dishes in the middle of the table.

● There are many different types of public eating places throughout the Arab world. Some of these are restaurants that specialize in particular kinds of food, such as charcoal-grilled lamb, fish and seafood, or pigeon. *kafiterya* are snack bars that sell sweets and desserts, and/or fresh fruit drinks, such as sugar cane and mango drinks.

● Some eating places open all day, and some open for lunch and then from 6.00 p.m. till late in the evening.

● The most popular foods for a sit-down or take-away snack are *fool* and *falafel*.

fool is a kind of broad bean that is soaked overnight and boiled. It's served in small bowls or in Arabic bread, with salad and tahini paste.

falafel is made from the same beans, but they are minced and mixed with herbs and garlic, made into small balls, fried, and served with Arabic bread and salad. Another common name for *falafel* is *Ta^amaya*.

● *koshari* (brown lentils mixed with rice, fried onions and chili sauce) is another popular cheap dish. *bamya* (okra), *molokhaya* (a green leaf cooked in rabbit, chicken or meat stock) and stuffed peppers or aubergines (*maHshi*) are also very popular.

● In Egypt and elsewhere in the Arab world there are many coffee houses (*'ahwa*), which are open all day and offer their guests only strong black tea, Turkish coffee and the 'hubbly bubbly' (*sheesha*). Here men meet to chat and play backgammon, cards and dominoes.

● Vegetarians will find they're well catered for since meat-free dishes are part of the regular weekly diet for rich and poor alike in the Arab world.

● There's a great deal of similarity and overlap between Mediterranean food (such as Greek, Italian and Turkish dishes) and Arab food, especially in Egypt, Lebanon, Syria, Morocco, Algeria and Tunisia. Pasta dishes, soups, moussaka, baklava, *kataifi* and *konaefa* are some examples.

● Muslims do not eat pork. In those countries such as Egypt and Lebanon which have sizeable Christian populations, pork is available in some shops.

● A staple part of the Arab diet is bread, of which there are three main kinds: 'Arabic bread' (*^aaysh baladi*) which is made of wheat dough and is flat (like pitta bread); 'foreign' or French bread (*^aaysh fino*); and Lebanese bread (*^aaysh shami*) which is also like pitta bread but is thicker.

• Tea and coffee are drunk extensively in the Arab world. Tea (*shay*) is brewed until it is black and is served very sweet, either plain or with mint (*bine^ana^a*), milk (*bilaban*), or with a variety of roots and spices such as ginger, caraway or cinnamon. If you want it without sugar, ask for *shay saeda*. English-style tea may be found in 4- and 5-star hotels and restaurants.

• The thick black Turkish coffee is served in small cups and saucers; be sure not to stir it once it arrives, or you will end up with a mouthful of grains! It comes ready-sugared (if you want it that way) and will automatically be made extremely sweet unless you ask for it the way you like it: *'ahwa saeda* – without sugar; *'ahwa ^aalal reeHa* – with very little sugar; *'ahwa mazbooT* – medium sweet; *'ahwa ziyaeda* – very sweet. Instant coffee (*neskafay*) is also available but is not widely drunk in most Arab countries.

• Alcohol is prohibited by Islam and is usually not available in shops in Muslim countries. In practice, attitudes towards alcohol vary considerably: in Saudi Arabia, the sale or public consumption of alcohol is severely punished; in other countries such as Egypt, Morocco and Jordan – where there are sizeable populations of non-Muslims – it's not so frowned upon. In most Arab countries you'll find alcoholic beverages in 4- and 5-star hotels, nightclubs and duty-free shops. In some countries it is also available in some grocery stores and restaurants.

• Juice bars are very popular throughout the Arab world. They have a wide range of fruits to choose from, and the juice is freshly squeezed while you wait.

You may see

أخدم نفسك	Self-service
بار	Bar
تواليت	Toilets, cloakroom
حلويات شاميه	Lebanese and Syrian sweets
سماك	Fish and seafood restaurant
قائمة السياح	Tourist menu
قهوه	Coffee shop
كافيتيريا	Café (or similar)
كبابجي	Charcoal-grilled lamb
محل أيس كريم	Ice-cream parlour
محل عصير	Juice bar
مطعم	Restaurant
مطعم ساندوتشات	Sandwich bar
مطعم فول و فلافل	Fool and falafel restaurant
مطعم كشرى	Koshari restaurant
نقبل كروت الأثمان	We accept credit cards

91

You may want to say

Are there any inexpensive
   restaurants around here?
fi maTaªim rekheeSa hena

One . . . please
*waHid . . . min faDlak/
   faDlik*

Another/More . . .
   . . . *kamaen*

A little more, please
*showaya kamaen
   min faDlak/faDlik*

A little less
a'al showaya

For me
ªashaeni

For him
ªashano

For her
ashanha

For them
ashanhom

For the baby
alashaen il baybi

This, please
da min faDlak/faDlik

Two of these, please
itnayn . . . min faDlak/faDlik

Do you have . . .?
andak (to m)/*andik* (to f) . . .

What do you have to eat?
andak/andik ay lil akl

What do you have for dessert?
andak/andik ay lil Helw

Is/Are there any . . .?
fi . . .

What do you recommend?
tinsaH bi ay

Do you have any typical local dishes?
*andak/andik aTba' sha*baya*

What is this?
ay da

How do you eat this?
bitaeklo da izay

Cheers!
fi seHetak (to m)/
fi seHetik (to f)/
fi seHetkom (to group)

Enjoy your meal!
bilhana wishefa

Thank you, same to you
shokran winto kamaen

Nothing else, thanks
il Hamdoo lilla shokran

The bill, please
il fatoora min faDlak/faDlik

Where are the toilets?
fayn itowalit

Bars and cafés

A coffee, please
'ahwa min faDlak/faDlik

A white coffee, please
'ahwa bilaban min faDlak/faDlik

Two Turkish coffees, please
itnayn 'ahwa torki min faDlak/faDlik

With sugar
bil sokkar

Without sugar
saeda

A mint tea
shay bineᵃnaᵃ

A hot chocolate
kakaw

Mineral water
maiya maᵃdanaya

Fizzy water
maiya fawaara

Still water
maiya ᵃada

A fizzy orange
ᵃaSeer borto'an fawar

What fruit juices do you have?
ᵃandak/ᵃandik ᵃaSeer ay

A mango juice, please
ᵃaSeer manga min faDlak/faDlik

A milk-shake
milk shayk

A beer/Two beers
beera/itnayn beera

A glass of (local) red wine
kaes nebeet aHmar (maHaeli)

A gin and tonic
jin wi tonik

With ice
bil talg

A cake
kayka

Some mezza, please
mezza min faDlak/faDlik

A toasted sandwich, please
sandawich towst min faDlak/faDlik

What rolls do you have?
ᵃandak/ᵃandik sandawichaet ay

A chicken roll, please
sandawich firaekh min faDlak/faDlik

Two (white) cheese rolls, please
itnayn sandawich gebna (bayDa) min faDlak/faDlik

Two falafel sandwiches, please
itnayn sandawich falafel min faDlak/faDlik

Do you have ice-creams?
ᵃandak/ᵃandik 'ays kreem

Chocolate, coffee and banana, please
kakaw 'ahwa wi mowz min faDlak/faDlik

A little of . . .
showayit . . .

93

Booking a table

I want to reserve a table for two people
^aayiz (m)/*^aayza* (f) *aHgiz tarabayza linafarayn*

For nine o'clock
issa^aa tes^aa

For tomorrow at half past eight
bokra issa^aa tamanya wi noS

I have booked a table
Hagazt tarabayza

My name is . . .
ismi . . .

In restaurants

A table for four, please
tarabayza li arba^aa tinfar min faDlak/faDlik

Outside/On the terrace, if possible
fil tiras law samaHt

Excuse me! *(to call the waiter/waitress)*
^aan iznak/iznik

The menu, please
il menyoo min faDlak/faDlik

The wine list, please
listit inebeet min faDlak/faDlik

Do you have a set price menu?
^aandak/^aandik menyoo bilistit il as^aar

Do you have vegetarian dishes?
^aandak/^aandik aTbaa' nabataya

The tourist menu (at 12 pounds), please
menyoo isoyaH (bi itnashar ginay) min faDlak/faDlik

For the starter . . .
lil aperateef . . .

Kofta, please
kofta min faDlak/faDlik

Tuna and olives, please
*toona wi zatoon
min faDlak/faDlik*

For the first course . . .
lil kors il awalaeni . . .

The fish soup, please
*shorbit issamak
min faDlak/faDlik*

Kebab, please
kabaeb min faDlak/faDlik

For the second course . . .
lil kors itaeni . . .

The roast chicken, please
*firaekh fil forn min faDlak/
faDlik*

The okra, please
il bamya min faDlak/faDlik

Are vegetables included?
bil khoDar

With rice
bil roz

With chips
bil baTaaTis il miHammar

And a mixed/green salad
wi SalaTit khoDar

For dessert . . .
lil Helw . . .

Semolina cake, please
*basboosa min faDlak/
faDlik*

Baklava, please
baqlaewa min faDlak/faDlik

A peach, please
khowkha min faDlak/faDlik

What cheeses are there?
*ªandak/ªandik geban
nowª ay*

Excuse me, where is the
moussaka?
*law samaHt fayn Talab il
misa'aªa*

More bread, please
*ªaysh kamaen min faDlak/
faDlik*

More chips, please
*baTaaTis miHammar
kamaen min faDlak/
faDlik*

A bottle of red wine
izaezit nebeet aHmar

A litre of white wine
litr nebeet abyaD

Half a litre of red wine
noS litr nebeet aHmar

*(for ordering coffee, see
page 90)*

It's very good
Helw 'awi

It's really delicious
lazeez 'awi

This is burnt
da maHroo'

This is not cooked
da mish maTbookh

No, I ordered the chicken
la'a ana Talabt il firaekh

The bill, please
il fatoora min faDlak/faDlik

Do you accept credit cards?
bite'bal karnay i'timaen

Can I pay with travellers' cheques?
momkin adfaᵃ bi shikaet siyaHaya

Excuse me, the bill is wrong
law samaHt fi ghalaT fil fatoora

You may hear

Bars and cafés

ay khedma
Can I help you?

teHib taekol ay/teHibi taekli ay
What would you like to eat?

teHib tishrab ay/teHibi tishrabi ay
What would you like to drink?

teHib/teHibi talg
Would you like ice?

fawar walla ᵃaedi
Fizzy or still?

HaDir
Right away

ᵃandena . . .
We have . . .

. . . Helw 'awi inaharda
The . . . is very delicious today

Tabbakhna biyeᵃmil . . . lazeez/lazeeza 'awi
Our chef makes very tasty . . .

Restaurants

kaem nafar
How many are you?

likaem nafar
For how many people?

*laHza waHda min faDlak/
faDlik*
Just a moment, please

teHib/teHibi ay
What would you like?

lil aperateef
For the starter

lil kors il awalaeni
For the first course

lil kors itaeni
For the second course

*teHib tishrab ay/teHibi
tishrabi ay*
What would you like to
drink?

meen Talab . . .
Who is the . . . for?

*teHib/teHibi Helw walla
'ahwa*
Would you like dessert, or
coffee?

teHib/teHibi likayr
Would you like a liqueur?

khedma tanya
Anything else?

MENU READER

All the words and phrases below are listed in Arabic alphabetical order.

General phrases

Hors d'œuvres	*aperateef*	أبراتيف
Breakfast	*ifTaar*	إفطار
Egg dishes	*aTbaq bayD*	أطباق بيض
À la carte	*a la kart*	الا كارت
Main courses	*il akla il ra'isaya*	الأكله الرئيسيه
Service included	*il khedma maDmoona fil Hissaeb*	الخدمه مضمونه فى الحساب
Tax included	*il Dareeba maDmoona fil Hissaeb*	الضريبه مضمونه فى الحساب
First courses	*il Talab il awil*	الطلب الأول
Second courses	*il Talab il taeni*	الطلب الثانى
Cheeses	*geban*	جبن
Desserts	*Halawayaet*	حلاويات
Vegetables	*khoDar*	خضار
Poultry	*dawaegin*	دواجن
Fish	*samak*	سمك
Snacks	*snak*	سناك

Salads	salaTaat	سلطات
Soups	shorba	شوربه
Dinner	ᵃasha	عشاء
Lunch	ghada'	غداء
Hors d'œuvres	faetiH lil shahaya	فاتح للشهيه
Fruit	fak-ha	فاكهه
Price list	qa'imit il asᵃaar	قائمةالأسعار
Tourist menu	qa'imit il Taᵃaam lil soyaH	قائمةالطعام للسياح
Menu of the day	qa'imit il yowm	قائمة اليوم
Coffees and teas	'ahwa wi shay	قهوه و شاى
Meat	laHm	لحم
Drinks	mashroobaet	مشروبات
Soft drinks	mashroobaet khafeefa	مشروبات خفيفه
Alcoholic drinks	mashroobaet koHoolaya	مشروبات كحولية
Alcoholic drinks	mashroobaet roHaya	مشروبات روحية
Wines	nebeet	نبيت

99

Soups

Vegetables, garlic and meat broth	molokhaya	ملوخيه
Pea soup	shorbit bisilla	شوربة بسله
Onion soup	shorbit baSal	شوربة بصل

Vegetable soup	*shorbit khoDar*	شوربة خضار
Fish soup	*shorbit samak*	شوربة سمك
Noodle soup	*shorba bil shi^araya*	شوربة بالشعريه
Tomato soup	*shorbit TamaTim*	شوربة طماطم
Lentil soup	*shorbit ^aads*	شوربة عدس
Chicken soup	*shorbit firaekh*	شوربة فراخ
Meat soup	*shorbit laHm*	شوربة لحم

Main meat and poultry dishes

Cutlet	*iskalob*	إسكالوب
Beefsteak	*boftaek*	بوفتيك
Pigeon	*Hamaem*	حمام
Stuffed pigeon	*Hamaem maHshi*	حمام محشى
Grilled pigeon	*Hamaem mashwi*	حمام مشوى
Turkey	*deek roomi*	ديك رومى
Roast beef	*rozbeef*	روز بيف
Lamb chops	*riyash*	ريش
Spicy sausages	*sogo'*	سجق
Strips of meat cooked on spit	*shawarma*	شاورمه
Chicken	*firaekh*	فراخ
Fillet	*filetto*	فيليتو
Chicken	*faerkha*	فرخه
Barbecued meat	*kebaeb*	كباب
Liver	*kibda*	كبده
Kidney	*kalaewi*	كلاوى

Meatballs with cracked wheat	*kobaeba*	كبيبه
Meatballs	**kofta**	كفته
Chops	**kostalaeta**	كستليته
Chicken broth and yoghurt	**kishk**	كشك
Meat	**laHm**	لحم
Veal	**laHm bitillo**	لحم بتلو
Lamb	**laHm Daani**	لحم ضاني
Camel	**laHm gamali**	لحم جلي
Beef	**laHm kandooz**	لحم كندوز
Minced meat	**laHm mafroom**	لحم مفروم
Stuffed	**maHshi**	محشى
Grilled	**mashwi**	مشوى
Meat and aubergines	**ma'looba**	مقلوبه
Moussaka	*misa'a^aa*	مسقعه
Vegetables, garlic and rabbit, chicken or beef broth	**molokhaya**	ملوخية
Shank, knuckle	**mowza**	موزه

Fish

Prawns	**gambari**	جمبرى
Oysters	**gaendofli**	جندوفلى
Fish	**samak**	سمك

Fish braised with onion, served with rice	*samak Sayadiyya*	سمك صياديه
Sole	*samak moosa*	سمك موسى
Nile perch	*qishr bayaD*	قشر بياض
Crab	*kaborya*	كابوريا
Charcoal-grilled chunks of fish	*kebaeb samak*	كباب سمك
Deep-fried fish balls	*koftit samak*	كفته سمك
Lobster	*kaeraekaend*	كبركند
Red mullet	*morgaen*	مرجان

Egg dishes

Eggs	*bayD*	بيض
Egg with pastoorma (beef cured with spices and garlic)	*bayD bil basToorma*	بيض بالبسطرمه
Egg mayonnaise	*bayD bil mayonayz*	بيض بالمايونيز
Hard boiled eggs, rice and tomato sauce	*shaekshooka*	شكشوكه
Omelette (thick)	*ªaegga*	عجه
Cheese omelette	*ªaegga bil gebna*	عجه بالجبنه
Omelette with mince	*ªaegga bil laHma*	عجه باللحمه

Vegetables, pulses and cereals

Asparagus	*asparagas*	أسباراجاس
Okra	*bamya*	باميه
Aubergine	*bitingaen*	بازنجان
Cracked wheat	*borghol*	برغل
Peas	*bisilla*	بسله
Onions	*baSal*	بصل
Potatoes	*baTaTis*	بطاطس
Beetroot	*bangar*	بنجر
Garlic	*towm*	ثوم
Watercress	*gargeer*	جرجير
Carrots	*gazar*	جزر
Chickpeas	*Homoos*	حمص
Artichokes	*kharshoof*	خرشوف
Rice	*roz*	ارز
Leeks	*koraat*	كرات
Lettuce	*khas*	خس
Cucumber	*khiyaar*	خيار
(Sweet)corn	*dora*	ذره
Olives	*zatoon*	زيتون
Spinach	*sabaenikh*	سبانخ
Pickled vegetables	*Torshi*	طرشى
Tomatoes	*TamaTim*	طماطم
Beans (pulses)	*faSolya*	فاصوليا
French (green) beans	*faSolya khaDra*	فاصوليا خضراء
Radishes	*figl*	فجل
Green peppers	*filfil akhDar*	فلفل أخضر

Pimento	*filfil Haemi*	فلفل حامى
Beans (brown)	*fool*	فول
Cauliflower	*'arnabeeT*	قرنبيط
Cabbage	*koronb*	كرنب
Celery	*karafs*	كرفس
Marrow/courgettes	*kowsa*	كوسه
Cracked wheat	*koskosi*	كسكسى
Lentils, rice and pasta	*koshari*	كشرى
Turnips	*lift*	لفت
Beans in tomato sauce (chilled)	*lobya bil zayt* (*mosalagga*)	لوبيا بالزيت (مثلجه)
Stuffed vegetables	*maHshi khoDar*	محشى
Vine leaves	*wara' ªinaeb*	ورق عنب

Salads

Salad	*salaTa*	سلطه
Egyptian salad	*salaTa baladi*	سلطه بلدى
Potato salad	*salaTit baTaTis*	سلطة بطاطس
Egg salad	*salaTit bayD*	سلطة بيض
Yoghurt, cucumber, mint and garlic salad	*salaTit zaebaedee*	سلطة زبادى
Mixed salad	*salaTa khaDra*	سلطه خضراء
Cucumber salad	*salaTit khiyaar*	سلطه خيار
Tomato salad	*salaTit TamaTim*	سلطه طماطم
Celery salad	*salaTit karafs*	سلطة كرفس
Cracked wheat salad	*taboola*	تبولة

Desserts

English	Transliteration	Arabic
Raisin cake with warm milk	*om ªali*	أم على
Ice cream	*ays kreem*	أيس كريم
Semolina cake	*basboosa*	بسبوسه
Nuts, raisins, wheat and milk	*bileela*	بليله
Flaky pastry with nuts (baklava)	*baqlaewa*	بقلاوه
Pastries dipped in rose water	*zalabiya*	زلابية
Shredded flaky pastry with nuts and honey	*konaefa*	كنافه
Pastry filled with nuts	*aTayif*	قطايف
Turkish delight	*malban*	ملبن
Rice or cornflour pudding	*mahalabaya*	مهلبيه

Cheeses

English	Transliteration	Arabic
White cheese	**gebna bayDa**	جبنه بيضاء
Cottage cheese	**gebna rikotta**	جبنه روكته
Hard cheese	**gebna roomi**	جبنه رومى
Thick, creamy cheese	**gebna qaerish**	جبنه قريش
Salted curd cheese	**gebna malHa**	جبنه مالحه

Goat's milk cheese	*gebna min laban almi^aeez*	جبنه من لبن المعيز
Curd cheese with olive oil	*labna*	لبنه
Hard, salty, mature cheese	*mish*	مش

Fruit

Pineapple	*ananaes*	أناناس
Oranges	*bortoqan*	برتقال
Plums	*baerqooq*	برقوق
Watermelon	*baTikh*	بطيخ
Dates	*balaH*	بلح
Apples	*toffaeH*	تفاح
Figs	*teen*	تين
Guava	*gawaefa*	جوافه
Peaches	*khowkh*	خوخ
Pomegranates	*rommaan*	رمان
Raisins	*zibeeb*	زبيب
Melon	*shammaem*	شمام
Grapes	*^ainaeb*	عنب
Strawberries	*firawla*	فراوله
Cherries	*kerayz*	كريز
Pears	*kommitra*	كمثرى
Lemons/Limes	*lamoon*	ليمون
Apricots	*mishmish*	مشمش
Mangoes	*manga*	مانجه

| Bananas | *mowz* | موز |
| Tangerines | *yostafaendi* | يوسف افندى |

Miscellaneous

Parsley	*baqdoonis*	بقدونس
Eggs	*bayD*	بيض
Garlic	*towm*	ثوم
Cheese	*gebna*	جبنه
Nutmeg	*gowzit iTeeb*	جوزةالطيب
Cardamon	*Habahaen*	حبهان
Mixed herbs	*khalTit a ªshaeb*	خلطة أعشاب
Basil	*reeHaen*	ريحان
Thyme	*za ªtar*	زعتر
Yoghurt	*zabaedi*	زبادى
Butter	*zebda*	زبده
Olive oil	*zayt zatoon*	زيت زيتون
Sesame seed	*semsem*	سمسم
Sugar	*sokkar*	سكر
Hot chilli	*shaTa*	شطة
Honey	*ªasal*	عسل
Bread	*ªaysh*	عيش
'Arabic' bread	*ªaysh baladi*	عيش بلدى
'French' bread	*ªaysh fino*	عيش فينو
'Lebanese' bread	*ªaysh shami*	عيش شامى
Spice	*ªoToor*	عطور
Pepper	*filfil*	فلفل
Sweet pepper	*filfil Helw*	فلفل حلو

Peanuts	*fool soodaeni*	فول سوداني
Cinnamon	*qerfa*	قرفة
Clove	*qoronfil*	قرنفل
Curry	*kary*	كاري
Cream	*kraym*	كريم
Coriander	*kozbara*	كزبره
Cumin	*kamoon*	كمون
Watermelon seeds	*leb*	لب
Jam	*mirabba*	مربى
Salt	*malH*	ملح
Rose water	*maiyit zahr*	ماء الزهر
Flower water	*maiyit ward*	ماء الورد
Mint	*ne^ana^a*	نعناع

Methods of cooking

Steamed	*bil bokhaar*	بالبخار
In sauce	*bil SalSa*	بالصلصه
Baked	*fil forn*	في الفرن
Marinated	*mitaebil*	متبل
Stuffed	*maHshi*	محشي
Chopped	*mikharraT*	مخرط
Smoked	*modaekhkhaen*	مدخن
Roasted	*rosto*	روستو
Braised	*misaebbik*	مسبك
Boiled, poached	*maeslooq*	مسلوق
Grilled	*mashwi*	مشوى

Barbecued	*mashwi ᵃalal faHm*	مشوى على الفحم
Creamed	*maDroob*	مضروب
Minced	*mafroom*	مفروم
Fried	*maqli*	مقلى
Cured	*mimaellaH*	مملح

Drinks

Brandy	*brandi*	براندى
Beer	*beera*	بيره
in a can	*fi ᵃelba*	فى علبه
bottled	*fi zogaega*	فى زجاجه
Flask	*tormos*	ترمس
Gin and tonic	*jin bi maiyit itonik*	جن بالماء التونيك
Sweet	*Helw*	حلو
Dry	*dray*	دراى
Herb drink	*kharoob*	خروب
In the bottle	*fi zogaega*	فى زجاجه
Tea	*shay*	شاى
Herb tea	*shay aᵃshaeb*	شاى أعشاب
Camomile tea	*shay bil sheeH*	شاى بالشيح
Tea with milk	*shay bil laban*	شاى باللبن
Tea with lemon	*shay bil lamoon*	شاى بالليمون
Mint tea	*shay bil neᵃnaᵃ*	شاى بالنعناع
Iced tea	*shay mosalag*	شاى مثلج
Still	*ᵃada*	عاده

Arak	*arak*	عرق
(Fresh) fruit juice	*aSeer fawakih (Taza)*	عصير فواكه (طازه)
Pineapple juice	*aSeer ananaes*	عصير اناناس
Orange juice	*aSeer borto'an*	عصير برتقال
Tamarind juice	*aSeer tamrhindi*	عصير تمرهندي
Grapefruit juice	*aSeer grebfroot*	عصير جريب فروت
Sugar cane juice	*aSeer qaSab*	عصير قصب
Lemon juice	*aSeer lamoon*	عصير ليمون
Apricot juice	*aSeer mishmish*	عصير مشمش
Mango juice	*aSeer manga*	عصير منجه
Banana juice	*aSeer mowz*	عصير موز
Sparkling, fizzy	*fawaar*	فوار
Fizzy soft drinks	*mashroobaet fawaara*	مشروبات فواره
Fizzy orange	*borto'al fawaar*	برتقال فوار
Fizzy lemon	*lamoon fawaar*	ليمون فوار
Vodka	*vodka*	ڤودكا
Coffee	*'ahwa*	قهوه
coffee with milk	*'ahwa bil laban*	قهوه باللبن
long black coffee, less strong than traditional Turkish coffee	*'ahwa khafeefa*	قهوه خفيفه
without sugar	*'ahwa saeda*	قهوه ساده
medium-sweet	*'ahwa mazboot*	قهوه مظبوط

very sweet	'ahwa ziyaeda	قهوه زياده
iced coffee	'ahwa mosalagga	قهوه مثلجه
instant coffee	'ahwa neskafay	قهوه نسكافيه
Hot chocolate	kakaw	كاكاو
Glass	koob	كوب
Coca cola	koka kola	كوكا كولا
Milk	laban	لبن
Liqueurs	likayr	ليكير
almond liqueur	likayr lowz	ليكير اللوز
Lemonade	limonada	ليموناده
Martini	marteenee	مارتينى
Soft drinks	mashroobaet khafeefa	مشروبات خفيفه
Water	maiya	مياه
tonic water	maiya il tonik	مياه التونيك
soda water	maiya il Sowda	مياه الصودا
mineral water	maiya maᵃdanaya	مياه معدنيه
Milk shake	milk shayk	ملك شيك
Wines	nebeet	نبيت
white (wine)	(nebeet) abyaD	(نبيت) ابيض
red (wine)	(nebeet) aHmar	(نبيت) أحمر
sparkling (wine)	(nebeet) fawaar	(نبيت) فوار
rosé (wine)	(nebeet) rozay	(نبيت) روزاى
table (wine)	(nebeet) sofra	(نبيت) سفره
Whisky	wiski	ويسكى

SHOPPING

● You'll probably do most of your shopping in small shops, bazaars *(sooq)*, open markets, from street merchants and a few supermarkets.

● In general shops are likely to be open from 9.00 a.m. until 10.00 p.m. Some close during the afternoon between 3.00 and 6.00 p.m., especially during the hotter months. They are closed one day a week, either Friday or Sunday, depending on whether the proprietor is Muslim or Christian. Opening times may be different during Ramadan.

● In most countries in the Arab world, you can buy stamps at post offices, from anywhere that sells postcards, from general stores *(khordawaeti)*, or from street corner kiosks. The style of postboxes varies from country to country: you may need to ask where your local postbox is. Alternatively mail can be posted at post offices and major hotels.

● Fruit and vegetables can be bought from small shops, or from market stalls. You will also find individuals – usually on street corners – who will sell you one or more particular type of vegetable out of a basket. If you buy from them or from markets you will have to haggle over the prices. As a rough guide, start off by offering half the asking price.

● You will also come across markets, called *sooq*, *bazaar* or *kasba*, throughout the region. They sell a variety of goods, from clothes, jewellery, antiques, artefacts and souvenirs to fruit and vegetables.

● In Arab countries it's essential to be prepared to haggle over the price of purchases. Traders aim to get as high a price as possible for their goods – and they also see bargaining as something of a game, which both sides should join in and enjoy.

If you don't participate, you'll end up paying much more than you should.

The main rule of haggling is to keep your sense of humour and smile at all times. All tactics may be employed to disarm your 'opponent', such as: flattery (of the person/their country), emotional blackmail, expressions of horror and disappointment, feigned departure, and so on. You may also be able to improve your side of the deal by asking for a similar item with a better standard of finish, asking for another small item to be included in the price, or even just by walking away shaking your head. You can always come back later, if they don't come after you.

● Kiosks selling local and foreign cigarettes, films, postcards, newspapers, sweets and soft drinks are found all over the towns and cities of the Arab world. They open all hours and often, in the bigger cities, the proprietors speak English.

● Always be prepared to pay for your purchases in cash. Travellers' cheques may be acceptable in bazaar shops selling tourist goods. Cheques and credit cards are not widely used outside hotels, railway stations, travel agents and airports.

● A *makwagi* is someone who irons your clean clothes for you. Their small shops are found all over town. Neither dry cleaners nor launderettes are common in the Arab world.

● When you go shopping, make sure you take a bag for your purchases; few shops or stalls provide them.

You may see

أجزجى	Duty chemist
اجزاخانه	Pharmacy
أخدم نفسك	Self-service

أدوات كهربائيه	Electrical goods
اسطوانات كاسيت	Records, cassettes
الدور الأول	First floor
الدور الثانى	Second floor
الدور الثالث	Third floor
الدور الرابع	Fourth floor
انتيكات	Antiques
اوكازيون	Sales
بدرون	Basement
بقاله	Grocer's
بائع الورد	Florist's
بائع السجاير	Tobacconist's
تخفيضات	Reductions
جزاره	Butcher's
جواهرجى	Jeweller's
حداد	Ironmonger's
خباز	Baker's
خرداواتى	Stationer's
خروج (طوارئ)	(Emergency) exit
خضرى	Greengrocer's
ساعاتى	Watchmaker's
سعر القطعه	Retail price
سماك	Fishmonger's
سمك	Fish
سوبر ماركت	Supermarket
سوق	Shopping centre
صراف	Cashier
صندوق بريد	Postbox
طوابع	Stamps on sale

عرض خاص	Special offer
عطور	Perfumery
فاتح	Open
فكهانى	Fruiterer's
كوافير	Hairdresser's
لبان	Dairy
مأكولات صحيه	Health foods
مشروبات روحيه	Off-licence
مصنوعات جلديه	Leather goods
مغلق	Closed
مكتب بريد	Post Office
مكتبه	Bookshop
ملابس	Clothes
منتجات رياضيه	Sports goods
موبيليا	Furniture
نظاراتى	Optician
هدايا	Gifts
هدايا تذكارية	Souvenirs

You may want to say

General phrases

(*see also* Directions, *page 33*; Problems and complaints, *page 151*; Numbers, *inside front cover*)

Where is the main shopping area?
fayn il soo'

Where is the pharmacy?
fayn il agzakhaena

Is there a grocer's shop around here?
fi ba'ael hena

Where can I buy batteries?
ayiz (m)/*ayza* (f) *ashteri baTarayaet*

What time does the baker's open?
il khabaez biyeftaH issaa kaem

What time does the post office close?
il bosTa bite'fil issaa kaem

What time do you open in the morning?
bitiftaHoo issaa kaem iSobH

What time do you close in the afternoon?
biti'filo issaa kaem bad iDohr

What time do you re-open?
bitiftaHoo issaa kaem

What time do you close in the evening?
biti'filo issaa kaem bilayl

Do you have . . .?
andak (to m)/
andik (to f) . . .

Do you have stamps?
andak/andik Tawaabi

Do you have any halva?
andak/andik Halaewa

How much is it?
bikaem

How much is this?
bikaem da

How much are these?
bikaem dowl

I don't understand
mish fahim (m)/*mish fahma* (f)

Can you write it down (here) please?
momkin tiktibha (hena) min faDlak/faDlik

It's too expensive
da ghaeli 'awi

Have you got anything cheaper?
andak/andik Haga arkhaS

I don't have enough money
maandeesh filoos kifaya

That's still too much
la' da kiteer 'awi

It's cheaper over there
isser arkhaS hinaek

I won't give you more than . . .
Hadilak/Hadilik . . . aekhir kalaem

I will give you two pounds only
Hadilak/Hadilik itnayn ginay bas

Is this your best price?
aekhir kalaem

It's a deal
itafa'na

Can you keep it for me?
momkin teHgizhaeli

I'm just looking
ana bas bakhod fekra

That one, please
da min faDlak/faDlik

Two, please
itnayn min faDlak/faDlik

Three, please
talaeta min faDlak/faDlik

Not that one – this one
mish da – da

There's one in the window
fi waHid fil vatreena

That's fine
kwayyis

Nothing else, thank you
bas keda shokran

I'll take it
Hashteree

I'll think about it
Hafakkar showaya

Do you have a plastic bag, please?
ªandak/ªandik shanTa blastik min faDlak/faDlik

Can you wrap it, please?
momkin tilefhaeli min faDlak/faDlik

With plenty of paper
bi wara' kiteer

I'm taking it to England
Hakhdoo ingilterra

It's a gift
hidaya

Where is the cashier?
fayn iSaraaf

Do you take credit cards?
bitakhod karnay i'timaen

Do you take travellers' cheques?
bitakhod shikaet siyaHaya

I'm sorry, I don't have any change
aesif (m)/*asfa* (f)
maªandeesh fakka

Can you give me a receipt, please?
iddeenee waSl min faDlak/faDlik

Buying food and drink

A kilo of . . .
keeloo . . .

A kilo of grapes, please
*keeloo ªenab min faDlak/
faDlik*

Two kilos of oranges, please
*itnayn keeloo borto'an
min faDlak/faDlik*

Half a kilo of tomatoes,
please
*noSikeeloo TamaTim
min faDlak/faDlik*

A hundred grams of . . .
meet graam . . .

A hundred grams of white
cheese, please
*meet graam gebna bayDa
min faDlak/faDlik*

Two hundred grams of
olives, please
*meetayn graam zatoon
min faDlak/faDlik*

A piece of cheese, please
*Hetit gebna min faDlak/
faDlik*

Five slices of corned beef,
please
*khamas transhaat bolobeef
min faDlak/faDlik*

A bottle of mineral water,
please
*izaezit maiya maªdanaya
min faDlak/faDlik*

Fizzy water
maiya fawaara

A (small) carton of milk,
please
*kartownit laban (Soghayara)
min faDlak/faDlik*

Two cans of beer, please
*ªelbitayn beera min faDlak/
faDlik*

A bit of that, please
*Hetta min da min faDlak/
faDlik*

A bit more
kamaen Hetta

A bit less
Hetta a'al

What is this?
ay da

What's in this?
da fi ay

Can I try it?
momkin adoo'

At the chemist's

Aspirins, please
asbireen min faDlak/faDlik

Plasters, please
blaster min faDlak/faDlik

Do you have something
for . . .?
ªandak (to m)/*ªandik*
(to f) *dawa li . . .*

Do you have something for
diarrhoea?
*ªandak/ªandik dawa lil
is-hael*

Do you have something for
mosquito bites?
*ªandak/ªandik dawa Ded
ªaDit ibaªooD*

Do you have something for
period pains?
*ªandak/ªandik dawa lil
ªaeda ishahraya*

Buying clothes and shoes

I want a skirt
ªayiz (m)/*ªayza* (f) *gonella*

I want a shirt
ªayiz/ªayza 'amees

I want some sandals
ªayiz/ªayza Sandal

Size 40
ma'aaes arbiªeen

Can I try it on?
momkin 'a' eesoo

Do you have a mirror?
fi miraya

I like it
ªagibni

I like them
ªagbinni

I don't like it
mish ªagibni

I don't like them
mish ªagbinni

I don't like the colour
ilown mish ªagibni

Do you have it in other
colours?
*ªandak/ªandik 'alwaen
tanya*

It's too big
kibeer 'awi

Have you got a smaller size?
*ªandak/ªandik m'aaes
aSghar*

It's too small
Soghayar 'awi

Have you got a bigger size?
*ªandak/ªandik m'aaes
akbar*

They're too big
kobar 'awi

They're too small
Soghayareen 'awi

Miscellaneous

Five stamps for England,
  please
*khamas Tawaabiª lingilterra
  min faDlak/faDlik*

A box of matches, please
*ªelbit kabreet min faDlak/
  faDlik*

A film like this, please
*film zay da min faDlak/
  faDlik*

For postcards
li koroot bosTa

For letters
li gawabaet

A film for this camera
film lil kamira di

Three postcards, please
*talat koroot bosTa
  min faDlak/faDlik*

Do you have any English
newspapers?
*ªandak/ªandik garayid
  ingleezi*

You may hear

ay khedma
May I help you?

'ad ay
How much would you like?

teHib/teHibi ay
What would you like?

kaem waHid/waHda
How many would you like?

tamaem
Is that all right?

ay khedma tanya
Anything else?

aesif/asfa khaeliS
I'm sorry, we're sold out

aesif/asfa iHna 'afleen
I'm sorry, we're closed now

HaniftaH (taeni) kamaen
robᵃ saᵃa
We (re-)open in fifteen
minutes

teHib alifo/alifaha lak (to m)
teHibi alifo/alifaha lik (to f)
Do you want me to wrap it
for you?

idfaᵃ ᵃand iSaraaf
min faDlak/faDlik
Please go to the cashier

ᵃandak/ᵃandik fakka
Do you have any change?

inta miHtaeg/inti
miHtaega roshetta
You need a prescription

m'aaesak/m'aaesik kaem
What size are you?

kart bosTa walla gawaeb
For postcard or letter?

. . . nowᵃ/noᵃha ay
What sort of . . .?

il kamira noᵃha ay
What sort of camera do
you have?

ᵃayiz/ᵃayza anhi nowᵃ film
What sort of film do you
want?

da bi khamsa ginay bas
This is for five pounds only

ᵃashaenak/ᵃashaenik
arbaᵃa ginay bas
For you, it's only four
pounds

la'a mish momkin
No, that's not possible

121

BUSINESS TRIPS

● Business hours in the Arab world are roughly from 7.30 a.m. until 2.30 p.m.; businesses are closed on Fridays and sometimes Sundays.

● The public sector keeps the same hours, but offices may also be closed on Saturdays.

● You'll probably be doing business with the help of interpreters or in a language everyone speaks, but you may need a few Arabic phrases to cope at a company's reception desk.

● When you arrive for an appointment, all you need do is say who you've come to see and give your name or hand over your business card. However, if you're not expected you may need to make an appointment or leave a message.

● Generally speaking, once you have met a business contact you will address them by their job title, plus first name, e.g. *doktowr ahmad* (Doctor Ahmed), *mohandis awad* (Engineer Awad), *ostaeza fawzaya* (Professor Fawzaya).

You may see

استعلامات	Information
استقبال	Reception
البدرون	Basement
الدورالأرضى	Ground floor
الدورالأول	First floor
الدورالثانى	Second floor
الدورالثالث	Third floor
الدورالرابع	Fourth floor

خروج (طوارئ)	(Emergency) exit
سلم	Stairs
شركه محدوده	Limited liability company
عاطل	Out of order
مدخل	Entrance
مصعد	Lift
ممنوع التدخين	No smoking
ممنوع الدخول	No entry
ممنوع الدخول لغيرالمسموح لهم	No entry to unauthorised persons

You may want to say

(see also Days, months, dates, page 168; Time, page 172)

Mr Ibrahim, please
*isayid ibraheem
min faDlak/faDlik*

Mrs Fathaya, please
*isayida fatHaya
min faDlak/faDlik*

Miss Fatima Mubarak,
please
*il'aenisa fatma moobarak
min faDlak/faDlik*

The manager, please
*il modeer min faDlak/
faDlik*

My name is . . .
ismi . . .

My company is . . .
shirketi . . .

I have an appointment with
Mr Sami Awad
*ªandi maªaed maªa isayid
sami ªawad*

I don't have an appointment
maªandeesh maªaed

I'd like to make an
appointment with Miss
Khadiga Mahmood
*ªayiz (m)/ªayza (f) aHadid
maªaed maªa il'aenisa
khadeega maHmood*

I am free this afternoon at one thirty
ana faaDi (m)/*faDya* (f) *inaharda ba*ᵃ*d iDohr issa*ᵃ*a waHda wi noS*

I'd like to talk to the export manager
ᵃ*ayiz/*ᵃ*ayza akalim modeer itaSdeer*

What is his name?
ismo ay

What is her name?
ismaha ay

When will he be back?
*Hayerga*ᵃ *imta*

When will she be back?
*Hatirga*ᵃ *imta*

Can I leave a message?
momkin aseeb risaela

Can you ask him/her to call me?
momkin yeTlobni/teTlobni

My telephone number is . . .
nemreti . . .

I am staying at the Hotel Luxor
ana naezil (m)/*nazla* (f) *fi hotayl lo'Sor*

Where is his/her office?
maktaebo/maktaebha fayn

I am here for the exhibition/trade fair
ana hena ᵃ*alashan aHDar il ma*ᵃ*raD itogaeri*

I am here for the conference
ana hena ᵃ*alashan aHDar il mo'tamar*

I have to make a phone call (to Britain)
laezim akalim (briTanya)

I have to send a telex
*laezim ab*ᵃ*at teleks*

I have to send a fax
*laezim ab*ᵃ*at faks*

I need someone to type this letter for me
ᵃ*ayiz/*ᵃ*ayza Had yeTba*ᵃ*li igawaeb da*

I want to send this by post/courier
ᵃ*ayiz/*ᵃ*ayza Had yeb*ᵃ*at da bil bosTa/kooryer*

I need to photocopy this
ᵃ*ayiz/*ᵃ*ayza aSawar da*

I need an interpreter
ᵃ*ayiz/*ᵃ*ayza motargim*

You may hear

*ismak/ismik ay
    min faDlak/faDlik*
Your name, please?

*ism ishirka ay min faDlak/
    faDlik*
The name of your company,
please

ªandak/ªandik maªaed
Do you have an
appointment?

ªandak/ªandik kart
Do you have a card?

*laHza waHda min faDlak/
    faDlik*
(Wait) one moment, please

*Ha'ollo inak waSalt/
    inik waSalti*
I'll tell him you're here

*Ha'ollaha inak waSalt/
    inik waSalti*
I'll tell her you're here

*Haykoon maªaek/maªaeki
    Haelan*
He will be with you in a
moment

*Hatkoon maªaek/maªaeki
    Haelan*
She will be with you in a
moment

*itfaDal o'ªod/itfaDali
    o'ªodi*
Please sit down

*itfaDal idkhol/itfaDali
    idkholi*
Go in, please

min hena
Come this way

isayid ªali mish mawgood
Mr Ali is not here

il'aenisa nadya kharagit
Miss Nadia is out

*isayida zakaraya Hatergaª
    issaªa Hidashar*
Mrs Zacharaya will be back
    at eleven o'clock

kamaen noS issaªa
In half an hour

kamaen saªa
In an hour

*khod il asansayr lil dowr
    italit*
Take the lift to the third
    floor

imshi fil mamar
Go along the corridor

awil/taeni baeb
It's the first/second door

125

ªalal shimael/yemeen
On the left/right

itfaDal/itfaDali
Come in!

'owda raqam toltomaya wi
  ªishreen
Room number 320

SIGHTSEEING

● You can get information about all the sights worth seeing in most countries from the relevant national tourist office in London (see Useful addresses, page 184) and from local tourist offices. The latter should also be able to tell you about sightseeing tours in cities and tourist areas, some with English-speaking guides.

● Opening hours for historic sites vary throughout the region, but are mostly around 9.00 a.m. to 5.00 p.m. They are usually closed on Fridays.

● Cairo is known as the city of a thousand minarets, but there are beautiful mosques all over the Arab world which you could visit. However, note that in the Gulf States and Libya you must ask permission.

To enter a mosque, your shoulders, arms and legs should be fully covered. Women should wear a headscarf, and avoid wearing tight clothing. Shoes must be taken off at the entrance. Photographs can usually be taken outside prayer times, with permission. During prayers avoid walking in front of standing or kneeling worshippers, and talk quietly. Watch what other people are doing and you'll soon learn what you can and cannot do inside a mosque.

You may see

استعلامات	Information
تذاكر	Tickets
خريطه	Map
خطر	Danger

ركوب الجمال	Camel rides
رحلات بمرشد	Guided tours
مغلق	Closed
فاتح	Open
ممنوع التصوير	No photography
ممنوع الدخول	No entry
ممنوع اللمس	Do not touch
منطقه خاصه	Private area
مواعيدالزياره	Visiting hours
هدايا تذكاريه	Souvenirs

You may want to say

(see also At the tourist office, *page 70, for asking for information, brochures etc.*)

Opening times

(see Time, *page 172*)

When is the museum open?
il matHaf biyeftaH issaᵃa kaem

What time do the Pyramids open?
il ahraam biteftaH issaᵃa kaem

What time does the gallery close?
il maᵃraD biye'fil issaᵃa kaem

Is it open every day?
biyeftaH kol yowm

Can we visit the mosque?
momkin nezoor il gameᵃ

Visiting places

One/Two, please
waHid/itnayn
min faDlak/faDlik

For two adults and one
child, please
itnayn ªadee wi Tefl
min faDlak/faDlik

Are there reductions for
children?
fi takhfeeD lil aTfaal

For students
lil Talaba

For pensioners
lili ªalal maªash

For the disabled
lil moªawaqeen

For groups
lil magmooªaet

Are there guided tours (in
English)
fi raHalaet bi morshid
bilogha (il ingleezaya)

Can I take photos?
momkin akhod Sowar

Would you mind taking a
photo of us, please?
momkin takhod Soora lena
min faDlak/faDlik

When was this built?
itbana imta

Who painted that picture?
min rasam iSoora di

In what year?
fi sanat kaem

What is this flower called?
il warda di ismaha ay

What is that bird called?
il ªasfoora di ismaha ay

Where are the toilets?
fayn itowalit

Where can I get a drink?
ashteri mashroob minayn

129

Sightseeing excursions

What tourist excursions are
there?
ay anwaª ireHlaet
issayaHaya ªandokom

Are there any excursions to
the Aswan dam?
fi reHlaet lisad aswan

What time does it leave?
tebda' issa^a kaem

How long does it last?
ireHla 'ad ay

What time does it get back?
Hanerga^a issa^a kaem

Where does it leave from?
bitebda' minayn

Does the guide speak English?
il morshid biyetkalim ingleezi

How much is it?
bikaem

Are there camel rides?
fi rekoob gimael

You may hear

il matHaf maftooH kol yowm ma^ada yowm il gom^a
The museum is open every day except Friday

ma'fool yowm isabt
It is closed on Saturdays

il ma^abad itbana fil ^asr il klasseekee
The temple was built in the Classical period

il ahraam itbanat talat talaef sana abl il milaed
The Pyramids were built in the third millennium BC

di ayqoona li . . .
It's an icon by . . .

fi reHlaet kol yowm talat wi khamees
There are excursions every Tuesday and Thursday

il otobees Hayemshi issa^a ^ashra min . . .
The coach leaves at ten o'clock from . . .

130

ENTERTAINMENTS

● The most popular spectator sport throughout the Arab world is football. Most professional sports fixtures take place on Fridays and Sundays.

● Evening performances at theatres, cinemas, musical events etc. usually start late – around 9.00 p.m. It is customary to give a small tip to theatre and cinema ushers.

● Many British and American films are shown throughout the Arab world, usually subtitled.

● The most common venues for entertainment are 'casinos' which are not gambling houses, but places where the whole family goes to have a meal and watch a small orchestra, stand-up comedian, belly dancer or folk dancing troupe. Most of these are found in the centre of the larger cities throughout the Arab world, in 5-star international hotels, on Nile cruise boats and at the seaside. They usually stay open till 2.00 a.m. or even later.

● Nightclubs offer music, dancing, dinner, belly dancing and so on for couples and single men. These are found mainly in Rabat, Marrakesh, Damascus, Amman, Cairo and Alexandria.

● Gambling is illegal in the Gulf States. If you fancy a flutter elsewhere in the Arab world, try one of the big international hotels.

You may see

إستاد	Stadium
استراحه	Interval
الحجز مقدماً	Advance booking

اوبرا	Opera house
باب	Door
مترجم بالعربيه	With Arabic subtitles
بحر	Sea
بلكون	Balcony, circle
تذاكر لحفله اليوم	Tickets for today's performance
تواليت	Toilets
ديسكو	Discothèque
درجه اولى	Stalls
ارض السباق	Racecourse
سباق الخيل	Horse racing
سيرك	Circus
سينما	Cinema
صف	Row
عرض مسائى	Evening performance
عرض مستمر	Continuous performance
فيلم	Film
كازينو	'Casino' nightclub
كومبليه	Sold out
لوج	Boxes
ماتينيه	Matinée
مسرح	Theatre
ممنوع الدخول بعد بدايةالعرض	No entry once the performance has begun
منصه	Stand

You may want to say

What's on

(*see* Time, *page 172*)

Where can we go tonight?
nis-har fayn ilayla

Is there a discothèque
around here?
fi disko hena

Is there any entertainment
for children?
fi tarfi lil aTfaal

What's on tonight?
fi ay ilayla

What's on tomorrow?
fi ay bokra

At the cinema
fil sinema

At the theatre
fil masraH

Who is performing?
meen biyemasil

Who is singing?
meen biyghani

Does the film have subtitles?
il film motargam

Is there a football match on
Sunday?
fi matsh kowra yowm il Had

Who are playing?
meen biyel*ab

What time does the show
start?
Hayebda' il*arD issa*a kaem

What time does the concert
end?
il Hafla tintehi issa*a kaem

How long does the
performance last?
il Hafla modet-ha 'ad ay

Tickets

Where can I get tickets?
ageeb tazakir minayn

Can you get me tickets for the concert?
momkin tigebli tazakir lil Hafla

For the football match
limatsh korit il qaddam

For the theatre
lil masraH

Two, please
itnayn min faDlak/faDlik

Three for tonight, please
talaeta ilayla di min faDlak/faDlik

Two for the eight o'clock screening, please
itnayn lil saªa tamanya min faDlak/faDlik

Are there any seats left for Saturday?
fi tazakir faDla liyowm isabt

I want to book a box for four people
ªayiz (m)/ªayza (f) aHgiz loj li arbaª tinfaar

I want to book two seats
ªayiz/ªayza aHgiz korsiyayn

For Friday
yowm il gomªa

In the stalls
fil daraga il 'oola

In the balcony
fil balkon

What price are the tickets?
bikaem il tazakir

Do you have any cheaper seats?
fi tazakir arkhaS

That's fine
kwayyis

At the show/game

Where is this seat, please?
fayn il korsi da min faDlak/faDlik

Where is the bar?
fayn il bar

Where are the toilets?
fayn il towalit

A programme, please
brogram min faDlak/faDlik

Where can I get a programme?
ashteri brogram minayn

A cushion, please
makhadda min faDlak/ faDlik

Is there an interval?
fi istiraHa

You may hear

momkin tishteri tazakir hena fil hotayl
You can buy tickets here in the hotel

fi maktaeb isiyaHa
At the tourist office

fil istaed
At the stadium

biyebda' issa^aa tamanya
It begins at eight o'clock

limodit sa^atayn wi rob^a
It lasts two and a quarter hours

yentehi issa^aa tes^aa wi noS
It ends at half past nine

fi istiraHa ^aishreen de'ee'a
There is a twenty-minute interval

^aayizhom li imta
When would you like them for?

fil daraga il' oola walla fil balkon
In the stalls or in the balcony?

(indicating on seating plan)
fi korsiyayn hena
There are two here

aesif/asfa . . . komplay
I'm sorry, the tickets are sold out

momkin ashoof tazkartak/ tazkartik
May I see your ticket?

135

SPORTS AND ACTIVITIES

• In Egypt water sports are widely practised in the region around the Red Sea, on the river Nile, near Suez and along the Mediterranean. In Morocco and Tunisia water sports are available on the Atlantic and Mediterranean coasts. In Jordan deep-sea diving is available in Aqaba.

• There is plenty of freshwater fishing along the Nile Delta and the Euphrates. There is also fishing in the Red Sea and along the Mediterranean.

• Sports clubs offering facilities for swimming, tennis, squash, volleyball, basketball, table tennis and golf are available for tourists in and around the larger cities and tourist areas. Ask at the local tourist information centre or at your hotel for details.

Sports activities for women are not available in the Gulf States, except on sites owned by multi-national companies. Female tourists can go swimming in the Gulf away from public view.

• Some of the many fine beaches along the Mediterranean and Red Sea are privately owned, but the majority are open to the public. There are no clothing restrictions for men or women in Egypt, Syria, Tunisia or Morocco, as long as costumes worn are not *too* revealing. Elsewhere, take your cue on dress and behaviour from the locals (see Religion and culture, page 8).

You may see

بلاچ	Beach
بلاچ خاص	Private beach
بلياردو	Billiards

تنس	Tennis
جنازيوم	Gymnasium
حمام سباحه (داخلى)	(Indoor) swimming pool
خاص	Private
خطر	Danger
ركوب الجمال	Camel rides
سكواش	Squash
كرةالسله	Basketball
(مدرسة) التزحلق الشراعى	Windsurfing (school)
مراكب للأيجار	Boat hire
مراكب شراعيه للأيجار	Sailboats for hire
ممنوع السباحه	No swimming
ممنوع الصيد	No fishing
ملعب كرة قدم	Football pitch
نادى	Sports centre

You may want to say

General phrases

Can I/we . . . ?
momkin . . .

Can we hire bikes?
momkin ni'aggar ªagal

Can I go fishing?
momkin arooH aStaaD

Can I go horse-riding?
momkin arkab HiSena

Can I go on a camel ride?
momkin arkab gamal

Can I go canoeing?
momkin a'adif

Where can I/we . . . ?
. . . fayn

Where can we play tennis?
momkin nelªab tenis fayn

I don't know how to . . .
mish ba^araf . . .

I don't know how to ride a camel
mish ba^araf arkab gamal

Do you give lessons?
momkin akhod derooS

I'm a beginner
ana lessa mobtadi'

I'm quite experienced at . . .
ana khabeer fi . . .

How much is it per hour?
bikaem fil sa^aa

How much is it for the whole day?
bikaem fil yowm

How much is it per game?
bikaem il matsh

Are there special rates for children?
fi takhfeeD lil aTfaal

Can I hire a boat?
momkin a'agar markib

Can I hire rackets?
momkin a'agar maDarib

Can I hire fishing lines?
momkin a'agar sinnara

Is a licence needed?
ana miHtaeg rokhSa

Where can I get a licence?
ageeb rokhSa minayn

Is it necessary to be a member?
hal Daroori akoon ^aodw

Beach and pool

Can I swim here?
momkin a^aoom hena

Can I swim in the sea?
momkin anzil il baHr

Is the sea dangerous?
il baHr khaTar

Can children swim in the sea safely today?
momkin ilaTfaal yenzelool baHr inaharda

You may hear

inta/inti mobtadi'
Are you a beginner?

te^araf ti'adif/te^arafi ti'adifi
Do you know how to canoe?

issa^aa bi khamsa ginay
It's five pounds per hour

laezim tedfa^a/tedfa^ai mo'addam ^aashra ginay
You have to pay a deposit of ten pounds

aesif/asfa mafeesh makaen
I'm sorry, we're booked up

momkin terga^a/terga^ai kamaen showaya
You'll have to come back later

laezim tegeeb/tegeebi Soora
You need a photograph

laezim rokhSa
You need a licence

HEALTH

Medical details - to show to a doctor

(Tick where appropriate, or fill in details)

		Self الطالب		Other members of family/party عائلته/ اصدقائه	
Blood group فصيلة الدم					
Asthmatic ربو					
Blind أعمى					
Deaf أطرش					
Diabetic سكر					
Epileptic صرع					
Handicapped معوق					
Heart condition أمراض القلب					
High blood pressure ارتفاع ضغط الرم					
Pregnant حامل					

Allergic to: ضد حساسيه

Antibiotics مضادات حيويه					
Penicillin بنسلين					
Cortisone كورتيزون					

Medicines أدويه

Self الطالب _____

Others عائلته/ أصدقائه _____

• Before travelling, make sure you have had the necessary immunisations, and don't forget to take vaccination certificates with you (see Arriving in an Arab country, page 30).

• Your local Department of Health office can provide information about medical and dental care abroad. Make sure you have good medical insurance if you're travelling to the Arab world. If you need treatment, you'll have to pay in cash and reclaim the payment from your insurance company when you return to Britain, so be sure to obtain receipts.

• Make sure you take supplies of medicines you need regularly, as well as something for the treatment of common travellers' complaints such as diarrhoea and mosquito bites.

• Chemists are generally highly trained and can often help with minor disorders and injuries. In an emergency, drugs which are available only on prescription in Britain may be obtainable over the counter at chemists in most Arab countries, but you should ensure that you know exactly what you need and the dosage. If in doubt, go to a doctor.

• Most hospitals in the region are state-owned and run, but there are also many private hospitals. There's a significant difference between the two in levels of hygiene, standards of service, degree of attention given, and comfort.

Hospitals in the Gulf are of the highest standards, often boasting state-of-the-art medical equipment and staffed by Egyptian, Palestinian and sometimes European doctors.

• Throughout the Arab world all doctors will have studied medicine in English and should therefore be able to communicate reasonably well with you.

• If you need to indicate where pain is, you can simply point and say 'it hurts here' (*andi waga* *hena*) – if necessary adding the Arabic for the appropriate part of the body (see list, page 148).

● Most complaints experienced by visitors are related to food and drink. You should avoid drinking anything but boiled or bottled water – and remember that also applies to ice in drinks. Refrain also from swimming in rivers or canals.

It is usually best to avoid eating salads or fruit salads in restaurants. Where possible, peel fruit yourself immediately before eating it, or else wash it carefully in bottled water.

Be wary of eating food sold in open markets, especially in summer. If you buy food to prepare yourself, make sure it's kept in a well-sealed container – cockroaches are a particular nuisance, especially in humid areas and by the sea.

● The other main cause of problems is the sun – take a hat, sunglasses and sunblock cream with you and avoid over-exposure.

You may see

استعمل قبل	Use before (*date*)
اسعاف	Ambulance
اسعافات اوليه	First aid post
العياده الخارجيه	Surgery, Out-patients
خدمات الطوارئ	Emergency services
دكتور	Doctor
دكتور إسنان	Dentist
عياده	Clinic
سموم	Poison
قسم الحوادث	Casualty
لاتبلع	Do not swallow
للأستعمال الخارجي فقط	For external use only

مستشفى	Hospital
مواعيد العياده	Surgery hours
رج قبل الأستعمال	Shake before use

You may want to say

At the doctor

I need a doctor
ayiz (m)/*ayza* (f) *doktowr*

Please call a doctor
iTlobli doktowr
  min faDlak/faDlik

Is there a female doctor?
fi doktowra

It's my husband
gowzi

It's my wife
miraati

It's my friend
SaHbi (m)/*SaHbiti* (f)

It's my son
ibni

It's my daughter
binti

Your symptoms

I feel unwell
ana ᵃayaen (m)/*ᵃayaena* (f)

It hurts here
biyewgaᵃ hena

I have earache
widaeni bitewgaᵃni

Someone else's symptoms

He/She feels unwell
howa ᵃayaen/haya ᵃayaena

He/She is unconscious
oghma ᵃalay/ᵃalayha

It hurts here
biyewgaᵃ hena

He/She has earache
widno bitewgaᵃo/
  widnaha bitewgaᵃha

I have a sore throat *zowri biyewga^ani*	He/She has a sore throat *zoro biyewga^ao/* *zorha biyewga^aha*
I have a temperature *^aandi Haraara*	He/She has a temperature *^aando/^aandaha Haraara*
I have diarrhoea *^aandi is-hael*	He/She has diarrhoea *^aando/^aandaha is-hael*
I feel dizzy *Hasis* (m)/*Hassa* (f) *bi dowkha*	He/She feels dizzy *^aando/^aandaha dowkha*
I have been sick *istafraght*	He/She has been sick *istafragh/istafraghit*
I can't sleep *mish 'aedir* (m)/ *'aedra* (f) *anaem*	He/She can't sleep *mish 'aedir yinaem/* *'aedra tinaem*
I can't breathe *mish 'aedir/'aedra atnafis*	He/She can't breathe *mish 'aedir yitnafis/* *'aedra titnafis*
My . . . is bleeding *^aandi nazeef fi . . .*	
It's broken *itkasar*	
It's sprained *itlawa*	
I have cut myself *^aawart nafsi*	
I have burnt myself *Hara't nafsi*	
I have been stung by an insect *Hashara lasa^aitni*	He/She has been stung by an insect *lasa^aito/lasa^ait-ha Hashara*

I have been bitten by a
    dog/snake
ªaDeni kalb/tiªbaen

He/She has been bitten
    by a dog/snake
ªaDoo/ªaDaha kalb/tiªbaen

I have been bitten by a
    scorpion
ªaDetni ªa'rabba

He/She has been bitten by
    a scorpion
ªaDetoo/ªaDetha ªa'rabba

You may hear

fayn il wagaª
Where does it hurt?

biyewgaª/bitewgaª hena
Does it hurt here?

biyewgaª/bitewgaª 'awi
Does it hurt a lot?

b'aelak ªayaen/
*   b'aelik ªayaena 'ad ay*
How long have you been
   feeling ill?

ªandak/ªandik kaem sana
How old are you?

ªando/ªandaha kaem sana
How old is he/she?

iftaH bo'ak/iftaHi bo'ik
Open your mouth

i'laª hedoomak min faDlak/
*   i'laªi hedoomik min faDlik*
Get undressed, please

bitakhod/bitakhdi adwaya
Are you taking any
   medicines?

ªandak/ªandik Hasasaya li
*   ay adwaya*
Are you allergic to any
   medicine?

khadt/khadti taTªeem Ded
*   il tetnas*
Have you been vaccinated
   against tetanus?

akalt/akalti ay inaharda
What have you eaten today?

Hadilak/Hadilik roshetta
I am going to give you a
   prescription

khod/khodi Habaya talat
*   marraat fil yowm*
Take a tablet three times a day

baªd il akl
After meals

'abl il nowm
At bedtime

molawas/molawassa
It is infected

145

Hadilak/Hadilik Ho'na
I have to give you an
injection

meHtaeg/meHtaega ghoraz
I have to give you some
stitches

*laezim takhod/takhdi
isha^a*
It is necessary to do an X-ray

*^ayiz/^ayza ^ayenit dam/
bowl*
I need to take a blood/
urine sample

galak/galik Sadma 'albaya
You have had a heart attack

^andak/^andik tasamom
You have food poisoning

^andak/^andik gafaef
You are dehydrated

*laezim tishrab/tishrabi
sawa'il kiteera*
You must drink plenty of
liquids

Soom limodit yowm waHid
Don't eat for a day

*laezim testerayaH/
testerayaHi*
You must rest

*laezim tor'od/tor'odi talat
tiyaem*
You must stay in bed for
three days

*irga^/irga^i kamaen
khamas tiyaem*
You must come back in
five days' time

*laezim teroH/teroHi il
mostashfa*
You will have to go to hospi

Hala khafeefa
It is nothing serious

inta saleem/inti saleema
There is nothing wrong
with you

*ilbis hedoomak/ilbisi
hedoomik*
You can get dressed again

You may want to say

At the dentist

I need a dentist
*ayiz (m)/*ayza (f)
doktowr sinaen

I have toothache
sinaeni bitewga*ni

This tooth hurts
sineti di bitewga*ni

I have broken a tooth
sineti itkasarit

I have lost a filling
il Hashw Tele*

I have lost a crown/cap
il taeg Tele*

He/She has toothache
*ando/*andaha waga* fi
issinaen

He/She has broken a tooth
kasar/kasarit sinna

He/She has lost a filling
il Hashw Tele*

He/She has lost a crown/cap
il taeg Tele*

Can you fix it temporarily?
momkin tiSalaH-ha
mo'aqatan

Can you give me an
injection?
momkin teddeenee Ho'na

Can you give him/her an
injection?
momkin tedeelo/tedelha
Ho'na

This denture is broken
il sinna di maksoora

Can you repair it?
momkin tiSalaH-ha

How much will it cost?
bikaem

You may hear

iftaH bo'ak min faDlak/
iftaHi bo'ik min faDlik
Open your mouth, please

meHtaeg/meHtaega Hashw
You need a filling

Hadilak/Hadilik Ho'na
I'll give you an injection

Hakhla*ha lak/lik
I have to extract it

Parts of the body

ankle	*rosgh ilqaddam* (m)	رسغ القدم
appendix	*moSraan a^{a}war* (m)	مصران أعور
arm	*derae^a* (m)	ذراع
back	*Dahr* (m)	ظهر
bladder	*il masaena* (f)	مثانه
blood	*dam* (m)	دم
body	*gism* (m)	جسم
bone	*^{a}aDma* (f)	عظمه
bottom	*deryer* (m)	ديرير
bowels	*ilaHsha'* (pl)	الأحشاء
breast	*Sadr* (m)	صدر
buttocks	*ardaef* (m)	ارداف
cartilage	*kartlij* (m)	كارتلاج
chest	*Sadr* (m)	صدر
chin	*da'n* (m)	ذقن
ear	*wedn* (f)	ودن
elbow	*koo^a* (m)	كوع
eye	*^{a}ayn* (f)	عين
face	*wag-h* (m)	وجه
finger	*Soba^a* (m)	صباع
foot	*qaddam* (m)	قدم
genitals	*a^{a}Da' ginsaya* (m pl)	أعضاء جنسيه
gland	*ghodda* (f)	غدة
hair	*sha^{a}r* (m)	شعر
hand	*yad* (f)	يد
head	*ras* (m)	رأس

English	Transliteration	Arabic
heart	*'alb* (m)	قلب
heel	*ka°b* (m)	كعب
hip	*redf* (m)	ردف
jaw	*fak* (m)	فك
joint	*mafSal* (m)	مفصل
kidney	*kelwa* (f)	كلوه
knee	*rokba* (f)	ركبه
leg	*regl* (m)	رجل
ligaments	*arbeTa* (m pl)	أربطه
lip	*sheffa* (f)	شفة
liver	*kebd* (m)	كبد
lung	*re'a* (m)	رئه
mouth	*fam* (m)	فم
muscle	*°aDala* (f)	عضله
nail	*Dofr* (m)	ظفر
neck	*ra'aba* (f)	رقبة
nerve	*°aSab* (m)	عصب
nose	*manakheer* (f)	مناخير
penis	*°oDw izzkoora* (m)	عضوالذكوره
private parts	*ala°Da' il ginsaya* (m pl)	الأعضاءالجنسيه
rectum	*fatHit il sharag* (f)	فتحةالشرج
rib	*Del°* (m)	ضلع
shoulder	*ketf* (m)	كتف
skin	*geld* (m)	جلد
spine	*°amood il fa'ri* (m)	العمودالفقرى
stomach	*me°da* (f)	المعده
tendon	*awtar* (m pl)	اوتار

testicles	*khawaSi* (f pl)	خواصى
thigh	*fakhd* (m)	فخد
throat	*zowr* (m)	زور
thumb	*Soba il ibhaem* (m)	صباع الأبهام
toe	*Soba iregl* (m)	صباع الرجل
tongue	*lisaen* (m)	لسان
tonsils	*lewaz* (f pl)	لوز
tooth	*sinna* (f)	سنه
vagina	*raHim* (m)	رحم
wrist	*rosgh* (m)	رسغ

PROBLEMS AND COMPLAINTS

● Generally, there are two police forces in Arab countries, one dealing with traffic control and the other with law and order. In Egypt, for example, the main police force wear green uniforms, while the traffic police wear black in winter and white in summer.

● Special 'tourist police' may be found at some archaeological sites.

● If you're attacked or have something stolen, you should contact the police immediately. Ask for the nearest police station (*fi ism bolees orayyib*), and if possible find someone who speaks English to help you – unless you're near a tourist site it's unlikely that any policeman will be able to speak English. In Morocco, Tunisia and Algeria, however, you may find one who understands French.

● If you're a woman and are assaulted, you may want to find another woman to talk to. In this case it's probably best to go to the nearest hospital and ask to see a female doctor (who will probably speak at least some English) or nurse. She will advise you what to do and may also be willing to accompany you to the police station. Arab women are very helpful and supportive, and will nearly always respond positively to a fellow woman in distress.

● In case of emergencies, check what the local emergency telephone numbers are when you arrive.

You may see

اسعاف	Ambulance station
البوليس السياحى	Tourist police

عاطل	Out of order
قسم البوليس	Police station
مستشفى	Hospital
مطافئ	Fire station

You may want to say

(for car breakdowns, see page 44; Emergencies, page 300)

General phrases

Can you help me?
momkin tisaªidni

Can you fix it (quickly)?
momkin tiSalaHoo (bisorªa)

When can you fix it?
HatiSalaHoo imta

Can I speak to the manager?
momkin akalim il modeer

There's a problem with . . .
fi moshkila . . .

There isn't/aren't any . . .
mafeesh . . .

I want (need) . . .
ªayiz (m)/*ªayza* (f) . . .

. . . doesn't work
. . . *bayiZ* (m)/*bayZa* (f)

. . . is broken
. . . *maksoor* (m)/*maksoora* (f)

I can't . . .
mish 'aedir (m)/
'aedra (f) . . .

It wasn't my fault
mish ghalTiti

I have forgotten my . . .
neseet . . .

(My) . . . is lost
. . . *Daª* (m obj)/
Daªit (f obj)

Someone has stolen (my) . . .
Had sara' . . .

I can't find . . .
mish laeªee (m)/*laªya* (f) . . .

This isn't mine
mish bitaªee (m)/*bitaªti* (f)

152

Where you're staying

There isn't any (hot) water
mafeesh maiya (sokhna)

There isn't any toilet paper
mafeesh wara' towalit

There isn't any electricity
mafeesh kahraba

There aren't any towels
mafeesh fowaT

I want another pillow
*ªayiz/ªayza kamaen
makhadda*

I want another blanket
*ªayiz/ªayza kamaen
baTanaya*

I want a light bulb
ªayiz/ªayza lamba

The light doesn't work
inoor bayiZ

The shower doesn't work
idosh bayiZ

The lock is broken
itirbaes maksoor

The switch on the lamp is
broken
moftaeH inoor maksoor

I can't open the window
*mish ªarif (m)/ªarfa (f)
aftaH ishibaek*

I can't close the window
*mish ªarif/ªarfa a'fil
ishibaek*

I can't turn the tap off
*mish ªarif/ªarfa a'fil il
Hanafaya*

I can't turn the tap on
*mish ªarif/ªarfa aftaH il
Hanafaya*

The toilet doesn't flush
isafown bayiZ

The wash-basin is blocked
il HowD masdood

The wash-basin is dirty
il HowD wesikh

The room is . . .
il 'owda . . .

The room is too dark
il 'owda Dalma 'awi

The room is too small
il 'owda Soghayara 'awi

There's a lot of noise
fi dawsha kiteer 'awi

It's too hot in the room
il 'owda Har 'awi

The air conditioning
doesn't work
itakyeef bayiZ

153

The air conditioning is too cold
itakyeef baerid 'awi

There is a smell of gas
fi reeHit gaez

The bed is not comfortable
il sereer mish moreeH

In cafés and restaurants

This is raw
da nay

This glass is cracked
il kobbaya di maksoora

This is burnt
da maHroo'

This is dirty
da wesikh

This is cold
da baerid

This smells bad
reHto weHsha

I didn't order this, I ordered . . .
ana maTalabtish da ana Talabt . . .

This tastes bad
*Ta*amo weHish*

This bill is wrong
il fatoora di ghalaT

In shops

I bought this here (yesterday)
ishtarayt da hena (imbariH)

I want to exchange this
ayiz/ ayza aghaiyyar da

Can you change this for me?
momkin tighaiyyarli da

Can you give me a refund?
momkin astarid filoosee

Here is the receipt
il waSl aho

I want to return this
ayiz (m)/ ayza (f) araga da*

The material has a flaw
il 'omash fi ayb

There is a hole	This isn't fresh
fi khorm	*da mish Taza*

There is a stain/mark	The lid is missing
fi ᶜalaema	*il ghaTa mish mawgood*

Forgetting and losing things and theft

I have forgotten my ticket	Where is the lost property office?
neseet itazkara	*fayn maktaeb il mafqoodaet*

I have forgotten the key	Where is the police station?
neseet il moftaeH	*fayn ism ibolees*

I have lost my wallet
il maHfaZa Daaᶜit

I have lost my driving licence
irokhSa Daaᶜit

We have lost our rucksacks
shonaaT iDahr Daaᶜoo

Someone has stolen my handbag
Had sara' shanTit eedee

Someone has stolen my car
Had sara' ᶜarabeetee

155

Someone has stolen my money
Had sara' filoosee

If someone is bothering you

Leave me alone!
sebni fi Haelee

Go away, or I'll call the police
Hatemshi walla aTlob ibolees

There is someone bothering me
fi waHid biyedaye'ni

There is someone following me
fi waHid biyemshi waraya

You may hear

Helpful and unhelpful replies

laHza min faDlak/ faDlik
Just a moment, please

Tab^aan
Of course

Hageeb lak waHid
I'll bring you one

Hageeb lak kamaen waHid
I'll bring you another one

Haelan
Right away

HaSalaHoo lak/lik bokra
I'll fix it for you tomorrow

aesif/asfa mish momkin
I'm sorry, it's not possible

mish shoghli ana
I am not the person responsible

iHna malnaesh da^awa
We are not responsible

ballagh ibolees
You should report it to the police

aham shay' te^amelo . . .
The best thing you can do is . .

insha' alla
God willing!

il Hamdoo lilla
Thanks be to God!

(*The last two are both common, positive replies*)

Questions you may be asked

ishtarayto imta
When did you buy it?

ma^aaek il waSl
Do you have the receipt?

HaSalit imta
When did it happen?

Da^ait minak/minik fayn
Where did you lose it?

itsara'it fayn
Where was it stolen?

momkin towSifli/towSifili . . .
Can you describe . . .?

momkin towSifli shanTitak/towSifili shanTitik
Can you describe your bag?

momkin towSifli/towSifili il ᵃarabaya
Can you describe the car?

noᵃha ay
What make is it?

nemrit-ha ay
What is the registration number?

sakin fayn
Where are you staying?

ᵃenwaenak/ᵃenwaenik ay
What is your address?

nemrit 'owdtak/'owdtik ay
What is your room number?

raqam basborak/basborik ay
What is your passport number?

ᵃandak/ᵃandik ta' meen
Have you got insurance?

momkin temla iTalab da
Please fill in this form

BASIC GRAMMAR

Classical Arabic, the language in which the Muslim holy book the Koran was written, dates back to the seventh century. All 23 Arab nations use this written form of the language, with only minor variations from country to country. The colloquial – spoken – language, used in this book, is used in Egypt and will be understood in most Arabic-speaking countries, and the basic rules of grammar which follow apply wherever you are.

Arabic is written from right to left. Each word is based on three 'root' letters, from which as many as ten different forms of the word may be derived (although some of them seem very far removed in meaning from the original word).

If you learn to read the Arabic script, you'll find that you'll often be able to guess the meaning of a word from its root letters. For example, the root letters of the word for book, *kitaeb*, are *k*, *t* and *b*. 'Write' is *katab*, 'writer' is *kaetib* and 'office' is *maktaeb* – all based on the same three letters.

Nouns

Arabic nouns are either masculine or feminine. As a rule, feminine nouns end in *-a*, or less commonly *-at*. Often the feminine form of a word is formed by adding one of these endings to the masculine, e.g.:

Masculine	**Feminine**	
Taalib	*Taaliba*	student
moddaris	*moddarissa*	teacher

However, there are many 'irregular' feminine nouns, such as:

bint	girl	*'om*	mother

Names of towns and countries are nearly always feminine.

Plurals

In Arabic the endings of nouns change in the plural. For 'regular' nouns you add *-een* to masculine nouns, and *-aet* to feminine nouns, e.g.:

Masculine	Feminine	
mohandis	*mohandissa*	engineer
mohandiseen	*mohandissaet*	engineers

'Irregular' nouns have no set rules for forming the plural – it's a matter of learning them as you go along, e.g.:

Singular		Plural	
kart	card	*koroot*	cards
bayt	house	*biyoot*	houses
baSala	onion	*baSal*	onions
shanTa	bag	*shonaaT*	bags

NB: There's a special plural for when you are referring to two of something: you add *-ayn* to the end of masculine words, and *-tayn* to feminine ones, e.g.:

layla	night	*layltayn*	two nights
sereer	bed	*sereerayn*	two beds
tazkara	ticket	*tazkartayn*	two tickets

Articles

The definite article ('the') in Arabic is *il*. This is the same for masculine and feminine, singular and plural. There is no indefinite article ('a' or 'an').

Meanings often depend on the position of *il* – and whether it is used at all. For example:

bayt	a house
il bayt	the house
il bayt il kibeer	the big house
il bayt kibeer	the house is big

Possessives ('my', 'your', 'his', 'her', etc.)

Arabic adds a range of endings to nouns to denote possession:

	Masculine	Feminine
my	*-i*	*-ti*
your (s)	*-ak*	*-ik*
his/her/its	*-o*	*-ha*
our	*-na*	*-tna*
your (pl)	*-kom*	*-kom*
their	*-hom*	*-t-hom*

For example:
shanTiti	my bag
basboro	his passport
reHlatna	our trip
kamirat-hom	their cameras

If the 'possessive' noun is accompanied by an adjective, this must be preceded by the definite article (*il*), e.g.:

kitaeb kibeer   a big book   *kitaebi il kibeer*   my big book

Adjectives

In Arabic, adjectives come after the noun. They 'agree' with it – that is, they have different endings according to whether the noun is masculine or feminine, singular or plural.

For 'regular' adjectives, you add *-a* to the masculine singular to make the feminine singular, e.g.:

il otobees il kibeer (m)	the big bus
il Taiyaara il kibeera (f)	the big aeroplane

For plurals, when referring to things (as opposed to people), adjectives have the feminine singular ending, e.g.:

Singular	Plural	
maTᵃam (m)	*maTaaᵃim*	cheap
rakheeS	*rakheeSa*	restaurant(s)
shanTa (f) *khaDra*	*shonaaT khaDra*	green bag(s)

When referring to people, adjectives have plural endings as appropriate: *-een* for masculine, *-aat* or *-aet* for feminine, e.g.:

walad (m) *Soghayar*	*aewlad Soghayareen*	little boy(s)
bint (f) *Helwa*	*banaet Helwaet*	pretty girl(s)

There are also 'irregular' adjectives, in which the whole word changes according to gender and number, e.g.:

tarabayza (f) *kibeera*	*tarabizaat kobaar*	big table(s)
walad (m) *shaeb*	*aewlad shabaeb*	young boy(s)

Personal pronouns

Subject pronouns are often omitted in Arabic, the context usually making it clear who or what is being referred to. They're sometimes used to give special emphasis, and it's also useful to learn them so that you can avoid misunderstandings.

I	*ana*
you (*masculine singular*)	*inta*
you (*feminine singular*)	*inti*
he/it	*howa*
she/it	*haya*
we	*iHna*
you (*plural*)	*intoo*
they	*homma*

Object pronouns ('me', 'him', 'her', 'us', etc.) are the same as the subject pronouns.

Indirect object pronouns ('to me', 'to him', etc.) are added to the ends of verbs. They are:

to me	*li*
to you (*masculine singular*)	*lo*
to you (*feminine singular*)	*liha*
to him/it	*lo*
to her/it	*liha*
to us	*lina*
to you (*plural*)	*lokom*
to them	*lohom*

For example:

olli min faDlak	Tell me please
Hab^a*atlokom gawabaet*	I'll send you (*pl*) letters

Demonstratives ('this', 'that')

Arabic doesn't differentiate between 'this' and 'that' but there are masculine and feminine forms, depending on the gender of the noun. There is also a plural form.

da	this/that (*masculine*)
di	this/that (*feminine*)
dowl	these/those

For example:

il bayt da kibeer	That house is big
di madeena qadeema	This is an old city
il madeena di qadeema	This city is old
bikaem dowl	How much are these?

Verbs

Verbs in Arabic have different forms according to the subject of the verb, the gender of the subject, and the tense. All verbs are derived from a 'root' of three letters (see page 158), and the different forms are made by changing the beginning, middle and/or end of the root. For example, the root of 'travel' is the letters **s**, **f**, **r**. Once you know the root of a verb, you can work out the various forms – most follow the pattern below.

There is no infinitive form of Arabic verbs (the equivalent of 'to . . .'), so in the Dictionary verbs are given in the 'he' and 'she' present tense forms.

Present tense

I travel	*asaefir*
You (*m*) travel	*tisaefir*
You (*f*) travel	*tisafri*
He/it travels	*yisaefir*
She/it travels	*tisaefir*
We travel	*nisaefir*
You (*pl*) travel	*tisafroo*
They travel	*yisafroo*

Past tense

I travelled	*safirt*
You (*m*) travelled	*safirt*
You (*f*) travelled	*safirti*
He/it travelled	*safir*
She/it travelled	*safrit*
We travelled	*safirna*
You (*pl*) travelled	*safirtom*
They travelled	*safrom*

Future tense

The future tense of most verbs is formed by placing *Ha-* in front of the present tense form:

I will travel	*Hasaefir*
You (*m*) will travel	*Hatsaefir*
You (*f*) will travel	*Hatsafri*
He/it will travel	*Haiysaefir*
She/it will travel	*Hatsaefir*
We will travel	*Hansaefir*
You (*pl*) will travel	*Hatsajroo*
They will travel	*Haiysafroo*

To give another example, the root letters of 'book' ('make a reservation') are **H**, **g**, **z**. Using the patterns above, 'I book', for instance, is *aHgiz*; 'we booked' is *Hagezna*; 'she will book' is *HateHgiz*.

Irregular verbs

There are a number of 'irregular' verbs in Arabic, which do not follow the pattern above. Two of the most useful are given below, in their present tense.

'To want'

I want	*ªawez*
You (*m*) want	*ªawza*
You (*f*) want	*ªawza*
He/it wants	*ªawez*
She/it wants	*ªawza*
We want	*ªawzeen*
You (*pl*) want	*ªawzeen*
They want	*ªawzeen*

'To come'

I come	*gay*
You (*m*) come	*gay*
You (*f*) come	**gaya**
He/it comes	*gay*
She/it comes	**gaya**
We come	*gayeen*
You (*pl*) come	*gayeen*
They come	*gayeen*

'To be'

Arabic has no verb 'to be'; the subject is simply followed by the rest of the sentence, without a verb. For example:

I am a student	*ana Taalib*
He is a doctor	*howa doktowr*

To say 'there is' or 'there are' you use the word *fi*, e.g.:

fi korsi   There is a chair   *fi tazakir*   There are tickets

The past tense of 'to be' is:

I was	*kont*
You (*m*) were	*kont*
You (*f*) were	**konti**
He/it was	*kaen*
She/it was	**kaenit**
We were	**konna**
You (*pl*) were	**kontom**
They were	**kaeno**

'To have'

Arabic has no verb 'to have' either. Instead, one of two words can be used to indicate possession. These are *^aand* meaning 'have' ('possess') and *ma^a* meaning 'have with . . .' (at the present time). They are used with a suffix:

	'have'	'have with . . .'
I have	*^aandi*	*ma^aaya*
You (m) have	*^aandak*	*ma^aaek*
You (f) have	*^aandik*	*ma^aaeki*
He/it has	*^aando*	*ma^aa*
She/it has	*^aandaha*	*ma^aaha*
We have	*^aandena*	*ma^aaena*
You (pl) have	*^aandokom*	*ma^aakom*
They have	*^aandohom*	*ma^aahom*

^aandi ^aarabaya	I own a car
ma^aaya ^aarabaya	I've got a car with me

momkin

One useful word to remember is ***momkin***. Used with the present tense of any verb, it means 'can I?', 'is it permitted?', e.g.:

momkin arkin hena	Can I park here?
momkin tiSawar di	Can she photocopy this?

Negatives

The negative in Arabic is formed in one of two main ways. With verbs *ma-* is put in front of the verb, and *-sh* after it, e.g.:

fi kalb	There is a dog	*mafeesh kalb*	There is no dog

With adjectives and adverbs *mish* is put before the word, e.g.:

da momkin   This is possible
da mish momkin   This is not possible

Questions

Questions in written Arabic end with a back-to-front question mark: ؟ . In speech a question is usually indicated simply by the voice rising at the end of the statement. However you can also make a sentence into a question by putting *hael* at the beginning:

il gaw Helw   The weather is good
hael il gaw Helw   Is the weather good?

Question words can come at the beginning or end of a sentence, e.g:

What is your name?   *ismak ay*
              or   *ay ismak*

167

Question words include:

fayn	where?	*lay*	why?
imta	when?	*izzay*	how?
ay	what?	*ay*	which?
meen	who?		

Prepositions

Some of the most frequently used prepositions in Arabic are:

ªala	on/over	*'abl*	before
min	from	*baªd*	after
fi	in(to)/in/at	*li*	to
fo'	over	*wara*	behind
taHt	under	*amaem*	before
ªan	about		

DAYS, MONTHS, DATES

Days

Monday	*yowm il itnayn*
Tuesday	*yowm italaet*
Wednesday	*yowm il arba^a*
Thursday	*yowm il khamees*
Friday	*yowm il gom^aa*
Saturday	*yowm isabt*
Sunday	*yowm il **Had***

Months

January	*yanayer*
February	*fabrayer*
March	*maeris*
April	*ibreel*
May	*mayo*
June	*yonyo*
July	*yolyo*
August	*aghostos*
September	*sebtambir*
October	*oktobar*
November	*novambir*
December	*disambir*

Seasons

Spring	*irabee^a*
Summer	*iSayf*
Autumn	*il khareef*
Winter	*isheta*

General phrases

day	*yowm*
week	*izboo^a*
fortnight (two weeks)	*izboo^aayn*
month	*shahr*
six months	*set osh-hor*
year	*sana*
today	*inaharda*
tomorrow	*bokra*
day after tomorrow	*ba^ad bokra*
yesterday	*imbariH*
day before yesterday	*awil imbariH*
(in the) morning	*iSobH*
(in the) afternoon	*ba^ad iDohr*
(in the) evening	*il maghrib*
(at) night	*bilayl*
this morning	*inaharda iSobH*
this afternoon	*inaharda ba^ad iDohr*
this evening	*inaharda il maghrib*
tomorrow morning	*bokra iSobH*
tomorrow afternoon	*bokra ba^ad iDohr*
tomorrow evening	*bokra il maghrib*
yesterday morning	*imbariH iSobH*
yesterday afternoon	*imbariH ba^ad iDohr*
yesterday evening	*imbariH il maghrib*
on Monday	*yowm il itnayn*
on Tuesdays	*kol yowm talaet*
every Wednesday	*kol yowm arba^a*
in August	*fi aghostos*
at the beginning of March	*awil maeris*

169

in the middle of June	*fi noS yonyo*
at the end of September	*fi akhir sebtambir*
during the summer	*fil Sayf*
two years ago	*min sanatayn*
in the nineties	*fil tes^aeenaet*
last Monday	*il itnaen ili faet*
last week	*il izboo^a ili faet*
last month	*ishahr ili faet*
last year	*isana ili faetit*
next Tuesday	*italaet ili gay*
next week	*il izboo^a ili gay*
next month	*ishahr ili gay*
next year	*isana igaya*
before Saturday	*abl yowm isabt*
after Tuesday	*ba^ad yowm italaet*
until/by Friday	*lighayit yowm igom^aa*
two days ago	*min yowmayn*
three days ago	*min talat tiyaem*
What day is it today?	*inaharda ay*
What is the date today?	*inaharda kaem fishahr*
When is your birthday?	*^aeed milaedak/milaedik imta*
On the first of January	*awil yanayer*
On Tuesday 10 May	*yowm italaet ^aashra mayo*
1993	*sanat alf tos^aomaya wi talaeta wi tes^aeen*
In the 15th century	*fil qarn il khamastashar*

The Muslim year

The Islamic calendar is a lunar one, and moves forward around eleven days in each 'Western' year. The year itself is dated from A.D. 580, and this means that, according to the Muslim calendar, 1993 for example falls half into the Islamic year 1413, and half into 1414. You may see the Islamic year written on documents (such as hotel registration forms), especially in the Gulf region.

The Islamic year is divided into twelve lunar months, as follows:

1st	*moHaram*	7th	*ragab*
2nd	*saffar*	8th	*sha*ᵃ*baen*
3rd	*rabee*ᵃ *ilawal*	9th	*ramadan*
4th	*rabee*ᵃ *itaeni*	10th	*shawael*
5th	*gamadee ilawal*	11th	*zool qe*ᵃ*da*
6th	*gamadee itaeni*	12th	*zool Haga*

TIME

one o'clock	*issa*ᵃ*a waHda*
two o'clock	*issa*ᵃ*a itnayn*
three o'clock	*issa*ᵃ*a talaeta*
quarter past . . .	*. . . wi rob*ᵃ
half past . . .	*. . . wi noS*
five past . . .	*. . . wi khamsa*
twenty past . . .	*. . . wi tilt*
twenty-five past . . .	*. . . wi noS ila khamsa*
quarter to . . .	*. . . ila rob*ᵃ
ten to . . .	*. . . ila* ᵃ*ashra*
twenty to . . .	*. . . ila tilt*
half past three	*talaeta wi noS*
half past seven	*saba*ᵃ*a wi noS*
five past nine	*tes*ᵃ*a wi khamsa*
quarter to five	*khamsa ila rob*ᵃ
ten to eleven	*Hidashar ila* ᵃ*ashra*
noon/midday	*iDohr*
midnight	*noS ilayl*
in the morning	*iSobH*
in the afternoon	*ba*ᵃ*d iDohr*
in the evening	*il maghrib*
a quarter of an hour	*rob*ᵃ *sa*ᵃ*a*
three quarters of an hour	*talatirba*ᵃ *sa*ᵃ*a*
half an hour	*noS sa*ᵃ*a*

The 24-hour clock is not generally used in the Arab world.

soon	*qareeban*
early	*badri*
late	*mit'akhar*
on time	*fi miado*
half an hour ago	*min noS saa*
in ten minutes' time	*kamaen ashar d'ayi'*
in a quarter of an hour	*kamaen rob saa*
What time is it?	*issaa kaem*
It's . . .	*issaa . . .*
It's nine o'clock	*issaa tesa*
It's six o'clock	*issaa setta*
It's quarter past eight	*issaa tamanya wi rob*
(At) what time . . .?	*. . . issaa kaem*
At . . .	*issaa . . .*
At half past one	*issaa waHda wi noS*
At quarter to seven	*issaa saba ila rob*
(At) exactly two o'clock	*issaa itnayn tamaeman*
About half past six	*Hawaeli setta wi noS*
Nearly quarter to five	*Hawaeli khamsa ila rob*

COUNTRIES AND NATIONALITIES

Country/Continent		Nationality & Adjective (*masculine/feminine*)
Africa	*afriqya*	*afreeqee/afreeqaya*
Algeria	*il gaza'ir*	*gaza'iri/gaza'iraya*
America	*amreeka*	*amreeki/amreekaya*
Asia	*asya*	*asyawi/asyawaya*
Austria	*inemsa*	*nemsawi/nemsawaya*
Australia	*ostralya*	*ostorali/ostoralaya*
Bahrain	*il baHrayn*	*baHrani/baHranaya*
Belgium	*baljeeka*	*biljeeki/biljeekaya*
Canada	*kanada*	*kanadi/kanadaya*
China	*iSeen*	*Seeni/Sennaya*
Denmark	*idenmark*	*denmarki/denmarkaya*
Egypt	*maSr*	*maSri/maSraya*
England	*ingilterra*	*ingleezi/ingleezaya*
Europe	*orobba*	*orobbi/orobbaya*
Finland	*finlanda*	*finlandi/finlandaya*
France	*faransa*	*faransawi/faransawaya*
Germany	*almanya*	*almaeni/almanaya*
Gibraltar	*gabal Tari'*	*min gabal Tari'*
Great Britain	*briTanya il°ozma*	*briTani/briTanaya*
Greece	*il yonaen*	*yonaeni/yonaenaya*
Holland	*holanda*	*holandi/holandaya*
India	*il hind*	*hindi/hindaya*
Iran	*iraan*	*iraani/iranaya*
Iraq	*il °iraq*	*°iraqi/°iraqaya*
Ireland	*ayrlanda*	*ayrlandi/ayrlandaya*
Israel	*isra'eel*	*isra'eeli/isra'eelaya*
Italy	*iTaliya*	*Tilyani/Tilyanaya*

Japan	*il yabaen*	*yabaeni/yabanaya*
Jordan	*ilordon*	*ordonni/ordonnaya*
Kuwait	*ikoweet*	*kweeti/kweetaya*
Lebanon	*libnaen*	*libnaeni/libnaenaya*
Libya	*libya*	*leebee/leebaya*
Malta	*malTa*	*malTi/malTaya*
Mauritania	*moritanya*	*moritaeni/moritaenaya*
Morocco	*il maghreb*	*maghrebi/maghrebaya*
New Zealand	*nyozeelanda*	*nyozeelandi/*
		nyozeelandaya
Norway	*inorweeg*	*norweegi/norweegaya*
Oman	*ᵃoman*	*ᵃomani/ᵃomanaya*
Palestine	*filisTeen*	*filisTeeni/filisTeenaya*
Portugal	*il bortoghael*	*bortoghaeli/*
		bortoghaelaya
Qatar	*qaTar*	*qaTari/qaTaraya*
Russia	*rosya*	*roosee/roosaya*
Saudi Arabia	*isoᵃodaya*	*soᵃoodi/soᵃoodaya*
Scotland	*skotlanda*	*iskotlandi/iskotlandaya*
Spain	*asbaniya*	*asbaeni/asbanaya*
Sudan	*isoodaen*	*soodaeni/soodanaya*
Sweden	*isoweed*	*soweedi/soweedaya*
Switzerland	*swisra*	*siwesri/siwesraya*
Syria	*sorya*	*sooree/sooraya*
Tunisia	*toonis*	*tonsi/tonsaya*
Turkey	*torkaya*	*torki/torkaya*
United Arab Emirates	*il imaraat il ᵃarabaya*	*min ilmaraat il ᵃarabaya*
United States of America	*il wilayaet il motaHida il amreekaya*	*amrikaeni/ amrikaenaya*
Wales	*waylz*	*min waylz*
Yemen	*il yaman*	*yamani/yamanaya*

PLACE NAMES

Abu Dhabi	*aboo Zabi*	أبوظبى
Aleppo	*Halab*	حلب
Alexandria	*iskinderayya*	الأسكندريه
Algiers	*algazaeir*	الجزائر
Amman	*ᵃamaen*	عمان
Cairo	*ilqahira*	القاهره
Casablanca	*idar ilbayDa*	الدار البيضاء
Damascus	*dimash'*	دمشق
Dubai	*doobay*	دبى
Fez	*faes*	فاس
Jeddah	*gadda*	جده
Luxor	*lo'Sor*	الأقصر
Karnak	*alkarnak*	الكرنك
Khartoum	*alkharToom*	الخرطوم
Marrakesh	*maraakish*	مراكش
Mecca	*makka*	مكه
Medina	*imadeena*	المدينه
Petra	*betra*	بترا
Riyadh	*ariyaaD*	الرياض
Suez	*isoways*	السويس
Tangier	*Tanga*	طنجه
Tripoli	*Tarablos*	طرابلس
Tunis	*toonis*	تونس
Valley of the Kings	*waedi imolooq*	وادى الملوك

GENERAL SIGNS AND NOTICES

Arabic	English
إجذب	Pull
إحذر	Caution
إحذرالكلب	Beware of the dog
إدفع	Push
اسعافات أوليه	First aid
الدخول مجاناً	Admission free
أطرق الباب من فضلك	Please knock
الدورالأرضى	Ground floor
اوكازيون	Sale, For sale
بارد	Cold
بوليس	Police
بويه	Wet paint
جرس حريق	Fire alarm
حجرات للأيجار	Rooms to let
خدمات الزبائن	Customer service
خروج	Exit
خروج (طوارئ)	(Emergency) exit
خطر	Danger
خطرالموت	Danger of death
دخول	Entrance
دق الجرس من فضلك	Please ring
رجال	Gentlemen
ساخن	Hot
سلم كهربائى	Escalator
سيدات	Ladies
صراف	Cashier

ضريبه	Tax, VAT
طريق خاص	Private road
عاطل	Out of order
عرض مسائى	Late performance
فاضى	Free, vacant
عرض خاص	Special offer
للأيجار	To let, For hire
محجوز	Reserved
مرحبا	Welcome
مشغول	Engaged
مصعد	Lift
مغلق	Closed
مغلق بمناسبة الأعياد	Closed for holidays
مغلق بمناسبة الأجازة الرسميه	Closed on public holidays
مغلق طول اليوم	Closed all day
مفتوح	Open
مفتوح خلال الأسبوع	Open on weekdays
مكان للوقوف فقط	Standing room only
ممنوع	Forbidden, prohibited
ممنوع الأزعاج	Do not disturb
ممنوع التجاوز	No trespassing
ممنوع التدخين	No smoking
ممنوع الدخول	No entrance
ممنوع اللمس	Do not touch
ممنوع المرور للمشاه	No thoroughfare for pedestrians
منطقه عسكريه	Military zone
مياه غيرصالحه للشرب	Not drinking water
مياه صالحه للشرب	Drinking water

CONVERSION TABLES (approximate equivalents)

Linear measurements

centimetres	*santimetr*	سینتیمتر
metres	*metr*	متر
kilometres	*keeloometr*	کیلومتر

10 cm = 4 inches	1 inch = 2.45 cm
50 cm = 19.6 inches	1 foot = 30 cm
1 metre = 39.37 inches	1 yard = 0.91 m
(just over 1 yard)	
100 metres = 110 yards	
1 km = 0.62 miles	1 mile = 1.61 km

To convert: km to miles: divide by 8 and multiply by 5
            miles to km: divide by 5 and multiply by 8

Miles		Kilometres
0.6	1	1.6
1.2	2	3.2
1.9	3	4.8
2.5	4	6.4
3	5	8
6	10	16
12	20	32
19	30	48
25	40	64
31	50	80
62	100	161
68	110	177
75	120	193
81	130	209

Liquid measures

| litre | *litr* | لتر |

1 litre = 1.8 pints   1 pint = 0.57 litres
5 litres = 1.1 gallons   1 gallon = 4.55 litres

'A litre of water's a pint and three quarters'

Gallons		Litres
0.2	1	4.5
0.4	2	9
0.7	3	13.6
0.9	4	18
1.1	5	23
2.2	10	45.5

Weights

gram	*gram*	جرام
100 grams	*meet gram*	١٠٠ جرام
200 grams	*meetayn gram*	٢٠٠ جرام
kilo	*keeloo*	كيلو

100 g = 3.5 oz   1 oz = 28 g
200 g = 7 oz   1/4 lb = 113 g
1/2 kilo = 1.1 lb   1/2 lb = 227 g
1 kilo = 2.2 lb   1 lb = 454 g

Pounds		Kilos (Grams)
2.2	1	0.45 (450)
4.4	2	0.9 (900)
6.6	3	1.4 (1400)
8.8	4	1.8 (1800)
11	5	2.3 (2300)
22	10	4.5 (4500)

Area

The unit of area used in the Arabic-speaking world is the
fedaen, which is slightly larger than an acre, or about half a
hectare. In some countries, hectares are also used.

Hectares		Acres
0.4	1	2.5
2	5	12
4	10	25
10	50	124
40.5	100	247

Clothing and shoe sizes

Women's dresses and suits

UK	10	12	14	16	18	20
Arab world	36	38	40	42	44	46

Men's suits and coats

UK	36	38	40	42	44	46
Arab world	46	48	50	52	54	56

Men's shirts

UK	14	$14^1/_2$	15	$15^1/_2$	16	$16^1/_2$	17
Arab world	36	37	38	39	41	42	43

Shoes

UK	2	3	4	5	6	7	8	9	10	11
Arab world	35	36	37	38	39	41	42	43	44	45

Waist and chest measurements

inches	28	30	32	34	36	38	40	42	44	46	48	50
centimetres	71	76	81	87	91	97	102	107	112	117	122	127

Tyre pressures

lb/sq in	15	18	20	22	24	26	28	30	33	35
kg/sq cm	1.1	1.3	1.4	1.5	1.7	1.8	2.0	2.1	2.3	2.5

NATIONAL HOLIDAYS

(*see* Religion and culture, *page 8*)

Christian and Islamic feasts are celebrated at different times each year according to the Muslim (lunar) or Christian (Coptic) calendar.

The main religious holidays are:

Muslim

ᵃeed il fiTr	The Breakfast Feast (3 days, after Ramadan)
ᵃeed il aDHa	The Biram Feast (4 days)
il moolid il nabawi	The Prophet's Birthday (1 day)

The timing of all these feasts depends upon the sighting of the New Moon.

Christian

krismas	Christmas (25 December)
ras il sana	New Year (31 December)
krismas	Coptic Christmas (7 January)
ᵃeed il qiyama	Easter

Other days mark political and military achievements and each country will have its own particular public days of celebration or holiday. It is advisable to check with the relevant tourist office before planning a visit, to ensure that you do not arrive at a time when everything is closed!

USEFUL ADDRESSES

In the UK and Ireland

(Where no separate address is given, Ireland is accredited to the London embassies.)

Egypt

Egyptian Embassy
26 South Street, London W1 *Tel:* 071-499 2401

Eygptian Consulate (*for visas*)
2 Lowndes Street, London SW1 *Tel:* 071-235 9777

Egyptian Embassy
12 Clyde Road, Ballsbridge, Dublin *Tel:* 01 606 566

Egyptian Tourist Authority
168 Piccadilly, London W1 *Tel:* 071-493 5282

Jordan

Jordanian Embassy
6 Upper Phillimore Gardens, London W8 *Tel:* 071-937 3685

Tourist information on Jordan is supplied through:

Royal Jordanian Airlines
211 Regent Street, London W1 *Tel:* 071-437 9465

Morocco

Moroccan Embassy
49 Queensgate Gardens, London SW7 *Tel:* 071-581 5001

Moroccan Consulate
97 Praed Street, London W2 *Tel:* 071-724 0719

Ireland is accredited to the Moroccan Embassy in Brussels:
29 Boulevard St Michel, 1040 Brussels
Tel: 376 1100/5

Moroccan Tourist Office
174 Regent Street, London W1 *Tel:* 071-437 0073

Saudi Arabia

Saudi Arabian Embassy
15 Curzon Street, London W1 *Tel:* 071-917 3000

Bahrain

Bahraini Embassy
98 Gloucester Road, London SW7 *Tel:* 071-370 5132

Syria

Syrian Embassy
8 Belgrave Square, London W1 *Tel:* 071-245 9012

In the Arab world

Egypt

British Embassy
Ahmed Ragheb Street, Garden City, Cairo *Tel:* 02 354 0850

There are British consulates in Alexandria, Luxor, Suez and Port Said.

There is no Irish Embassy in Egypt, only an honorary consul. Find out details before travelling, since they are liable to change.

Egyptian Tourist Authority (*headquarters*)
Misr Travel Tower, Abbassia Square, Cairo *Tel:* 02 823510/ 02 824858

Jordan

British Embassy
P.O.B. 87, Abdoun, Amman *Tel:* 06 823100

There is an Irish honorary consul in Amman. Check details before travel.

Tourist information is available from the Ministry of Tourism in Amman. *Tel:* 06 642311.

Morocco

British Embassy
17 Boulevard de la Tour, Hasan Rabat *Tel:* 0727 20905/6

There are also British Embassy representatives in Tangier, Casablanca and Agadir.

Morocco is accredited to the Irish Embassy in Paris:
Embassy of Ireland, 12 Avenue Foch, 75116 Paris
Tel: 45 00 20 87

Tourist Information Centre
22 Avenue d'Alger, Rabat *Tel:* 0773 0562

Saudi Arabia

British Embassy
P.O.B. 94351, Riyadh 11693 *Tel:* 01 488 0077

There is also a British consulate in Jeddah.

Irish Embassy
Diplomatic Quarter, Riyadh *Tel:* 01 488 2300

ENGLISH - ARABIC DICTIONARY

There is a list of car and bicycle parts on pages 46, parts of the body on page 148, and Menu reader on page 98; see also the lists on pages 168–176. Numbers are inside the front cover and on page 188.

Verbs are given in the third person singular (*m* and *f*). (*See* Basic grammar, *page 158*.)

A

about (*relating to*)	*ªan*	عن
(*approximately*)	*Hawaeli*	حوالي
above	*fo'*	فوق
abroad	*barra*	بره
abscess	*waram* (m)	ورم
accept: he/she accepts	*ye'bal* (m)/*te'bal* (f)	يقبل/ تقبل
accident	*Hadsa* (f)	حادثه
accommodation	*sakan* (m)	سكن
according to	*Hasab*	حسب
account (*bank; bill*)	*Hissaeb* (m)	حساب
accountant	*moHaesib* (m)/ *moHasba* (f)	محاسب/ محاسبه
ache	*wagaª* (m)	وجع
acid	*Haamid* (m)	حامض
across	*ªabr*	عبر
acrylic	*akrilik* (m)	اكريليك
act (*on stage*): he/she acts	*yemassel* (m)/ *temassel* (f)	يمثل/ تمثل
activity	*nashaat* (m)	نشاط

Bahrain

British Embassy
21 Government Avenue, Manama, Bahrain *Tel:* 534404

Bahrain is accredited to the Irish Embassy in Riyadh.

Syria

British Embassy
Quarter Malki, 11 Mohammad Kurd Ali Street, Imm Kotob, Damascus *Tel:* 011 712561

There is also a British consulate in Aleppo.

Tourist information is available from Damascus airport, and from the Ministry of Tourism, Damascus.

NUMBERS

0	*Sefr*	٠
1	*waHid, waHda*	١
2	*itnayn*	٢
3	*talaeta*	٣
4	*arbaa*	٤
5	*khamsa*	٥
6	*setta*	٦
7	*saba*	٧
8	*tamanya*	٨
9	*tesa*	٩
10	*ashra*	١٠
11	*Hidashar*	١١
12	*itnashar*	١٢
13	*talatashar*	١٣
14	*arbatashar*	١٤
15	*khamastashar*	١٥
16	*setashar*	١٦
17	*sabatashar*	١٧
18	*tamantashar*	١٨
19	*tesatashar*	١٩
20	*ishreen*	٢٠
21	*waHid wi ishreen*	٢١
22	*itnayn wi ishreen*	٢٢
23 *etc.*	*talaeta wi ishreen*	٢٣
30	*talaeteen*	٣٠
31	*waHid wi talaeteen*	٣١
32 *etc.*	*itnayn wi talaeteen*	٣٢
40	*arbeen*	٤٠
50	*khamseen*	٥٠
60	*seteen*	٦٠
70	*sabeen*	٧٠

188

80	*tamaneen*	٨٠
90	*teseen*	٩٠
100	*maya*	١٠٠
101	*maya wi waHid*	١٠١
102 *etc.*	*maya wi itnayn*	١٠٢
150	*maya wi khamseen*	١٥٠
200	*mitayn*	٢٠٠
300	*toltomaya*	٣٠٠
400	*robomaya*	٤٠٠
500	*khomsomaya*	٥٠٠
600	*sotomaya*	٦٠٠
700	*sobomaya*	٧٠٠
800	*tomnomaya*	٨٠٠
900	*tosomaya*	٩٠٠
1,000	*alf*	١٠٠٠
1,100 *etc.*	*alf wi maya*	١١٠٠
2,000	*alfayn*	٢٠٠٠
3,000	*talatalaef*	٣٠٠٠
4,000	*arbatalaef*	٤٠٠٠
5,000	*khamastalaef*	٥٠٠٠
6,000	*setalaef*	٦٠٠٠
7,000	*sabatalaef*	٧٠٠٠
8,000	*tamantalaef*	٨٠٠٠
9,000	*tesatalaef*	٩٠٠٠
100,000	*mit alf*	١٠٠,٠٠٠
1,000,000	*miliown*	١,٠٠٠,٠٠٠
2,000,000	*itnayn miliown*	٢,٠٠٠,٠٠٠

The number one has two forms, for use with masculine and feminine nouns: *waHid* (m) and *waHda* (f).

Compound numbers in Arabic are written from left to right, as in English. For example, 1993 = ١٩٩٣; 1414 = ١٤...

● Years

1993	*alf wi tosomaya talaeta wi te...*
2000	*alfayn*

English	Transliteration	Arabic
actor	*momassil* (m)	ممثل
actress	*momassilla* (f)	ممثله
adaptor (*electrical*)	*moHawil* (m)	محول
add (*count*): he/she adds	*ye^ad* (m)/*te^ad* (f)	يعد / تعد
addicted	*modmin* (m)/ *modmina* (f)	مدمن / مدمنه
address	*^aenwaen* (m)	عنوان
adhesive tape	*wara' lazza'* (m)	ورق لزاق
admission	*dekhool* (m)	دخول
admission charge	*tazkarit dekhool*	تزكرة دخول
adopted	*tabaenna* (m)/ *tabaennat* (f)	تبنى / تبنت
adult	*raashid* (m)/ *rashida* (f)	رشيد / رشيده
advance: in advance	*mo'addam:* *mo'addaman*	مقدم / مقدماً
advanced (level)	*(mestawa) ^aaeli*	مستوى عالى
advertisement	*i^alaen* (m)	إعلان
advertising	*de^aaya* (f)	دعايه
aerial	*erial* (m)	إيريال
aeroplane	*Taiyaara* (f)	طياره
afford: I/we can't afford it	*mish 'addena*	مش قدنا
afraid: he/she is afraid	*khayef* (m)/*khayfa* (f)	خايف / خايفه
after(wards)	*ba^adayn*	بعدين
afternoon	*ba^ad iDohr* (m)	بعدالظهر
aftershave	*ba^ad il Hela'a*	بعدالحلاقه
again	*taeni*	تانى
against	*Ded*	ضد
age	*^aomr* (m)	عمر
agency	*wikaela* (f)	وكاله
ago	*min*	من
a week ago	*min izboo^a*	من اسبوع

191

English	Transliteration	Arabic
agree: he/she agrees	*yewafe'* (m)/ *tewafe'* (f)	يوافق / توافق
I agree	*ana metefe'* (m)/ *ana metefa'* (f)	أنامتفق / أنامتفقه
I don't agree	*ana mish mewafe'* (m)/*ana mish mewaf'a* (f)	انامش موافق / انامش موافقه
AIDS	*aidz* (m)	أبدز
air	*hawa* (m)	هواء
by air	*bil gaw*	بالجو
(by) air mail	*bareed gawi*	بريد جوي
air conditioning	*takyeef hawa* (m)	تكييف هواء
air force	*selaH eTayaran* (m)	سلاح الطيران
airline	*khaT gawi* (m)	خط جوي
airport	*maTaar* (m)	مطار
aisle	*Tor'a* (f)	طرقه
alarm	*inzaar* (m)	إنزار
alarm clock	*menabbeh* (m)	منبه
alcohol	*khamra* (f)	خمره
alcoholic (*content*)	*fi khamra*	فيه خمره
(*person*)	*khamorggi* (m)/ *khamorggaya* (f)	خمرجي / خمرجيه
alive	*Hai* (m)/*Haiya* (f)	حي / حيه
all	*kol*	كل
allergic (to)	*Hasassayya (Ded)*	حساسيه ضد
alley	*Hara* (f)	حاره
allow: he/she allows	*yesmaH* (m)/ *tesmaH* (f)	يسمح / تسمح
(not) allowed	*(mish) masmooH*	(مش) مسموح
all right	*kwayyis* (m)/ *kwayissa* (f)	كويس / كويسه
almond	*lowz* (pl)	لوز
alone	*lewaHdi*	لوحدي
also	*kamaen*	كمان
although	*belraghm min*	بالرغم من
always	*dayman*	دائما
am (*see* 'to be', p. 165)		

192

English	Transliteration	Arabic
ambassador	*safeer* (m)/*safeera* (f)	سفير/ سفيره
ambition	*TomooH* (m)	طموح
ambitious	*TamooH* (m)/ *TamooHa* (f)	طموح/ طموحه
ambulance	*es^aaaf* (m)	إسعاف
among	*min Demn*	من ضمن
amount	*kemayya* (f)	كميه
amusement arcade	*Salit le^ab*	صالة لعب
amusement park	*malaehee* (pl)	ملاهى
anaesthetic	*beng* (m)	بنج
general anaesthetic	*beng ^aam*	بنج عام
and	*wa*	و
angry	*ghaDbaan* (m)/ *ghaDbaana* (f)	غضبان/ غضبانه
animal	*Hayaewaen* (m)	حيوان
anniversary	*zekra* (f) *sanawaya*	ذكرى سنويه
annoyed	*metdaye'* (m)/ *metday'a* (f)	متدايق/ متدايقه
anorak	*jaketta* (f)	جاكته
another (one)	*kamaen (waHid* (m)/ *waHda* (f))	كمان (واحد/ واحده)
answer	*gawaeb* (m)	جواب
answer: he/she answers	*yigaewib* (m)/ *tigaewib* (f)	يجاوب/ تجاوب
antibiotic	*moDaad Hayawee* (m)	مضاد حيوى
antique	*'adeem* (m)/ *'adeema* (f)	قديم/ قديمه
antiseptic	*mo^aaqam* (m)/ *mo^aaqama* (f)	معقم/ معقمه
anxious	*'al'aen* (m)/ *'al'aena* (f)	قلقان/ قلقانه
anyone	*ay Had*	أى حد
anything	*ay Haga*	أى حاجة
anything else?	*Haga tanya*	حاجه تانيه؟
anyway	*^aalla 'ay Haal*	على أى حال
anywhere	*ay makaen*	أى مكان
apart (from)	*biSarf inaZar (^aan)*	بصرف النظر (عن)

193

English	Transliteration	Arabic
apartment	*sha'a* (f)	شقه
aperitif	*fatH nefs* (m)	فتح نفس
appendicitis	*il moSran ela ª war* (m)	المصران الأعور
apple	*tofaHa* (f)	تفاحه
appointment	*mi ª aed* (m)	ميعاد
approximately	*Hawaeli*	حوالي
apricot	*mishmish* (m)	مشمش
Arab	*ª arabi* (m)/ *ª arabaya* (f)	عربي/عربيه
Arabic	*ª arabi* (m)	عربي
arch	*qoos* (m)	قوس
archaeology	*ª ilm il athaar* (m)	علم الآثار
architect	*mohandis me ª maeri* (m)/*mohandissa me ª maraya* (f)	مهندس معماري/مهندسه معماريه
are (*see* 'to be', *p. 165*)		
argument	*mona'sha* (f)	مناقشه
arm	*dera ª* (m)	ذراع
army	*gaysh* (m)	جيش
around	*Hawalayn*	حول
arrange: he/she arranges		
(*appointment*)	*yewaDab* (m)/ *tewaDab* (f)	يوضب/توضب
(*flowers etc.*)	*yenassa'* (m)/ *tenassa'* (f)	ينسق/تنسق
arrivals	*woSool* (m)	وصول
arrive: he/she arrives	*waSal* (m)/*waSalit* (f)	وصل/وصلت
art	*faen* (m)	فن
fine arts	*faenoon gameela* (pl)	فنون جميله
art gallery	*matHaf* (m)	متحف
artichoke	*kharshoof* (m)	خرشوف
article	*maqala* (f)	مقاله
artificial	*Senaa ª i* (m)/ *Senaa ª iya* (f)	صناعي/صناعيه
artist	*faennaen* (m)/ *faennaena* (f)	فنان/فنانه

194

artistic	*faenni* (m)/	فنى/ فنيه
	faennaya (f)	
as (*like*)	*zai*	زى
(*while*)	*baynama*	بينما
ash	*Tafye* (f)	طفيه
ashtray	*Taffaya* (f)	طفايه
ask: he/she asks	*yes'al* (m)/*tes'al* (f)	يسأل/ تسأل
aspirin	*asbereen* (m)	اسبرين
assistant (*in shop*)	*baya^a* (m)/*baya^aa* (f)	بياع/ بياعه
asthma	*raboo* (m)	ربو
Aswan Dam	*isad il^aaeli*	السد العالى
at	*fi*	فى
athletics	*gombaaZ* (m)	جباز
atmosphere	*gaw* (m)	جو
attack: he/she	*yehgem* (m)/	يهجم/ تهجم
attacks	*tehgem* (f)	
attendant (*garage*)	*baya^a* (m)/*baya^aa* (f)	بياع/ بياعه
(*museum*)	*mowaZaf* (m)/	موظف/ موظفه
	mowaZafa (f)	
attractive	*gaZaeb* (m)/	جذاب/ جذابه
	gaZaeba (f)	
aubergine	*betingaen* (m)	باذنجان
auction	*maezaed* (m)	مزاد
aunt (*mother's side*)	*khaela* (f)	خاله
(*father's side*)	*^aamma* (f)	عمه
author	*mo'allif* (m)/	مؤلف/ مؤلفه
	mo'allifa (f)	
automatic	*tomateeki* (m)/	اوتوماتيكى/
	tomateekaya (f)	اوتوماتيكيه
autumn	*khareef* (m)	خريف
avenue	*share^a* (m)	شارع
avocado	*avokaeta* (f)	افوكاته
avoid: he/she avoids	*yatagannab* (m)/	يتجنب/ تتجنب
	tatagannab (f)	
away	*be^aeed*	بعيد
. . . away (*distance*)	. . . *min hena*	من هنا
awful	*weHish* (m)/	وحش/ وحشه
	weHsha (f)	

195

B

English	Transliteration	Arabic
baby	*baybi* (m)	بايبى
baby food	*akl* (m) *il baybi*	أكل البيبى
baby's bottle	*bazaezit* (f) *il baybi*	بزازيت البيبى
babysitter	*galeesit aTfaal* (f)	جليسةاطفال
back	*Dahr* (m)	ظهر
back: at the back (of)	*khalf*	خلف
backwards	*khalfi*	خلفى
bad	*weHish* (m)/ *weHsha* (f)	وحش/ وحشه
bag	*shanTa* (f)	شنطة
baggage	*aafsh* (pl)	عفش
baker's	*khabbaez* (m)	خباز
balcony	*balakowna* (f)	بلكونه
bald	*aSlaa* (m)	أصلع
ball	*kora* (f)	كوره
ballet	*ra's il balay* (m)	رقص الباليه
ballpoint pen	*alam gaef* (m)	قلم جاف
banana	*mowza* (f)	موزه
band (*music*)	*fer'a* (f)	فرقه
bandage	*rabTa* (f)	ربطه
bank	*bank* (m)	بنك
bank (*i.e. public*) holiday	*'agaeza rasmaya* (f)	اجازه رسميه
bar	*baar* (m)	بار
barber	*Hallae'* (m)	حلاق
bargain	*lo'Ta* (f)	لقطه
bargain: he/she bargains	*yizaewid* (m)/ *tizaewid* (f)	يذايد/ تذايد
baseball	*bayzbowl* (m)	بايزبول
basement	*badrown* (m)	بدرون
basin	*HowD* (m)	حوض
basket	*sabat* (m)	سبت
basketball	*korit il salla*	كورة السلة
bath	*banyo* (m)	بانيو

196

bathe: he/she bathes	*yestaHamma* (m)/	يستحمى / تستحمى
	testaHamma (f)	
bathing costume	*mayo* (m)	مايوه
bathroom	*Hammaem* (m)	حمام
battery	*baTarayya* (f)	بطاريه
bay	*sharm* (m)	شرم
bazaar	*sooq* (m)	سوق
be (*see* 'to be', *p. 165*)		
beach	*shaati'* (m)	شاطئ
beans (*dried brown*)	*fool* (m)	فول
(*French/green*)	*faSolya khaDra* (f)	فاصوليا خضراء
beard	*da'n* (f)	دقن
beautiful	*gameel* (m)/	جميل / جميله
	gameela (f)	
because	*bisabab*	بسبب
bed	*sereer* (m)	سرير
bedroom	*otil* (f) *nowm*	حجرة النوم
bee	*naHla* (f)	نحله
beef	*ba'ari* (f)	بقرى
beer	*beera* (f)	بيره
beetroot	*bangar* (m)	بنجر
before	*'abl*	قبل
begin: he/she begins	*yabda'* (m)/*tabda'* (f)	يبدأ / تبدأ
beginner	*mobtade'* (m)/	مبتدى / مبتدئه
	mobtade'a (f)	
beginning	*bidaya* (f)	بدايه
behind	*wara*	وراء
beige	*bayj*	بيج
believe: he/she	*yeSada'* (m)/	يصدق / تصدق
believes	*teSada'* (f)	
bell	*garas* (m)	جرس
below	*taHt*	تحت
belt	*Hizaem* (m)	حزام
bend	*monHana* (m)	منحنى
bend: he/she bends	*yetnee* (m)/*tetnee* (f)	ينى / تنى
bent	*matni* (m)/*matnaya* (f)	متنى / متنيه
berries	*toot* (pl)	توت
berth	*sereer* (m)	سرير

English	Transliteration	Arabic
beside	*ganb*	جنب
besides	*bil eDaafa ila*	بالأضافة
best	*aHsan*	احسن
better (than)	*aHsan (min)*	أحسن من
between	*bayn*	بين
beyond (*place*)	*ba^ad*	بعد
bib	*maryala* (f)	مريله
Bible	*ingeel* (m)	إنجيل
bicycle	*^aagala* (f)	عجله
big	*kibeer* (m)/	كبير/ كبيره
	kibeera (f)	
bigger	*akbar*	أكبر
bill	*fatoora* (f)	فاتوره
bin (*rubbish*)	*SafeeHa* (f)	صفيحه
binoculars	*naDara* (f)	نضاره معظمه
	mo^aazzama	
biochemistry	*kemya Hayawaya* (f)	كيمياء حيويه
biology	*aHia'* (pl)	أحياء
bird	*^aaSfoora* (f)	عصفوره
birthday	*^aeed milaed* (m)	عيد ميلاد
biscuit	*baskaweet* (pl)	بسكويت
bishop	*osqof* (m)	أسقف
(a) bit	*showaya*	شويه
bite: he/she bites	*ye^aoD* (m)/*te'^aoD* (f)	يعض/ تعض
bitter	*morr* (m)/*morra* (f)	مُر/ مره
black	*eswid* (m)/*sowda* (f)	اسود/ سوده
black and white (*film*)	*abyaD wi eswid*	ابيض و أسود
black coffee	*'ahwa saeda*	قهوة ساده
blanket	*baTanaya* (f)	بطانيه
bleed: he/she bleeds	*yenzif* (m)/*tenzif* (f)	ينزف/ تنزف
blister	*qorHa* (f)	
blocked	*masdood* (m)/	ـود/ مسدوده
	masdooda (f)	
blond(e)	*ash'ar* (m)/	لمقر/ شقره
	sha'ara (f)	
blood	*dam* (m)	ادم

English	Transliteration	Arabic
blouse	*bilooza* (f)	بلوزه
blow: he/she blows	*yenfokh* (m)/ *tonfokh* (f)	ينفخ/ تنفخ
blue	*azra'* (m)/*zar'a* (f)	ازرق/ زرقاء
board: he/she boards (*bus etc.*)	*yerkab* (m)/*terkab* (f)	يركب/ تركب
boarding card	*biTa'it* (f) *isaffar*	بطاقه السفر
boat	*markib* (f)	مركب
boat trip (*by sea*)	*reHla baHaraya*	رحله بحريه
(*on river*)	*reHla nahraya*	رحله نهريه
body	*gesm* (f)	جسم
bodyguard	*Haris* (m)	حارس
boil: he/she boils	*yeghlee* (m)/*teghlee* (f)	يغلي/ تغلي
boiled egg	*bayDa masloo'a* (f)	بيضه مسلوقه
boiler	*sakhaen* (m)	سخان
bomb	*kombela* (f)	قنبله
bone	*ªaDma* (f)	عظمه
book	*kitaeb* (m)	كتاب
book: he/she books	*yeHgiz* (m)/ *teHgiz* (f)	يحجز/ تحجز
booking	*Hagz* (m)	حجز
booking office	*shibaek il Hagz* (m)	شباك الحجز
booklet	*kotayib* (m)	كتيب
bookshop	*maktaba* (f)	مكتبه
boots	*boot* (m)	بوت
border (*edge/ frontier*)	*Hedood* (pl)	حدود
bored	*zah'aen* (m)/ *zah'aena* (f)	زهقان/ زهقانه
boring	*momil* (m)/ *momila* (f)	ممل/ ممله
...s	*irayyis* (m)/ *irayissa* (f)	الريس/ الريسه
...oth	*ilitneen*	الأتنين
...ottle	*izaeza* (f)	قزازه
...ottle opener	*fataeHa* (f)	فتاحه
bottom	*qaaª* (m)	قاع

bow (*ship*)	*moqademit il markib* (f)	مقدمة المركب
(*knot*)	*babyowna* (f)	بابيونه
bowl	*Taba'* (m) *ghaweet*	طبق غويط
box	*ªelba* (f)	علبه
box office	*shibaek* (m) *il Hagz*	شباك الحجز
boy	*walad* (m)	ولد
boyfriend	*boyfrend* (m)	بوى فريند
bra	*sotyaen* (m)	سوتيان
bracelet	*isswera* (f)	إسوره
braces	*Hammaela* (f)	حماله
brain	*ªa'l* (m)	عقل
branch (*of tree*)	*farª* (m)	فرع
brand	*marka* (f)	ماركه
brandy	*brandi* (m)	براندى
brass	*naHaes* (m)	نحاس
brave	*shogaeª* (m)/ *shogaeªa* (f)	شجاع / شجاعه
bread	*ªaysh* (pl)	عيش
Arabic	*ªaysh baladi*	عيش بلدى
bread shop	*khabbaez* (m)	خباز
break: he/she breaks	*yeksar* (m)/*teksar* (f)	يكسر / تكسر
breakdown	*qoTl* (m)	عطل
breakfast	*fiTaar* (m)	أفطار
breast	*Sedr* (m)	صدر
breathe: he/she breathes	*yetanafis* (m)/ *tetanafis* (f)	يتنفس / تتنفس
bride	*ªaroosa* (f)	عروسه
bridegroom	*ªarees* (m)	عريس
bridge	*kobri* (m)	كوبرى
briefcase	*shanTa* (f)	شنطة
bright (*colour*)	*faeteH*	فاتح
(*light*)	*baree'*	بريق
bring: he/she brings	*yegeeb* (m)/*tegeeb* (f)	يجيب / تجيب
British	*briTani* (m)/ *briTanaya* (f)	بريطانى / بريطانيه

English	Transliteration	Arabic
broad	*ªareeD* (m)/ *ªareeDa* (f)	عريض/ عريضه
brochure	*katalowg* (m)	كتالوج
broken	*maksoor* (m)/ *maksoora* (f)	مكسور/ مكسوره
bronchitis	*iltihaeb re'awi* (m)	إلتهاب رئوى
bronze	*bronz* (m)	بروندز
brooch	*browsh* (m)	بروش
brother	*'akh* (m)	أخ
my brother	*akhooya* (m)	اخويا
brother-in-law	*neseeb* (m)	نسيب
my brother-in-law	*neseebi* (m)	نسيبى
brown	*bonni*	بنى
brown sugar	*sokkar* (m) *aSfar*	سكر اصفر
bruise	*khadsh* (m)	خدش
brush	*forsha* (f)	فرشه
bucket	*gardal* (m)	جردل
buffet	*boofay* (m)	بوفيه
build: he/she builds	*yebni* (m)/*tebni* (f)	يبنى/ تبنى
builder	*ªamil bonna* (m)	عامل بناء
building	*mabna* (m)	مبنى
bulb (*light*)	*lamba* (f)	لمبه
bull	*towr* (m)	ثور
bumper	*ekSidaam* (m)	إكصدام
burn	*Har'* (m)	حرق
burn: he/she burns	*yeHra'* (m)/*teHra'* (f)	يحرق/ تحرق
burnt	*maHroo'* (m)/ *maHroo'a* (f)	محروق/ محروقه
bus	*otobees* (m)	اوتوبيس
by bus	*bil otobees*	بالاوتوبيس
bus-driver	*sawa'* (m) *ilotobees*	سواق الأوتوبيس
bus station, stop	*maHaTit ilotobees*	محطةالاوتوبيس
business	*ma'mooraya* (f)	مأموريه
business trip	*reHlit aªmael* (f)	رحلة أعمال
on business	*fi ma'mooraya*	فى مأموريه
businessman	*ragil aªmael* (m)	رجل اعمال
businesswoman	*sayidit aªmael* (f)	سيدة اعمال

English	Transliteration	Arabic
business studies	*idarit a^amael*	إدارة أعمال
busy	*mashghool* (m)/ *mashghoola* (f)	مشغول/ مشغوله
but	*laekin*	لكن
butane gas	*botagaez* (m)	بوتاجاز
butcher's	*gazzaar* (m)	جزار
butter	*zebda* (f)	زبده
butterfly	*faraasha* (f)	فراشه
button	*zooraar* (m)	زرار
buy: he/she buys	*yeshteri* (m)/ *teshteri* (f)	يشترى/ تشترى
by (author)	*ta'leef*	تأليف
(train, bus etc.)	*bil*	بال

C

cabbage	*koronb* (f pl)	كرنب
cabin	*kabeena* (f)	كابينه
cable car	*metro mo^aallaq*	مترو معلق
café	*'ahwa* (pl)	قهوه
cake	*kayka* (pl)	كيكه
cake shop	*Halawaenni* (m)	حلوانى
calculator	*kalkoolaytor* (m)	كالكوليتر
call (telephone)	*mokalma* (f)	مكالمه
call: he/she calls	*yinaedee* (m)/ *tinaedee* (f)	ينادى/ تنادى
I am called	*ismi*	إسمى
calm	*haedi* (m)/*hadya* (f)	هادئ/ هادنه
camel	*gamal* (m & f)	جمل
camera	*kamira* (f)	كاميرا
camomile tea	*sheeH* (m)	شيح
campbed	*sereer khayma* (m)	سرير خيمه
camping	*ye^aaskar* (m)	يعسكر
campsite	*mo^aaskar* (m)	معسكر

can: he/she can		
(*is able to*)	*ye'dar* (m)/*te'dar* (f)	يقدر/ تقدر
(*knows how to*)	*ye^araf* (m)/*te^araf* (f)	يعرف/ تعرف
I could	*a'dar* (m & f)	أقدر
can (*tin*)	*^aelba* (f)	علبه
can opener	*fataHit il ^aelab* (f)	فتاحة العلب
cancel: he/she cancels	*yelghee* (m)/*telghee* (f)	يلغى/ تلغى
cancellation	*elgha'* (m)	إلغاء
cancer	*saraTaan* (m)	سرطان
candle	*sham^aa* (f)	شمعه
canoe	*'aerib* (m)	قارب
capital (*city*)	*^aaSima* (f)	عاصمه
captain	*kaptin* (m)	كابتن
car	*^aarabaya* (f),	عربيه/ سياره
	saiyaara (f)	
by car	*bil ^aarabaya*	بالعربيه
car hire	*saiyaraat lil*	سيارات للأيجار
	iygar (pl)	
car park	*maw'af*	موقف سيارات
	saiyaraat (m)	
caravan	*karavan* (m)	كارافان
(*of camels*)	*qafilat gimael*	قافلة جمال
caravan site	*mo^aaskar*	معسكر كارافانات
	karavanaat	
cardigan	*jaketta* (f)	جاكته
care: I don't care	*walla yehemennee*	ولا يهمنى
take care	*khod baelak* (m)/	خد بالك/
	khodi baelik (f)	خدى بالك
careful	*^aalla mahlak* (m)/	على مَهلك/ مهلك
	mahlik (f)	
careless	*mohmil* (m)/	مهمل/ مهمله
	mohmila (f)	
carpenter	*naggar* (m)	نجار
carpet	*seggaeda* (f)	سجاده
carriage (*railway*)	*^aarabaya* (f)	عربيه
carrier bag	*shanTa* (f)	شنطه
carrots	*gazar* (pl)	جزر

English	Transliteration	Arabic
carry: he/she carries	*yesheel* (m)/*tesheel* (f)	يشيل/ تشيل
car wash	*ghaseel* (m) *saiyaraat*	غسيل سيارات
case: in case	*fi haalit*	في حالة
cash	*kash* (m)	كاش
cash: he/she cashes	*yeSrif* (m)/*teSrif* (f)	يصرف/ تصرف
cash desk	*maktaeb* (m) *iSaraaf*	مكتب الصراف
cassette	*kassett* (m)	كاسيت
castle	*'al^aa* (f)	قلعه
cat	*'ot* (m)/*'otta* (f)	قط/ قطه
catalogue	*katalowg* (m)	كتالوج
catch: he/she catches		
(*train/bus; cold*)	*yakhod* (m)/*takhod* (f)	ياخد/ تاخد
(*ball*)	*yemsik* (m)/ *temsik* (f)	يمسك/ تمسك
cathedral	*katedr'aya* (f)	كاتدرائيه
Catholic	*katoleekee* (m)/ *katoleekaya* (f)	كاثوليكي/ كاثوليكيه
cauliflower	*'arnabeeT* (pl)	قرنبيط
cause: he/she causes	*yesabib* (m)/*tisabib* (f)	يسبب/ تسبب
caution	*HaZar* (m)	حذر
cave	*kahf* (m)	كهف
ceiling	*sa'f* (m)	سقف
celery	*karafs* (pl)	كرفس
cellar	*badrown* (m)	بدرون
cemetery	*'araafa* (f)	قرافه
centimetre	*santimetr* (m)	سنتمتر
central	*markazi*	مركزي
central heating	*tadfe'a markazaya* (f)	تدفئه مركزيه
centre	*markaz* (m)	مركز
century	*qarn* (m)	قرن
cereal (*crops*)	*Hoboob* (pl)	حبوب
certain	*moHadad*	محدد
certainly	*belta'keed*	بالتأكيد
certificate	*shahaeda* (f)	شهاده
chain	*selsela* (f)	سلسله
chair	*korsi* (m)	كرسي
chalet	*shalay* (m)	شاليه

champagne	*shambanya* (f)	شامبانيا
change (*small coins*)	*fakka* (pl)	فكه
change: he/she changes	*yeghaiyyar* (m)/ *teghaiyyar* (f)	يغير/ تغير
changing room	*Hammaem* (m)	حمام
chapel	*keneesa* (f)	كنيسه
charcoal	*faHm* (pl)	فحم
charge	*ogra* (f)	أجره
charge: he/she charges	*yeHaesib* (m)/ *teHaesib* (f)	يحاسب/ تحاسب
cheap	*rekheeS* (m)/ *rekheeSa* (f)	رخيص/ رخيصة
check: he/she checks	*yata'kad* (m)/ *tata'kad* (f)	يتأكد/ تتأكد
check-in (desk)	*maktaeb il tasgeel* (m)	مكتب التسجيل
cheek	*khad* (m)	خد
cheeky	*sha'i* (m)/*sha'aya* (f)	شقى/ شقيه
cheers!	*fi seHetak* (m)/ *fi seHetik* (f)/ *fi seHetkom* (pl)	فى صحتك/ فى صحتك/ فى صحتكم
cheese	*gebna* (f)	جبنه
chef	*Tabbakh* (m)/ *Tabbakha* (f)	طباخ/ طباخه
chemist	*agzagi* (m)	أجزجى
chemist's shop	*agzakhaena* (f)	أجزخانه
chemistry	*kemya* (f)	كيمياء
cheque	*sheek* (m)	شيك
cherries	*kerayz* (pl)	كريز
chess	*shaTarang* (m)	شطرنج
chewing gum	*lebaena* (f)	لبان
chicken	*faerkha* (f)/ *firaekh* (pl)	فرخه
chickenpox	*gowdayri* (m)	جديرى
child	*Tefl* (m)/*Tefla* (f)	طفل/ طفله
children	*aTfaal*	أطفال
chimney	*madkhana* (f)	مدخنه
china	*Seenee* (pl)	صينى

chips	baTaaTis miHammar (pl)	بطاطس محمر
chocolate	shokolaata (f)	شيكولاته
choose: he/she chooses	yekhtaar (m)/ tekhtaar (f)	يختار / تختار
chop (lamb)	riyash (Daani) (f)	ريش (ضاني)
Christian	maseeHee (m)/ maseeHaya (f)	مسيحى / مسيحيه
Christmas	krismas (m)	كريسماس
Christmas Eve	liltil ikrismas (f)	ليلة الكريسماس
church	keneesa (f)	كنيسه
cigar	sigaar (m)	سيجار
cigarette	sigaara (f)	سيجاره
cigarette papers	wara' sagayyer (pl)	ورق سجاير
cinema	sinema (f)	سينما
cinnamon	'erfa (f)	قرفه
circle	dayra (f)	دائره
circus	sirk (m)	سرك
city	madeena (f)	مدينه
civil servant	mowaZaf (m)/ mowaZafit (f) Hokooma	موظف / موظفة حكومه
class	faSl (m)	فصل
classical music	mazeeka klassiki (f)	مزيكه كلاسيك
claustrophobia	klostrofobya (f)	كلوستروفوبيا
clean: he/she cleans	yenaDaf (m)/ tenaDaf (f)	ينظف / تنظف
clean	neDeef (m)/ neDeefa (f)	نظيف / نظيفه
clear	waaDiH (m)/ waDHa (f)	واضح / واضحه
clerk	mowaZaf (m)/ mowaZafa (f)	موظف / موظفه
clever	shaaTir (m)/ shaaTra (f)	شاطر / شاطره
cliff	Sakhara (f)	صخره
climate	gaw (m)	الجو / طقس

climb: he/she climbs	*yatasala'* (m)/ *tatasala'* (f)	يتسلق / تتسلق
climber	*motasali'* (m)/ *motasali'a* (f)	متسلق / متسلقة
climbing	*tasalo'* (m)	تسلق
clinic	*ᵃeyaeda* (f)	عيادة
cloakroom	*Hammaem* (m)	حمام
clock	*saᵃa* (f)	ساعه
close (by)	*orayyib*	قريب
close to	*orayyib min*	قريب من
close: he/she closes	*ye'fil* (m)/*te'fil* (f)	يقفل / تقفل
closed	*ma'fool* (m)/ *ma'foola* (f)	مقفول / مقفوله
cloth	*o'maesh* (f)	قماش
clothes	*hedoom* (pl)	هدوم
clothes peg(s)	*mashbak* (s)/ *mashaabik* (pl)	مشبك / مشابك
cloud	*siHaebba* (f)	سحابه
cloudy (*weather*)	*meghayyim*	الجومغيم
club (*society*)	*naedi* (m)	نادي
coach (*bus*)	*otobees* (m)	اوتوبيس
(*railway*)	*ᵃarabayit sekka Hadeed* (f)	عربية سكة حديد
coal	*faHm* (pl)	فحم
coarse	*khishin* (m)/ *khishna* (f)	خشين / خشنه
coast	*shaaTi'* (m)	شاطئ
coat	*balToo* (m)	بالطو
coat-hanger	*shamaᵃit* (f) *hidoom*	شماعة هدوم
cocktail	*koktayl* (m)	كوكتيل
code (*telephone*)	*nemrit ilkowd* (f)	نمرة الكود
coffee	*'ahwa* (f)	قهوه
coin	*'ersh* (m)	قرش
cold	*baerid* (m)/*barda* (f)	بارد / بارده
cold: I have a cold	*ᵃandi bard* (m)	عندي برد
collar	*yaeᵃa* (f)	ياقه
colleague	*zimeel* (m)/*zimeela* (f)	زميل / زميله

collect: he/she collects	*yelem* (m)/*tilem* (f)	يلم / تلم
collection	*magmoo^aa* (f)	مجموعه
(*post*)	*gam^a il bareed*	جمع البريد
college	*kollaya* (f)	كليه
colour	*lown* (m)	لون
colour blind	*^aama alwaen* (m & f)	عماء ألوان
comb	*meshT* (m)	مشط
come: he/she comes	*gay* (m)/*gaya* (f)	جاى
he/she comes back	*yerga^a* (m)/ *terga^a* (f)	يرجع / ترجع
he/she comes in	*yedkhol* (m)/ *tedkhol* (f)	يدخل / تدخل
come in!	*'edkhol* (to m)/ *'edkholi* (to f)	إدخل / إدخلى
comedy	*komidia* (f)	كوميديا
comfortable	*moreeH* (m)/ *moreeHa* (f)	مريح / مريحه
comic (*magazine*)	*megallit karikatir* (f)	مجله كاريكاتير
(*funny*)	*moDhik* (m)/ *moDhika* (f)	مضحك / مضحكه
commercial	*togaeri* (m)/ *togaeraya* (f)	تجارى / تجاريه
common	*ma^aroof* (m)/ *ma^aroofa* (f)	معروف / معروفه
(*well-known*)		
(*shared*)	*moshtarak* (m)/ *moshtaraka* (f)	مشترك / مشتركه
(Holy) Communion	*^aasha' rabaennee* (m)	عشاء ربانى
communism	*shoyoo^aaya* (f)	شيوعيه
compact disc	*seedee* (f)	سى دى
company (*firm*)	*shirka* (f)	شركه
compared with	*bil moqarnna li*	بالمقارنه
compartment	*diwaen* (m)	ديوان
compass	*bargal* (m)	برجل
complain: he/she complains	*yeshteki* (m)/ *teshteki* (f)	يشتكى / تشتكى
complaint	*shakwa* (f)	شكوه

complete	*kaemil* (m)/*kamla* (f)	كامل/ كامله
complicated	*mi^aad* (m)/ *mi^aada* (f)	معقد/ معقده
composer	*mo'alif moseeqee* (m)/ *mo'alifa moseeqaya* (f)	مؤلف موسيقى/ مؤلفه موسيقيه
compulsory	*igbaeri* (m)/ *igbaeraya* (f)	إجبارى/ إجباريه
computer	*kombyootaar* (m)	كومبيوتر
operator	*^aamil* (m)/*^aamila* (f) *kombyootaar*	عامل/ عامله كومبيوتر
programmer	*mo^aid baramig kombyootaar* (m)	معد برامج كومبيوتر
studies	*deraasit il kombyootaar*	دراسة الكومبيوتر
concert	*Hafla moseeqaya* (f)	حفله موسيقيه
concert hall	*Saalit il Hafalaet* (f)	صالة الحفلات
concussion	*irtigaeg fil mokh* (m)	إرتجاج فى المخ
condition	*Hala* (f)	حاله
condom	*kabboot* (m)	كبوت
conference	*mo'tamar* (m)	مؤتمر
confirm	*yo'akid* (m)/ *to'akid* (f)	يؤكد/ تؤكد
conscious	*wa^aee* (m)/*wa^aya* (f)	داعى/ داعيه
conservation	*il moHafzaH* (f)	المحافظة
conservative	*moHaafiZ* (m)/ *moHaafZa* (f)	محافظ/ محافظه
constipation	*imsaek* (m)	إمساك
consul	*'onsol* (m & f)	قنصل
consulate	*'onsolaya* (f)	قنصليه
consultant	*mostashaar* (m)/ *mostashaara* (f)	مستشار/ مستشاره
contact lens	*^aadasa lasqa* (f)/ *^aadasaet lasqa* (pl)	عدسه لاصقه/ عدسات لاصقه
contact lens cleaner	*monazef il ^aadasaet*	منظف العدسات
continent	*qarra* (f)	قاره

English	Transliteration	Arabic
contraceptive	*man^a il Haml* (m)	منع الحمل
contract	*kontraatoo* (m), *^aaqd* (m)	كونتراتو/عقد
control (*passport*)	*gawazaet* (pl)	جوازات
convenient	*monaesib* (m)/ *monasba* (f)	مناسب/ مناسبه
convent	*dayr il rahibaet* (m)	ديرالراهبات
cook	*Tabbakh* (m)/ *Tabbakha* (f)	طباخ/ طباخه
cook: he/she cooks	*yaTbookh* (m)/ *toTbookh* (f)	يطبخ/ تطبخ
cooked	*maTbookh* (m)/ *maTbookha* (f & pl)	مطبوخ/ مطبوخه
cooker	*botagaez* (m)	بوتاجاز
cool	*baerid* (m)/*barda* (f)	بارد
cool box	*^aelbit talg* (f)	علبة ثلج
copper	*naHaes* (m)	نحاس
copy	*noskha* (f)	نسخه
copy: he/she copies	*yen'el* (m)/*ten'el* (f)	ينقل/ تنقل
cork	*fella* (f)	فله
corkscrew	*fataeHit il azayiz* (f)	فتاحة زجاجات
corner	*rokna* (f)	ركنه
correct	*SaaHeeH* (m)/ *SaaHeeHa* (f)	صحيح/ صحيحه
corridor	*Tor'a* (f)	طرقه
cosmetic	*saaT-Hi* (m)/ *SaaT-Haya* (f)	سطحى/ سطحيه
cosmetics	*makyaj* (pl)	ميكياج
cost	*takleffa* (f)	تكلفه
cost: it costs	*yetkallif* (m)/ *tetkallif* (f)	يتكلف/ تتكلف
cot	*sereer aTfaal* (m)	سرير أطفال
cottage	*kookh* (m)	كوخ
cotton	*'otn* (pl)	قطن
cotton wool	*'otna* (f)	قطنه
cough	*koHa* (f)	كحه

210

English	Transliteration	Arabic
cough: he/she coughs	*yekoH* (m)/*tekoH* (f)	يكح/ تكح
could (*see* 'can')		
count: he/she counts	*ye*ᵃ*id* (m)/*te*ᵃ*id* (f)	يعد/ تعد
counter (*shop*)	*maktaeb il biy*ᵃ (m)	مكتب البيع
country (*nation*)	*balaed* (f)	بلد
country(side)	*reef* (m)	ريف
in the country	*fil reef*	في الريف
couple (*pair*)	*zowg* (pl)	زوج
courgettes	*kowsa* (pl)	كوسه
course (*lessons*)	*kors* (m)	كورس
court (*law*)	*maHkama* (f)	محكمة
(*tennis etc.*)	*mal*ᵃ*ab* (m)	ملعب
cousin: my cousin		
father's brother's son	*ibn* ᵃ*amee*	ابن عمي
father's brother's daughter	*bint* ᵃ*amee*	بنت عمي
father's sister's son	*ibn* ᵃ*ameti*	ابن عمتي
father's sister's daughter	*bint* ᵃ*ameti*	بنت عمتي
mother's brother's son	*ibn khaeli*	ابن خالي
mother's brother's daughter	*bint khaeli*	بنت خالي
mother's sister's son	*ibn khaelti*	ابن خالتي
mother's sister's daughter	*bint khaelti*	بنت خالتي
cover	*ghaTa* (m)	غطاء
cow	*ba'ara* (f)	بقرة
crab	*kaboorya* (f)	كابوريا
cramp	*kramp* (m)	كرامب
crayons	*qalam alwaen* (m)	قلم ألوان
crazy	*magnoon* (m)/*magnoona* (f)	مجنون

cream (*food*)	*kreem* (m)	كريم
(*lotion*)	*kreem* (m)	كريم
(*colour*)	*kraym* (m)/*krayma* (f)	كريم / كريمه
cream cheese	*gebna bil krema* (f)	جبنه بالكريمه
credit card	*karnay i'timaen* (m)	كارنيه إمتحان
cricket	*krikit*	كريكيت
crisps	*baTaaTis miHammar* (pl)	بطاطس محمر
crescent	*hilael* (m)	هلال
Red Crescent	*il hilael laHmar* (m)	الهلال الأحمر
cross	*Saaleeb*	صليب
Red Cross	*iSaaleeb laHmar* (m)	الصليب لأحمر
cross: he/she crosses	*ye^aadee* (m)/	يعدى/ نعدى
(*border*)	*te^aadee* (f)	
crossing (*sea*)	*^aoboor* (m)	عبور
crossroads	*takaato^a* (m)	تقاطع
crowd	*ziHam* (m)	زحام
crowded	*mazHoom* (m & f)	مزحوم
crown	*taeg* (m)	تاج
cruise (*at sea*)	*reHla baHaraya*	رحله بحريه
(*on river*)	*reHla nahraya*	رحله نهريه
crutches	*^aokaez* (m)	عكاز
cry: he/she is crying	*ye^aaiyat* (m)/	يعيط/ تعيط
	te^aaiyat (f)	
crystal	*kristael* (m)	كريستال
cucumber	*khiyaar* (m)	خيار
cuff	*eswerra* (f)	إسوره
cup	*fingaen* (m)	فنجان
cupboard	*doolaab* (m)	دولاب
cure (*remedy*)	*^aelaeg* (m)	علاج
cure: he/she cures	*ye^aalig* (m)/*te^aalig* (f)	يعالج/ تعالج
curly	*memawig* (m & f)	موج
current (*electricity*)	*tayaar* (m)	تيار
curtain	*sitaara* (f)	ستاره
curve	*monHana* (m)	منحنى
cushion	*makhadda* (f)	مخده

customs	*gomrok* (m)	جمرك
cut	*'aTª* (m)	قطع
cut: he/she cuts	*ye'Taª* (m)/*te'Taª* (f)	يقطع/ تقطع
I've cut myself	*ªawart nafsi*	عورت نفسي
cycling	*rekoob il daragaat* (m pl)	ركوب الدراجات
cyclist	*raekib il daraga* (m)	راكب الدراجه
cylinder (*car*)	*soltanayya* (f)	سلطانيه
(*gas*)	*amboobit il botagaez* (f)	أمبوبة البوتاجاز
cystitis	*iltihaeb* (m) *imasaena*	التهاب المثانه

D

daily	*yowmi*	يومي
damage	*kasr* (m)	كسر
damage: he/she damages	*kassar* (m)/*kassarit* (f)	كسر/ كسرت
damp	*mablool* (m)/ *mabloola* (f)	مبلول/ مبلوه
dance	*ra'S* (m)	رقص
dance: he/she dances	*yor'oS* (m)/*tor'oS* (f)	يرقص/ ترقص
danger	*khaTar* (m)	خطر
dangerous	*khaTeer* (m)/ *khaTeera* (f)	خطير/ خطيره
dark	*Dalma* (f)	ظلمه
(*colour*)	*ghaemi'* (m)/ *ghami'a* (f)	غامق/ غامقه
darling	*Habeebee* (m)/ *Habibti* (f)	حبيبي/ حبيبتي
data (*information*)	*maªloomaet* (pl)	معلومات
date (*day*)	*taereekh* (m)	تاريخ
(*fruit*)	*balaH* (pl)	بلح
daughter	*ibna* (f)	ابنه
my daughter	*binti* (f)	بنتي
daughter-in-law	*miraat il ibn* (f)	مرات الأبن

213

English	Transliteration	Arabic
day	*yowm* (m)	يوم
day after tomorrow	*ba^ad bokra*	بعد بكره
day before yesterday	*awil imbariH*	اول إمبارح
dead: he/she is dead	*maeyit* (m)/ *maeyita* (f)	ميت / ميته
Dead Sea	*ibaHr ilmayit*	البحر الميت
deaf	*'aTrash* (m)/ *Tarsha* (f)	أطرش / طرشه
dealer	*baya^a* (m) *baya^aa* (f)	بياع / بياعه
dear (*precious*)	*aezeez* (m) *aezeeza* (f)	عزيز / عزيزه
(*expensive*)	*ghaelee* (m)/ *ghalya* (f)	غالى / غاليه
death	*mowt* (m)	موت
debt	*dayn* (m)	دين
decaffeinated coffee	*'ahwa min ghayr kafyeen* (f)	قهوه من غير كافيين
decide: he/she decides	*qarrar* (m)/*qararat* (f)	قرر / قررت
deck	*dek* (m)	دك
deckchair	*shez long* (m)	شيز لونج
declare: he/she declares	*yeSaraH* (m)/ *teSaraH* (f)	يصرح / تصرح
deep	*ghaweeT* (m & f)	غويط
deer	*ghazael* (m)	غزال
defect (*fault*)	*^aayb* (m)	عيب
defective	*bayiZ* (m)/*bayZa* (f)	بايظ / بايظه
definitely	*mo'akad*	مؤكد
defrost	*yesayaH* (m)/ *tesayaH* (f)	يسيح / تسيح
degree	*daraga* (f)	درجه
delay	*ta'kheer* (m)	تأخير
delicate	*ra'ee'* (m)/*ra'ee'a* (f)	رقيق / رقيقه
delicious	*lazeez* (m)/*lazeeza* (f)	لذيذ / لذيذه
deliver: he/she delivers	*yessaelim* (m)/ *tessaelim* (f)	يسلم / تسلم
delivery	*istilaem* (m)	استلام

demonstration	*moZahra* (f)	مظاهره
denim	*denim* (m)	دنم
dental	*sinaen* (pl)	سنان
dentist	*doktowr sinaen* (m) / *doktowrit sinaen* (f)	دكتور / سينان دكتورة سينان
dentures	*sinaen Sina^aaya* (pl)	سنان صناعيه
deodorant	*Ded el^aara'* (m)	ضد العرق
depart: he/she departs	*yesaefir* (m) / *tisaefir* (f)	يسافر / تسافر
department	*qism* (m)	قسم
department store	*soopar market* (m)	سوبر ماركت
departure	*saffar* (m)	سفر
departure lounge	*Salit il saffar* (m)	صالة السفر
deposit	*mo'addam* (m)	مقدم
describe: he/she describes	*yowSif* (m) / *towSif* (f)	يوصف / توصف
description	*waSf* (m)	وصف
desert	*SaHara* (f)	صحراء
design	*TaSmeem* (m)	تصميم
design: he/she designs	*yeSamim* (m) / *tiSamim* (f)	يصمم / تصمم
designer	*moSamim* (m) / *moSamaema* (f)	مصمم / مصممه
dessert	*Helw* (m)	حلو
destination	*nihaeyit il saffar* (m)	نهاية السفر
details	*tafaSeel* (pl)	تفاصيل
detergent	*monaZif* (m)	منظف
develop: he/she develops	*yeTawar* (m) / *teTawar* (f)	يتطور / تتطور
diabetes	*sokkar* (m)	سكر
diabetic: he is diabetic	*^aandoo sokkar*	عنده سكر
she is diabetic	*^aandaha sokkar*	عندها سكر
dial: he/she dials	*yoTlob* (m) / *toTlob* (f)	يطلب / تطلب
dialling code	*nemrit ilkowd* (f)	نمرة الكود
diamond	*maesa* (f)	ماسه
diarrhoea	*is-hael* (m)	إسهال
diary	*mozakkaraat* (pl)	مزكرات

dice	*Zahr* (pl)	زهر
dictator	*diktatoor* (m)/	دكتاتور/دكتاتوره
	diktatoora (f)	
dictionary	*qamoos* (m)	قاموس
die: he/she dies	*yemoot* (m)/*timoot* (f)	يموت/تموت
. . . died	. . . *maet* (m)/	. . . مات/ماتت
	maetit (f)	
diesel	*deezil* (m)	ديزل
diet	*rezheem* (m)	ريجيم
different	*mokhtilif* (m)/	مختلف/مختلفه
	mokhtilifa (f)	
difficult	*Sa\u1d43b* (m)/*Sa\u1d43ba* (f)	صعب/صعبه
dining-room	*otil akl* (f)	اودة السفره
dinner	*\u1d43asha* (m)	عشاء
dinner jacket	*takseedo* (m)	تاكسيدو
diplomat	*diblomaesee* (m)/	دبلوماسى/دبلوماسيه
	diblomaesaya (f)	
direct (*route*)	*dairekt* or	دايركت/مباشر
	mobaeshaer	
direction	*itigae* (m)	إتجاه
director	*ra'ees* (m)/*ra'eesa* (f)	رئيس/رئيسه
directory (*telephone*)	*daleel* (m)	دليل
dirty	*wesikh* (m)/*weskha* (f)	وسخ/وسخه
disabled	*mo\u1d43awaq* (m)/	معوق/معوقه
	mo\u1d43awaqa (f)	
disappointed (*upset*)	*za\u1d43laen* (m)/	زعلان/زعلانه
	za\u1d43laena (f)	
disc (*record*)	*isTiwaana* (f)	إسطوانه
(*token*)	*feesha* (f)	فيشه
disc jockey	*disk jokkey* (m)	ديسك جوكى
disco(thèque)	*disko* (m)	ديسكو
discount	*Takhfeed* (m)	تخفيض
dish	*Taba'* (m)	طبق
dishwasher	*ghasaelit* (f) *il itba'*	غسالة/لأطباق
disinfectant	*moTahir* (m)	مطهر
dislocated	*yekhla\u1d43* (m)/	يخلع/تخلع
	tekhla\u1d43 (f)	

English	Transliteration	Arabic
disposable	*mostahlak* (m)/ *mostahlaka* (f)	مستهلك/ مستهلكه
distance	*masaefa* (f)	مسافه
distilled water	*maiya ma'aTara* (f)	مياه مقطره
district (of country)	*moqaT°a* (f)	مقاطعه
(of town)	*DaHaya* (f)	ضاحيه
dive: he/she dives	*yeghooS* (m)/ *teghooS* (f)	يغوص/ تغوص
diversion	*taHweela* (f)	تحويله
diving	*ghawaSan* (m)	غوصان
diving-board	*minaSit* (f) *ghaTs*	منصة غطس
divorced	*meTala'* (m)/ *meTala.a* (f)	مطلق/ مطلقه
dizzy	*daeyikh* (m)/ *daeyikha* (f)	دايخ/ دايخه
do: he/she does	*ye°mil* (m)/ *te°mil* (f)	يعمل/ تعمل
done	*°amal* (m)/ *°amalit* (f)	عمل/ عملت
dock	*meena* (f)	ميناء
doctor	*doktowr* (m)/ *doktowra* (f)	دكتور/ دكتوره
documents	*mostanadaet* (pl)	مستندات
dog	*kalb* (m)/*kalba* (f)	كلب/ كلبه
doll	*°aroossa* (f)	عروسه
dollars	*dollaraat* (pl)	دولارات
dome	*'obba* (f)	قبه
dominoes	*domino* (m)	دومينو
donkey	*Homar* (m)/ *Homara* (f)	حمار/ حماره
door	*baeb* (m)	باب
double	*dobl*	دوبل
double bed	*sereer* (m) *dobl*	سرير دوبل
dough	*°ageena* (f)	عجينه
down	*taHt*	تحت
downstairs	*taHt*	تحت
drain	*magaeree* (pl)	مجارى

drama	*drama* (f)	دراما
draught (*air*)	*Taiyaar* (m)	تيار
draw: he/she draws	*yersim* (m)/*tersim* (f)	يرسم/ ترسم
drawer	*dorg* (m)	درج
drawing	*rasm* (m)	رسم
drawing-pin	*dabboos* (m)	دبوس
dreadful	*weHish* (m)/	وحش/ وحشه
	weHsha (f)	
dream	*Helm* (m)	حلم
dress	*foostaen* (m)	فستان
dress: he/she gets dressed	*yelbis* (m)/*telbis* (f)	يلبس/ تلبس
dressing (*medical*)	*gheyaar* (m)	غيار
(*salad*)	*Sows* (m)	صوص
drink	*mashroob* (m)	مشروب
drink: it drinks	*yishrab* (m)/*tishrab* (f)	يشرب/ تشرب
drip: it drips	*yena'aT* (m)/	ينقط/ تنقط
	tena'aT (f)	
drive: he/she drives	*yesoo'* (m)/*tesoo'* (f)	يسوق/ تسوق
driver	*sawae'* (m)/*sawae'a* (f)	سواق/ سواقه
driving licence	*rokhSa* (f)	رخصه
drown: he/she drowns	*yeghra'* (m)/	يغرق/ تغرق
	teghra' (f)	
drug(s)	*mokhaddar* (s)/	مخدر/ مخدرات
	mokhaddaraat (pl)	
drug addict	*modmin* (m)/	مدمن/ مدمنه
	modmina (f)	
drum	*Tabla* (f)	طبله
drunk	*sakraan* (m)/	سكران/ سكرانه
	sakraana (f)	
dry	*naeshif* (m)/	ناشف/ ناشفه
	naeshfa (f)	
(*wine*)	*draiy*	دراى
dry-cleaning	*tanZeef ªalal naeshif*	تنظيف على الناشف
dubbed	*doblaej* (m)	دوبلاج
duck	*baTa* (f)	بطه
dull (*weather*)	*weHish* (m)	وحش
dumb	*akhras* (m)/*kharsa* (f)	أخرس/ خرسه

218

dummy (*imitation*)	*ta'leed* (m)	تقليد
(*baby's*)	*bazaeza* (f)	بزازه
during	*khilael*	خلال
dust	*toraab* (pl)	تراب
dustbin	*safeeHit izibaela* (f)	صفيحة الزباله
dusty	*motrib* (m & f)	مترب
duty (*tax*)	*Dareeba* (f)	ضريبة
duty-free (*market*)	*(il soo') il Horra* (f)	السوق الحره
duvet	*liHaef* (m)	لحاف

E

each (one)	*kol (waHid)* (m)/	كل واحد/ كل واحده
	kol (waHda) (f)	
ear(s)	*wedn* (f)/*widaen* (pl)	ودن/ ويدان
earache	*waga*ᵃ (m) *fil wedn*	وجع فى الودن
eardrops	*'atra lil wedn* (f)	قطره للودن
early	*badri*	بدرى
earlier than	*badri* ᵃ*an*	بدرى عن
earn: he/she earns	*yeksaeb* (m)/	يكسب/ تكسب
	teksaeb (f)	
earrings	*Hel'aen* (pl)	حلقان
earth (*soil*)	*il torba* (f)	التربه
(*world*)	*il arD* (f)	الأرض
earthquake	*zilzael* (m)	زلزال
east	*shar'* (m)	شرق
eastern	*shar'ee*	شرقى
Easter	ᵃ*eed il qiyama*	عيدالقيامه
easy	*sahl* (m)/*sahla* (f)	سهل/ سهله
eat: he/she eats	*yaekol* (m)/*taekol* (f)	ياكل/ تاكل
economical	*iqtiSaadi* (m)/	إقتصادى/ إقتصاديه
	iqtiSaadaya (f)	
economy	*iqtiSaad* (m)	إقتصاد
edible	*yettaekil* (m)/	يتاكل/ تتاكل
	tettaekil (f)	
egg	*bayDa* (f)/*bayD* (pl)	بيضه/ بيض

either: either one	*'ay*	أى
either . . . or . . .	*ya . . . 'aw . . .*	يا . . . أو . . .
elastic	*astik* (m)	استيك
elections	*intikhabaet* (pl)	انتخابات
electric	*kahrobae'ee* (m)/	كهربائى/ كهربائيه
	kahrobae'aya (f)	
electrician	*kahrabae'ee* (m)	كهربائى
electricity	*kahraba* (f)	كهرباء
electronic	*iliktrowni* (m)/	الكترونى/
	iliktrownaya (f)	الكترونيه
else: anything else?	*ay khedma*	أى خدمة؟
embark: he/she	*yabda'* (m)/*tabda'* (f)	يبدأ/ تبدأ
embarks		
embarrassing	*yeksif* (m)/*teksif* (f)	يكسف/ تكسف
embassy	*sifaara* (f)	سفاره
emergency	*Tawari'* (pl)	طوارئ
emergency exit	*baeb* (m) *il tawari'*	باب الطوارئ
emergency	*tilifown* (m)	تليفون الطوارئ
telephone	*il Tawari'*	
empty	*faaDi* (m)/*faDya* (f)	فاضى/ فاضيه
empty: he/she	*yefaDi* (m)/*tefaDi* (f)	يفضى/ تفضى
empties		
enamel	*Tilae'* (m)	طلاء
end	*nehaya* (f)	نهايه
end: he/she ends	*yekhallaS* (m)/	يخلص/ تخلص
	tekhallaS (f)	
energetic	*nasheeT* (m)/	نشيط/ نشيطه
	nasheeTa (f)	
energy	*nashaaT* (m)	نشاط
engaged (*to be*	*makhToob* (m)/	مخطوب/ مخطوبه
married)	*makhTooba* (f)	
(*occupied*)	*mashghool* (m)/	مشغول/ مشغوله
	mashghoola (f)	
engine	*maTowr* (m)	ماتور
engineer	*mohandis* (m)/	مهندس/ مهندسه
	mohandissa (f)	
engineering	*handassa* (f)	هندسه

England	*ingilterra* (f)	إنجلترا
English	*ingleezi* (m)/	انجليزى/ انجليزيه
	ingleezaya (f)	
enjoy: he/she enjoys	*yetmatta^a* (m)/	يتمتع/ تتمتع
	tetmatta^a (f)	
enough	*kifaeya*	كفايه
is that enough?	*kifaeya kida*	كفايه كده؟
enter: he/she enters	*yedkhol* (m)/	يدخل/ تدخل
	tedkhol (f)	
entertainment	*taslaya* (f)	تسليه
enthusiastic	*motaHamis* (m)/	متحمس/ متحمسه
	motaHamissa (f)	
entrance	*madkhael* (m)	مدخل
envelope	*maZroof* (m)	مظروف
environment	*beey'a* (f)	بيئه
equal	*motasaewee* (m)/	متساوى/ متساويه
	motasaewaya (f)	
equipment	*^aedda* (f)	عده
escalator	*sellim* (m) *kahraba*	سلم كهرباء
especially	*bizzaet*	بالذات
essential	*Daroori* (m)/	ضرورى/ ضروريه
	Daroraya (f)	
estate	*^aiqaar* (m)	عقار
estate agent	*simsaar* (m)/	سمسار/ سمساره
	simsaara (f)	
evaporated milk	*laban* (m) *nesla*	لبن نسله
even (*including*)	*Hatta*	حتى
(*not odd*)	*zowgi*	زوجى
evening	*masae'* (m)	مساء
every	*kol*	كل
everyone	*kol waHid* (m)/	كل واحد/ كل واحده
	kol waHda (f)	
everything	*koli shay'*	كل شئ
everywhere	*koli makaen*	كل مكان
exact	*mazboot*	مظبوط
exactly	*biZabT*	بالظط
examination	*imtiHan* (m)	امتحان

example	*masal* (m)	مثل
for example	*masalan*	مثلاً
excellent	*momtaez* (m)/	ممتاز/ممتازه
	momtaeza (f)	
except	*illa*	إلا
excess luggage	*wazn* (m) *ziyaeda*	وزن زياده
exchange: he/she	*yeyghaiyyar* ^a*omla* (m)/	يغير عمله/
exchanges	*tighaiyyar* ^a*omla* (f)	تغير عمله
exchange rate	*nesbit* (f) *il taghyeer*	نسبة التغير
excited, exciting	*moseer* (m)/	مثير/ مثيره
	moseera (f)	
excursion	*reHla* (f)	رحله
excuse me (*sorry*)	*aesif* (to m)/	أسف/ أسفه
	asfa (to f)	
(*to attract attention*)	^a*an iznak* (to m)/	عن إذنك/
	^a*an iznik* (to f)	عن إذنك
executive	*idaeri* (m)/	إداري/ إداريه
	idaeraya (f)	
exercise	*tamreen* (n)	تمرين
exhibition	*ma*^a*raD* (m)	معرض
exit	*khoroog* (m)	خروج
expect: he/she	*montazir* (m)/	منتظر/ منتظره
expects	*montazira* (f)	
expensive	*ghaeli* (m)/*ghalya* (f)	غالي/ غاليه
experience	*khebra* (f)	خبره
expert	*khabeer* (m)/	خبير/ خبيره
	khabeera (f)	
explain: he/she	*yeshraH* (m)/	يشرح/ تشرح
explains	*teshraH* (f)	
explosion	*infigaar* (m)	انفجار
export	*taSdeer* (m)	تصدير
export: he/she	*yeSaddar* (m)/	يصدر/ تصدر
exports	*teSaddar* (f)	
express (*service*)	*mista*^a*gil* (m)/	مستعجل/
	mista^a*gila* (f)	مستعجله
(*train*)	*saree*^a (m)	سريع
extension (*to visa*)	*tamdeed* (m)	تمديد

English	Transliteration	Arabic
extra (*spare*)	*iDaafi* (m)/*iDafaya* (f)	إضافى / إضافيه
eye(s)	*ᵃayn* (f)/*ᵃayoon* (pl)	عين / عيون
eyebrow	*Hagib* (m)	حاجب
eyebrow pencil	*'alam* (m) *Hawagib*	قلم حاجب
eyelash	*remsh* (m)/ *remoosh* (pl)	رمش / رموش
eyeliner	*'alam* (m) *remoosh*	قلم رموش
eyeshadow	*Zil* (m) *ᵃayoon*	ظل عيون

F

English	Transliteration	Arabic
fabric	*'omaesh* (m)	قماش
a piece of fabric	*Hetit 'omaesha* (f)	حتة قماشة
face	*wesh* (m)	وش
face cream	*kreem* (m) *lil wesh*	كريم الوجه
face powder	*bodra* (f) *lil wesh*	بوده الوجه
facilities	*tas-heelaet* (pl)	تسهيلات
fact	*waqeᵃ* (m)	واقع
in fact	*fil waqeᵃ*	فى الواقع
factory	*maSnaᵃ* (m)	مصنع
failure	*fashal* (m)	فشل
faint: he/she faints	*oghma ᵃalay* (m)/ *oghma ᵃalayha* (f)	أغمى عليه / أغمى عليها
fair (*haired*)	*blond* (m)/ *blondaya* (f)	بلوند / بلوندايه
(*weather*)	*kwayyis*	كويس
fair	*maᵃraD* (m)	معرض
trade fair	*maᵃraD* (m) *togaeri*	معرض تجارى
faith	*eemaen* (m)	إيمان
fake	*mezawar* (m)/ *mezawara* (f)	مذور / مذوره
fall (down/over): he/she falls	*yoᵃaᵃ* (m)/*toᵃaᵃ* (f)	يقع / تقع
false	*falSo*	فالصو
false teeth	*sinaen* (pl) *falSo*	سنان فالصو
familiar	*maᵃroof* (m)/ *maᵃroofa* (f)	معروف / معروفه

223

English	Transliteration	Arabic
family	*ª a'ila* (f)	عائله
famous	*mashhoor* (m)/	مشهور/ مشهوره
	mashhoora (f)	
fan (*air*)	*marwaHa* (f)	مروحه
(*supporter*)	*moshaggeª* (m & f)/	مشجع/
	moshaggeªeen (pl)	مشجعين
fantastic	*modhish* (m)/	مدهش/ مدهشه
	modhisha (f)	
far (*away*)	*beªeed* (m)/*beªeeda* (f)	بعيد/ بعيده
is it far?	*beªeed*	بعيد؟
as far as I know	*ªala Hasab ªelmi*	على حسب علمى
fare	*ogra* (f)	أجره
farm	*mazraªa* (f)	مزرعه
farmer	*mozaereª* (m)	مزارع
fashion	*mowda* (f)	موده
fashionable	*mowda* (m & f)	موده
fast	*sareeª* (m)/*sareeªa* (f)	سريع/ سريعه
fat (*adj*)	*tekheen* (m)/	تخين/ تخينه
	tekheena (f)	
fat (*n*)	*tokhn* (m)	تخن
fatal	*momeet* (m)/	مميت/ مميته
	momeeta (f)	
father	*'ab* (m)	أب
my father	*'abooya* (m)	أبويا
father-in-law	*Hama* (m)	حما
my father-in-law	*Hamaeya* (m)	حمايا
fault	*ghalaT* (m)	غلط
it's not my fault	*mish ghalTiti*	مش غلطتى
faulty	*bayiZ* (m)/*bayZa* (f)	بايظ/ بايظه
favourite	*mofaDal* (m)/	مفضل/ مفضله
	mofaDala (f)	
fax	*faks* (m)	فاكس
feather	*reesha* (f)	ريشه
fed up	*zah'aen* (m)/	زهقان/ زهقانه
	zah'aena (f)	
fee	*ogra* (f)	أجره
feed: he/she feeds	*ye'akil* (m)/*te'akil* (f)	يأكل/ تأكل
she breastfeeds	*bitraDaª* (f)	بترضع

English	Transliteration	Arabic
feel: he/she feels		
(touch)	*yeHess* (m)/*teHess* (f)	يحس / تحس
(emotion)	*yash^aor* (m)/	يشعر / تشعر
	tash^aor (f)	
I don't feel well	*ana ta^abaen* (m)/	انا تعبان / تعبانه
	ta^abaena (f)	
female	*onsa* (f)	انثى
feminine	*Hareemee* (f)	حريمى
fence	*soor* (m)	سور
ferry	*markib* (m)	مركب
festival	*mahragaen* (m)	مهرجان
fetch: he/she fetches	*yegeeb* (m)/*tegeeb* (f)	يجيب / تجيب
fever	*Harara* (f)	حراره
a few	*'aleel*	قليل
fiancé(e)	*khaTeeb* (m)/	خطيب / خطيبه
	khaTeeba (f)	
fibres	*alyaef* (pl)	الياف
field	*ghayT* (m)	غيط
figs	*teen* (pl)	تين
fight: he/she fights	*yiHareb* (m)/	يحارب / تحارب
	tiHareb (f)	
file *(documents)*	*mallaf* (m)	ملف
(nail, DIY)	*mabraD* (m)	مبرد
fill (in): he/she fills	*yemla* (m)/*temla* (f)	يملأ / تملأ
filling *(dental, pie etc.)*	*Hashw* (m)	حشو
film	*film* (m)	فيلم
filter	*filtar* (m)	فلتر
finance: he/she finances	*yimawel* (m)/	يمول / تمول
	timawel (f)	
financial	*maeli* (m)/*maeliya* (f)	مالى / ماليه
find: he/she finds	*yelae'ee* (m)/	يلاقى / تلاقى
	telae'ee (f)	
fine *(OK)*	*kwayyis* (m)/	كويس / كويسه
	kwayissa (f)	
(weather)	*kwayyis*	كويس
(fabric)	*qayyim* (m)/	قيم / قيمه
	qayyima (f)	

English	Transliteration	Arabic
fine (*penalty*)	*gharama* (f)	غرامه
finger	*Soba*ᵃ (m)	صباع
finish: he/she finishes	*yekhallaS* (m)/ *tekhallaS* (f)	يخلص/ تخلص
fire	*Haree'a* (f)	حريقه
fire brigade	*maTaefi* (pl)	مطافئ
fire extinguisher	*Tafaiyit* (f) *Haree'a*	طفاية حريقه
firewood	*khashab* (pl) *lil Har'*	خشب للحرق
fireworks	*Sawareekh* (pl)	صواريخ
firm (*adj*)	*gaemid* (m)/*gamda* (f)	جامد/ جامده
firm (*n*)	*shirka* (f)	شركه
first	*awil* (m)/*awila* (f)	اول/ اوله
first aid	*isᵃaef* (m) *awalee*	اسعاف أولي
first-aid kit	*Sandoo' il isᵃaef* (m)	صندوق لأسعاف
fish	*samak* (pl)	سمك
fish/go fishing: he/she fishes	*yiSTaad* (m)/ *tiSTaad* (f)	يصطاد/ تصطاد
fishing	*Sayd samak* (m)	صيد سمك
fishing rod	*sinnara* (f)	سناره
fishmonger's	*samaek* (m)	سماك
fit (*healthy*)	*laye' Tebayan* (m)/ *laye'a Tebayan* (f)	لائق طبياً/ لائقه طبياً
fit: it fits me	*ma'aaesi*	مقاسي
this doesn't fit me	*mish ma'aaesi*	مش مقاسي
fitting room	*'odit* (m) *il borowva*	حجره البروفه
fix: he/she fixes	*yeSalaH* (m)/ *teSalaH* (f)	يصلح/ تصلح
fizzy	*fawaar* (m)/ *fawaara* (f)	فوار/ فواره
flag	*ᵃalam* (m)	علم
flash	*baree'* (m)	بريق
flashbulb	*flaesh* (m)	فلاش
flat (*apartment*)	*sha'a* (f)	شقه
flat (*level*)	*motasaewee* (m)/ *motasawya* (f)	متساوى/ متساويه
flat battery	*baTarayya* (f) *faDya*	بطاريه فاضيه

226

flavour	*ta^{a}m* (m)	طعم
flaw	*ghalaT* (pl)	غلط
flea	*barghoot* (m)	برغوت
flight	*reHla* (f)	رحله
flight bag	*shanTit* (f) *isaffar*	شنطة السفر
flood	*fayaDan* (pl)	فيضان
floor	*arD* (m)	أرض
on the first floor	*fil dowr il awil*	في الدور الأول
on the ground floor	*fil dowr il arDee*	في الدور الأرضى
flour	*de'ee'* (pl)	دقيق
flower	*warda* (f)	ورده
flu	*anfilwanza* (f)	انفلونزا
fluent	*Taleeq* (m)/	طليق/ طليقه
	Taleeqa (f)	
fluently	*biTaala'a*	بطلاقة
fluid (*n*)	*sae'il* (m)	سائل
fly	*dibaena* (f)	دبانه
fly spray	*rashaashit* (f)	رشاشة الدبان
	iddibaen	
fly: he/she flies	*yeTeer* (m)/*teTeer* (f)	يطير/ تطير
fog	*Dabaab* (pl)	ضباب
foil	*wara'* (pl)	ورق الألومنيوم
	alamonyom	
folding (*e.g. chair*)	*yeTaba'* (m)/	يطبق/ تطبق
	teTaba' (f)	
folk music	*mazeeka* (f) *baladi*	مزيكه بلدى
follow: he/she follows	*yetba^a* (m)/*tetba^a* (f)	يتبع/ تتبع
following (*next*)	*molHa'*	ملحق
food	*akl* (m)	أكل
food poisoning	*tasamom* (m)	تسمم
foot	*qaddam* (m)	قدم
on foot	*mashi*	مشى
football	*korit il qaddam*	كرة القدم
footpath	*Taree'* (m)	طريق
for	*li*	لى

forbidden	*mamnoo^a* (m)/ *mamnoo^a a* (f)	ممنوع/ ممنوعه
foreign, foreigner	*agnabi* (m)/ *agnabaya* (f)	اجنبي/ اجنبيه
forest	*ghaeba* (f)	غابه
forget: he/she forgets	*yensa* (m)/*tensa* (f)	ينسى/ تنسى
forgetfulness	*naesaeyaen* (m)	نسيان
forgive: he/she forgives	*yisaemeH* (m)/ *tisaemeH* (f)	يسامح/ تسامح
fork	*showka* (f)	شوكه
form (*document*)	*Talab* (m)	طلب
fortnight	*izboo^ayn* (m)	اسبوعين
forward (*direction*)	*motaqadim*	متقدم
fountain	*nafoora* (f)	نافوره
foyer	*Sala* (f)	صاله
fracture	*kasr* (m)	كسر
frankly	*biSaraHa*	بصراحه
freckles	*namash* (pl)	نمش
free (*of charge*) (*available, unoccupied*)	*bibalaesh* (m & f) *faaDi* (m)/ *faDya* (f)	بلاش فاضي/ فاضيه
freedom	*Horayya* (f)	حريه
freeze (*food*): he/she freezes	*yetalig* (m)/*tetalig* (f)	يثلج/ تثلج
freezer	*freezar* (m)	فريزر
frequently	*keteer*	كتير
fresh	*TaaZa*	طازه
fridge	*talaega* (f)	ثلاجه
fried	*miHammar* (m)/ *miHammara* (f)	محمر/ محمره
friend	*SaHib* (m)/*SaHba* (f)	صاحب/ صاحبه
frightened	*khayef* (m)/*khayfa* (f)	خايف/ خايفه
fringe (*hair*)	*'ossa* (f)	قصه
frog	*DofDa^a* (f)	ضفدعة
from	*min*	من

English	Transliteration	Arabic
front	*moqaddema* (f)	مقدمه
in front of	*'oddaem*	قدام
front door	*madkhal* (m)	مدخل
frontier	*gabha* (f)	جبهه
frost	*Saqee^a* (m)	صقيع
frozen (*food*)	*metalig* (m)/	مثلج/ مثلجه
	metaliga (f)	
fruit	*fak-ha* (pl)	فاكهة
fruit shop	*fakahaeni* (m)	فكهاني
fry: he/she fries	*yiHammar* (m)/	يحمر/ تحمر
	tiHammar (f)	
frying pan	*Taasa* (f)	طاسه
fuel	*benzeen* (m)	بنزين
full	*malyaen* (m)/	مليان/ مليانه
	malyaena (f)	
full board	*fool bord*	فول بورد
full up	*komplay*	كومبليه
fun: he/she has fun	*yestamta^a* (m)/	يستمتع/ تستمتع
	testamta^a (f)	
funeral	*ganaeza* (f)	جنازه
funfair	*malaehee* (pl)	ملاهي
funny (*amusing*)	*moDHik* (m)/	مضحك/ مضحكه
	moDHika (f)	
(*peculiar*)	*ghareeb* (m)/	غريب/ غريبه
	ghareeba (f)	
fur	*farw* (pl)	فرو
furniture	*^{a}afsh* (pl)	عفش
further on	*ab^{a}ad*	ابعد
fuse	*Samaam* (m)	صمام
fusebox	*^{a}elbit* (f) *iSamamaat*	علبةالصمامات

G

English	Transliteration	Arabic
gallery	maᵃraD (m)	معرض
gambling	'omaar (m)	قمار
game (*match*)	matsh (m)	ماتش
gangway	madkhal (m)	مدخل
garage (*for storage*)	garaj (m)	جراج
(*for repairs*)	warsha (pl)	ورشه
garden	ginayna (f)	جنينه
gardener	ganaynee (m)	جنايني
garlic	towm (m)	ثوم
gas	botagaez (m)	بوتاجاز
gas bottle, refill	amboobit (f) botagaez	انبوبة بوتاجاز
gastritis	iltihaeb (m) maᵃawi	إلتهاب معوى
gate	bawaeba (f)	بوابه
general	ᵃamm	عام
generally, in general	ᵃomoomaen	عموماً
generous	kareem (m)/ kareema (f)	كريم / كريمه
gentle	ra'ee' (m)/ra'ee'a (f)	رقيق / رقيقه
gentleman/men (*gents*)	jentilmaen	جنتلمان
genuine	'aSeel (m)/'aSeela (f)	أصيل / اصيله
geography	goghrafya (f)	جغرافيا
get: he/she gets (*receives*)	yestelim (m)/ testelim (f)	يستلم / تستلم
he/she gets off (*e.g. bus*)	yenzil (m)/tenzil (f)	ينزل / تنزل
he/she gets on (*e.g. bus*)	yerkaeb (m)/ terkaeb (f)	يركب / تركب
gift	hidaya (f)	هديه
gin	jin (m)	جن
gin and tonic	jin wi tonik	جن و تونيك
girl	bint (f)	بنت
girlfriend	gerlfrend (f)	صديقه
give: he/she gives	yedi (m)/tedi (f)	يعطي / تعطى

230

English	Transliteration	Arabic
glass (*for drinking*)	kobbaya (f)	كوب
(*substance*)	izaez (m)	زجاج
glasses (*spectacles*)	naDara (f)	نظاره
gloves	gowantee (m)	جوانتى
glue	Samgh (m)	صمغ
go: he/she goes	yerowH (m)/	يروح / تروح
	terowH (f)	
he/she goes away	yessaefir (m)/	يسافر / تسافر
	tissaefir (f)	
go away!	imshi	امشى!
he/she goes down	yinzil (m)/tinzil (f)	ينزل / تنزل
he/she goes in	yedkhol (m)/	يدخل / تدخل
	tedkhol (f)	
he/she goes out	yekhrog (m)/	يخرج / تخرج
	tokhrog (f)	
he/she goes up	yeTla^a (m)/	يطلع / تطلع
	teTla^a (f)	
let's go!	yalla	يالله
goal	gown (m)	جول
goat	me^aza (f)	معزه
God	alla	الله
gold	dahab (m)	ذهب
golf	golf (m)	جولف
golf clubs	maDrab (m) golf	مضرب جولف
golf course	mal^aab (m) golf	ملعب جولف
good	kwayyis (m)/	كويس / كويسه
	kwayyissa (f)	
good day	nahaarak sa^aeed (m)/	نهارك سعيد
	nahaarik sa^aeed (f)	نهارك سعيد
good morning	SabaH il kheer	صباح الخير
good evening	misa' il kheer	مساء الخير
good night	tiSbaH (to m)/	تصبح /
	tiSbaHi (to f)/	تصبحى /
	tiSbaHoo (to pl)	تصبحو
	^aala kheer	على خير
goodbye	ma^aassalaema	مع السلامه

English	Transliteration	Arabic
goods	boDaaªa (pl)	بضاعه
government	Hokooma (f)	حكومه
gram	graam (m)	جرام
grammar	qawaªid (pl)	قواعد
grandchildren	aHfaed (pl)	احفاد
granddaughter	Hafeeda (f)	حفيده
grandfather	ged (m)	جد
my grandfather	geddi (m)	جدى
grandmother	geda (f)	جده
my grandmother	gedetti (f)	جدتى
grandson	Hafeed (m)	حفيد
grandstand	minaSa (f)	منصه
grapes	ªenab (pl)	عنب
grapefruit	graypfroot (m)	جرايب فروت
grass	zarª (pl)	زرع
grateful: I am grateful	shakir faDlak (to m)/ shakir faDlik (to f)	شاكر فضلك/ شاكر فضلِك
greasy	mizayit (m & f)	مزيت
great!	ªazeem	عظيم
green	'akhDar (m)/ khaDra (f)	أخضر/ خضراء
greengrocer's	khoDari (m)	خضرى
greet: he/she greets	yessalim (m)/ tessalim (f)	يسلم/ تسلم
grey	romaadee (m & f)	رمادى
grilled	mashwi (m)/ mashwaya (f)	مشوى/ مشويه
grocer's	ba'ael (m)	بقال
ground	arD (f)	ارض
ground floor	il dowr (m) il arDi	الدور الأرضى
group	magmooªa (f)	مجموعه
grow (cultivate): he/she grows	yezraª (m)/ tezraª (f)	يزرع/ تزرع
guarantee	Damaan (m)	ضمان
guard (on train)	Haeris (m)	حارس

guest	*Dayf* (m)/*Dayfa* (f)	ضيف/ ضيفه
(*in hotel*)	*zeboon* (m)/	زبون/ زبونه
	zeboona (f)	
guest house	*bansyown* (m)	بنسيون
guide	*morshid* (m)/	مرشد/ مرشده
	morshida (f)	
guided tour	*ziyara* (f) *ma^aa*	زياره مع مرشد
	morshid	
guidebook	*daleel* (m)	دليل
guilty	*moznib* (m)/	مذنب/ مذنبه
	mozniba (f)	
guitar	*geeTar* (m)	جيتار
Gulf	*ilkhaleeg*	الخليج
gun	*bondo'aya* (f)	بندقيه
guy rope	*Habl* (m)	حبل
gymnastics	*gombaaz* (m)	جباز

H

habit	*^aada* (f)	عاده
hair	*sha^ar* (pl)	شعر
hairbrush	*forsha* (f)	فرشه
haircut	*Hila'a* (f)	حلاقه
hairdresser	*Halla'* (m)	حلاق
hairdrier	*seshwaar* (m)	سشوار
hairgrip	*bensa* (f)	بنسه
hairspray	*bakhaekhit* (f) *sha^ar*	بخاخة شعر
half	*noS*	نصف
half board	*hafbord*	هاف بورد
half price	*noS tazkara* (f)	نصف تزكره
half fare	*noS itaman*	نصف الثمن
half-hour/half an hour	*noSissa^aa*	نصف ساعه
half past . . .	*. . . wi noS*	. . . و نصف
(*see* Time, *p. 172*)		

233

English	Transliteration	Arabic
hall (*in house*)	*Saalla* (f)	صاله
(*concert*)	*qaªa* (f)	قاعه
ham	*jambon* (m)	جامبون
hamburger	*hamborger* (m)	همبورجر
hammer	*shakoosh* (m)	شاكوش
hand	*yad* (f)	يد
hand cream	*kreem aydayn*	كريم اليد
hand luggage	*shonaaT yad*	شنط يد
hand-made	*yadawi* (m)/ *yadawaya* (f)	يدوى/يدويه
handbag	*shanTit* (f) *yad*	شنطة يد
handicapped	*moªawaq* (m)/ *moªawaqa* (f)	معوق/معوقه
handkerchief	*mandeel* (m)	منديل
handle	*yad* (f)	يد
hang up: he/she hangs up	*yeªala'* (m)/*teªala'* (f)	يعلق/تعلق
happen: it happens	*HaSal* (m)/ *HaSalat* (f)	حصل/حصلت
234		
happy	*mabsooT* (m)/ *mabsooTa* (f)	مبسوط/مبسوطه
harbour	*meena* (f)	ميناء
hard	*gaemid* (m)/ *gaemda* (f)	جامد/جامده
(*difficult*)	*Saªb* (m)/*Saªba* (f)	صعب/صعبه
hat	*bornaeTa* (f)	برنيط/قبعه
hate: he/she hates	*yekra* (m)/*tekra* (f)	يكره/تكره
have: he/she has	*ªando* (m)/ *ªandaha* (f)	عنده/عندها
(*see p. 166*)		
I have	*ªandi*	عندى
I have with me	*maªaya*	معايا
hay	*'ash* (pl)	قش
hay fever	*Hasasaya* (f)	حساسيه
hazelnut	*bondo'* (m)	بندق
he (*see* Basic grammar, *p. 161*)	*howa*	هو

head	*raas* (m)	رأس
(*boss*)	*rayis* (m)/*rayisa* (f)	رئيس/ رئيسه
headache	*Soda* ^{a} (m)	صداع
headphone	*samae* ^{a}a (f)	سماعه
heal: he/she heals	*yekhafif* (m)/	يخفف/ تخفف
	tekhafif (f)	
health	*SeHa* (f)	صحه
health foods	*akl* (m) *SeHi*	أكل صحى
healthy, in good health	*seHa kwayissa*	صحه كويسه
hear: he/she hears	*yesma* ^{a} (m)/*tesma* ^{a} (f)	يسمع/ تسمع
hearing (*facility*)	*sama* ^{a} (m)	سماع
hearing aid	*samae* ^{a}a (f)	سماعه
heart	*'alb* (m)	قلب
heart attack	*sakta* (f) *'albaya*	سكته قلبيه
heat	*Harara* (f)	حراره
heater	*dafaya* (f)	دفايه
heating	*tadfe'a* (f)	تدفئه
heaven	*ganna* (f)	جنه
heavy	*ti'eel* (m)/*ti'eela* (f)	ثقيل/ ثقيله
heel	*ka* ^{a}b (m)	كعب
height	*Tool* (m)	طول
helicopter	*helikoptar* (f)	هليكوبتر
hell	*gohannam* (f)	جهنم
hello	*ahlan*	أهلا
helmet	*khowza* (f)	خوزه
help	*mosa* ^{a}da (f)	مساعده
help!	*ilHa'ooni*	الحقوني!
help: he/she helps	*yisa* ^{a}id (m)/*tisa* ^{a}id (f)	يساعد/ تساعد
her (*pronoun*)	*haya*	هى
(*adj.*) (*see Basic grammar, p. 160*)		
herb	*nabaeti* (m)	نباتى
herbal tea	*shay a* ^{a}shaeb	شاى أعشاب
here	*hena*	هنا
here is . . .	*aho . . .*	أهو . . .
hiccups	*zoghoTa* (f)	زغطه
high	^{a}*ali* (m)/^{a}*alya* (f)	عالى/ عاليه
high chair	*korsi* (m) ^{a}*ali*	كرسى عالى

hijack: he/she hijacks	*yekhTaf* (m)/ *tekhTaf* (f)	يخطف / تخطف
hill	*rabwa* (f)	ربوه
him *(see p. 161)*		
hire: he/she hires	*ye'aggar* (m)/*te'aggar* (f)	يأجر / تأجر
his *(see p. 160)*		
history	*tareekh* (m)	تاريخ
hit: he/she hits	*yeDrab* (m)/*teDrab* (f)	يضرب / تضرب
hobby	*howaya* (f)	هوايه
hold: he/she holds	*yemsik* (m)/*temsik* (f)	يمسك / تمسك
hole	*khorm* (m)	خرم
holidays	*'agaeza* (f)	أجازه
on holiday	*fi 'agaeza*	في أجازه
holy	*moqadas* (m)/ *moqadassa* (f)	مقدس / مقدسه
home	*bayt* (m)	بيت
at home	*fil bayt*	في البيت
home address	*^aenwaen* (m) *il bayt*	عنوان البيت
he/she goes home	*yerawaH* (m)/ *terawaH* (f)	يروح / تروح
homosexual	*shaez* (m) *ginsayan*	شاذ جنسياً
honest	*'ameen* (m)/ *'ameena* (f)	أمين / أمينه
honeymoon	*shahr ^aassal* (m)	شهر عسل
hope: he/she hopes	*yatamanna* (m)/ *tatamanna* (f)	يتمنى / تتمنى
I hope so	*atamanna*	أتمنى
horrible	*faZee^a* (m)/ *faZee^aa* (f)	فظيع / فظيعه
horse	*HoSaan* (m)	حصان
hose	*kharToom* (m)	خرطوم
hospital	*mostashfa* (f)	مستشفى
host	*imoDeef* (m)	المضيف
hot *(temperature)*	*Har* (m & f)	حر
(spicy)	*Harra'* (m)/ *Harra'a* (f)	حراق / حراقه

hotel	*hotayl* (m)	هوتيل
hour	*sa*^{a}*a* (f)	ساعه
half-hour	*noSissa*^{a}*a*	نصف ساعه
house	*bayt* (m)	بيت
housewife	*sit* (f) *bayt*	ست بيت
housework	*shoghl* (m) *il bayt*	شغل البيت
hovercraft	*hoverkraft*	هوفركرافت
how	*izzay*	إزاى
how long/many/ much?	*'ad ay*	قدايه؟
how much does it/do they cost?	*bikaem*	بكام؟
human	*insaeni* (m)/ *insaenaya* (f)	إنسانى/ إنسانيه
human being	*insaen* (m)/ *insaena* (f)	إنسان/ إنسانه
hungry	*ga*^{a}*aen* (m)/ *ga*^{a}*aena* (f)	جعان/ جعانه
hunt: he/she hunts	*yeSTaad* (m)/ *teSTaad* (f)	يصطاد/ تصطاد
hunting	*Sayd* (m)	صيد
hurry: he/she is in a hurry	*mista*^{a}*gil* (m)/ *mista*^{a}*gila* (f)	مستعجل/ مستعجله
hurt: he/she hurts	*yegraH* (m)/*tegraH* (f)	يجرح/ تجرح
it hurts	*biyewga*^{a} (m)/ *bitewga*^{a} (f)	بيوجع/ بتوجع
husband	*gowz* (m)	جوز
hut	*kookh* (m)	كوخ
hydrofoil	*haydrowfoyl* (m)	هيدروفويل

237

I

I (*see* Basic grammar, *p. 161*)	*ana*	أنا
ice	*talg* (m)	ثلج
ice-cream	*'ays kreem* (m)	أيس كريم

	icy	*mitalig* (m)/ *mitaliga* (f)	مثلج / مثلجه
	(*weather*)	*sa'e*ᵃ	ساقع
	idea	*fikra* (f)	فكره
	if	*izza*	إذا
	ill	ᵃ*ayaen* (m)/ ᵃ*ayaena* (f)	عيان / عيانه
	illness	*maraD* (m)	مرض
	imagination	*khayael* (m)	خيال
	imagine: he/she imagines	*yetkhayael* (m)/ *tetkhayael* (f)	يتخيل / تتخيل
	immediately	*Hallan*	حالاً
	immersion heater	*sakhaen* (m)	سخان
	impatient	*maᵃendoosh Sabr* (m)/ *maᵃendahaesh Sabr* (f)	معندوش صبر / معندهاش صبر
	important	*mohim* (m)/ *mohima* (f)	مهم / مهمه
238	impossible	*mostaHeel* (m)/ *mostaHeela* (f)	مستحيل / مستحيله
	impressive	*modhish* (m)/ *modhisha* (f)	مدهش / مدهشه
	in	*fi*	في
	included	*min Demn*	من ضمن
	income	*dakhl* (m)	دخل
	indeed	*Tabᵃan*	طبعاً
	independent	*mostaqil* (m)/ *mostaqila* (f)	مستقل / مستقله
	indigestion	*soo' haDm* (m)	سوء هضم
	indoors	*gowa*	جوا
	industrial	*Sinaaᵃi* (m)/ *Sinaaᵃiya* (f)	صناعي / صناعيه
	industry	*Sinaaᵃa* (f)	صناعه
	infected	*melawath* (m)/ *melawatha* (f)	ملوث / ملوثه
	infection	ᵃ*adwa* (f)	عدوى

English	Transliteration	Arabic
infectious	mo ªdee (m)/ mo ªdaya (f)	معدى/ معديه
inflamed	moltahib (m)/ moltahiba (f)	ملتهب/ ملتهبه
inflammation	iltihaeb (m)	إلتهاب
influenza	infilwanza (f)	انفلونزا
informal	ghayr rasmee (m)/ ghayr rasmaya (f)	غير رسمى/ غير رسميه
information	ma ªloomaet (pl)	معلومات
information desk/office	maktaeb il istiªlamaet	مكتب استعلامات
injection	Ho'na (f)	حقنه
injure: he/she injures	yegraH (m)/tegraH (f)	يجرح/ تجرح
injured	itgaraH (m)/ itgaraHit (f)	اتجرح/ اتجرحت
injury	garH (m)	جرح
ink	Hebr (m)	حبر
inner	dakhili (m)/ dakhilaya (f)	داخلى/ داخليه
innocent	baree' (m)/baree'a (f)	برىء/ بريئه
insect	Hashara (f)	حشره
insect bite	ªaDit Hashara	عضة حشره
insect repellent	Ded il Hasharaat	ضدالحشرات
inside	gowa	جوا
insist	yeSamim (m)/ tiSamim (f)	يصمم/ تصمم
inspector	mofatish (m)/ mofatisha (f)	مفتش/ مفتشه
instant coffee	neskafay (f)	نسكافيه
instead of	badal min	بدل من
instructor	moddarris (m)/ moddarissa (f)	مدرس/ مدرسه
insulin	insooleen (m)	إنسولين
insult	ihaena (f)	إهانه
insurance	ta'meen (pl)	تأمين
insurance certificate	shahaedit (f) ta'meen	شهاده تأمين

insure: he/she insures	ye'amin (m)/ te'amin (f)	يأمن/ تأمن
insured	mo'amin (m)/ mo'amina (f)	مؤمن/ مؤمنه
intelligent	nabee (m)/nabeeha (f)	نبيه/ نبيهه
interested, interesting	moseer lil ihtimam	مثير للاهتمام
interior	dakhili (m)	داخلي
intermediate	metawasiT (m)/ metawasiTa (f)	متوسط/ متوسطه
international	dawli (m)/dawlaya (f)	دولي/ دوليه
interpret: he/she interprets	yetargim (m)/ tetargim (f)	يترجم/ تترجم
interpreter	motargim (m)/ motargima (f)	مترجم/ مترجمه
interval (*theatre etc.*)	istiraHa (f)	إستراحه
interview	moqabla (f)	مقابله
into	fi	في
introduce: he/she introduces	ye'adim (m)/ te'adim (f)	يقدم/ تقدم
invitation	da'wa (f)	دعوه
invite: he/she invites	yad'o (m)/tad'ee (f)	يدعو/ تدعي
iodine	iodeen (pl)	أيودين
Ireland	ayrlanda (f)	ايرلندا
Irish	ayrlandi (m)/ ayrlandaya (f)	ايرلندي/ ايرلنديه
iron (*metal*)	Hadeed (pl)	حديد
(for clothes)	makwa (f)	مكوه
iron: he/she irons	yekwi (m)/tekwi (f)	يكوي/ تكوي
person who irons clothes	makwagi (m)	مكوجي
is (*see* 'to be', *p. 165*)		
is there . . .?	fi . . .	في . . . ؟
Islam	islaem (m)	أسلام
Islamic	Islaemi (m)/ islaemaya (f)	اسلامي/ اسلاميه
island	gizeera (f)	جزيره
it (*see* Basic grammar, *p. 161*)		

itch	*harsha* (f)	هرشه
its (*see* Basic grammar, *p. 160*)		

J

jacket	*jaketta* (f)	جاكته
jam	*mirabba* (f)	مربى
jar	*barTamaan* (m)	برطمان
jazz	*mazeeka gaez* (m)	موسيقى الجاز
jeans	*jeenz* (pl)	جينز
jelly (*food*)	*jellee* (m)	جلى
jellyfish	*qandeel il baHr* (m)	قنديل البحر
Jesus Christ	*il maseeH* (m)	المسيح
jetty	*marsa* (f)	مرسى
jeweller's	*gawahirgi* (m)	جواهرجى
Jewish	*yahoodee* (m)/	يهودى / يهوديه
	yahoodaya (f)	
job	*wazeefa* (f)	وظيفه
jog: he/she jogs	*yegri* (m)/*tegri* (f)	يجرى / تجرى
jogging	*gari* (m)	جرى
joke	*nokta* (f)	نكته
journalist	*SaHafi* (m)/	صحفى / صحفيه
	SaHafaya (f)	
journey	*reHla* (f)	رحله
judge	*qaadi* (m)	قاضى
jug	*shafsha'* (m)	شفشق
juice	*ªaSeer* (m)	عصير
jump: he/she jumps	*yenoT* (m)/*tenoT* (f)	ينط / تنط
jumper	*bolovar* (m)	بلوفر
junction	*moltaqa* (f)	ملتقى
just (*only*)	*bas*	بس

K

keep: he/she keeps	*yaHtafiZ* (m)/	يحتفظ / تحتفظ
	taHtafiZ (f)	

English	Transliteration	Arabic
kettle	*barraad* (m)	براد
key	*moftaeH* (m)	مفتاح
key ring	*midaiyit* (f) *mafateeH*	ميدالية مقاتيح
kidney	*kelwa* (f) / *kalaewi* (pl)	كلية / كلاوى
kill: he/she kills	*yeqtil* (m) / *teqtil* (f)	يقتل / تقتل
kilo(gram)	*keeloo* (m)	كيلو
kilometre	*keelomitr* (m)	كيلومتر
kind (*sort*)	*now*ᵃ (m)	نوع
(*generous*)	*kareem* (m) / *kareema* (f)	كريم / كريمه
king	*malik* (m)	ملك
kiss	*bosa* (f)	بوسه
kiss: he/she kisses	*yiboos* (m) / *tiboos* (f)	ييوس / تبوس
kitchen	*maTbakh* (m)	مطبخ
knickers	*libaes* (m)	لباس
knife	*sikkeena* (f)	سكينه
knitting	*tereeko* (m)	تريكو
knitting needle	*ibrit* (f) *tereeko*	إبرة تريكو
knock (*on door*): he/she knocks	*yekhabat* (m) / *tekhabat* (f)	يخبط / تخبط
knot	*ᵃoqda* (f)	عقده
know: he/she knows	*yeᵃraf* (m) / *teᵃraf* (f)	يعرف / تعرف
as far as I know	*ᵃala Hasab ᵃelmi*	على حسب علمى
Koran	*qor'an* (m)	قرآن

L

English	Transliteration	Arabic
label	*tikit* (m)	تيكت
lace	*dantayl* (f)	دانتيل
ladder	*sellem* (m)	سلم
lady	*sayeda* (f)	سيده
ladies	*sayedaet* (pl)	سيدات
lager	*beera* (f)	بيره
lake	*boHira* (f)	بحيره
lamb (*animal*)	*kharoof* (m)	خروف
(*meat*)	*Daani* (m)	ضانى

English	Transliteration	Arabic
lamp	*lamba* (f)	لمبه
lamp post	*ᵃamood noor* (m)	عمود نور
land	*arD* (f)	أرض
land: he/she lands	*yahbaat* (m)/ *tahbaat* (f)	يهبط/ تهبط
landing (*house*)	*dowr* (m)	دور
(*plane*)	*hobooT* (m)	هبوط
landlady	*SaHbit ilbayt* (f)	صاحبة البيت
landlord	*SaHb ilbayt* (m)	صاحب البيت
lane (*country road*)	*Taree'* (m)	طريق
language	*logha* (f)	لغه
large	*Dakhm* (m)/ *Dakhma* (f)	ضخم/ ضخمه
last	*akheer* (m)/ *akheera* (f)	أخير/ أخيره
last: he/she lasts	*yastaghriq* (m)/ *tastaghriq* (f)	يستغرق/ تستغرق
late: (it is) late	*met'akhar*	متأخر
later	*baᵃdayn*	بعدين
laugh	*DeHk* (m)	ضحك
laugh: he/she laughs	*yeDHak* (m)/ *teDHak* (f)	يضحك/ تضحك
launderette	*ghassaela* (f)	غساله
laundry	*ghaseel* (pl)	غسيل
law	*qanoon* (m)	قانون
lawyer	*moHaemi* (m)/ *moHaemaya* (f)	محامي/ محاميه
laxative	*mosahil* (m)	مسهل
lazy	*kaslaen* (m)/ *kaslaena* (f)	كسلان/ كسلانه
lead (*metal*)	*roSaaS* (pl)	رصاص
lead-free	*min ghayr roSaaS*	من غير رصاص
lead: he/she leads	*yaqood* (m)/ *taqood* (f)	يقود/ تقود
leaf	*wara'a* (f)	ورقه
leaflet	*manshoor* (m)	منشور

243

English	Transliteration	Arabic
lean: he/she leans (out)	yanHani (m)/ tanHani (f)	ينحني/ تنحني
learn: he/she learns	yetªalim (m)/ tetªalim (f)	يتعلم/ تتعلم
learner	motaªalim (m)/ motaªalima (f)	متعلم/ متعلمه
least: at least	ªalalaqal	على الأقل
leather	geld (m)	جلد
leave: he/she leaves (message etc.)	yeseeb (m)/teseeb (f)	يسيب/ تسيب
(goes away)	yemshi (m)/ temshi (f)	يمشي/ تمشى
lecturer	moHaaDir (m)/ moHaaDira (f)	محاضر/ محاضره
left	shimael	شمال
left-handed	ashwal (m)/ showla (f)	أشول/ شوله
leg	regl (m)	رجل
legal	qanooni (m)/ qanoonaya (f)	قانوني/ قانونيه
lemon	lamoona (f)/ lamoon (pl)	ليمونه/ ليمون
lemonade	lamonaeta (f)	ليموناده
lend: he/she lends	yisallif (m)/tisallif (f)	يسلف/ تسلف
length	Tool (m)	طول
lens (camera)	ªadasa (f)	عدسه
lentils	ªats (pl)	عدس
lesbian	shaeZa ginsayan (f)	شاذه جنسياً
less	a'al	أقل
lesson	dars (m)	درس
let: he/she lets (allows)	yesmaH (m)/ tesmaH (f)	يسمح/ تسمح
(rents)	ye'agar (m)/ te'agar (f)	يأجر/ تأجر
letter	gawaeb (m)	جواب
letterbox	Sandoo' bareed (m)	صندوق بريد

lettuce	*khas* (m)	خس
leukaemia	*saraTaan* (m) *fil dam*	سرطان فى الدم
level (*height, standard*)	*mistawa* (m)	مستوى
level (*flat*)	*misaTaH* (m)/ *misaTaHa* (f)	مسطح / مسطحه
level crossing	*ªoboor* (m) *sekka Hadeed*	عبور سكه حديد
library	*maktabba* (f)	مكتبه
licence (*driving etc.*)	*rokhSa* (f)	رخصه
lid	*ghaTa* (m)	غطاء
lie down: he/she lies down	*yastalqi* (m)/ *tastalqi* (f)	يستلقى / تستلقى
life	*Haiyae* (f)	حياه
lifebelt	*Toq nagae* (m)	طوق نجاه
lifeboat	*qarib nagae* (m)	قارب نجاه
lifeguard	*ªamil inqaaZ* (m)	عامل إنقاذ
lifejacket	*towb nagae* (m)	ثوب نجاه
lift	*asanser* (m)	اسانسير
light (*n*)	*noor* (m)	نور
light bulb	*lamba* (f)	لمبه
light (*coloured*) (*weight*)	*faetiH* (m)/*fatHa* (f) *khafeef* (m)/ *khafeefa* (f)	فاتح / فاتحه خفيف / خفيفه
light: he/she lights (*fire*)	*yewalaª* (m)/ *tewalaª* (f)	يولع / تولع
lighter (*cigarette*)	*walaªa* (f)	ولاعه
lighter fuel	*botagaez* (m)	بوتاجاز
lightning	*bar'* (m)	برق
like (*similar to*)	*zay*	زى
like this/that	*zay da* (m)	زى ده
what is . . . like?	*. . . zaya ay*	. . . زى إيه؟
like: he/she likes	*biHeb* (m)/*bitHeb* (f)	بيحب / بتحب
I like it	*ªagebni*	عاجبنى
likely	*gayiz*	جائز
limited	*maHdood* (m)/ *maHdooda* (f)	محدود / محدوده

245

line	*khaT* (m)	خط
lion	*asad* (m)	أسد
lioness	*labwa* (f)	لبوه
lip	*sheffa* (f)	شفه
lipstick	*'alam* (m) *rooj*	قلم روج
liqueur	*likayr* (m)	ليكير
liquid	*sae'il* (m)	سائل
list	*lista* (f)	لسته
listen: he/she listens (to)	*yesma^a* (m)/*tesma^a* (f)	يسمع / تسمع
litre	*litr* (m)	لتر
litter	*zibaela* (pl)	زباله
little	*Soghayar* (m)/ *Soghayara* (f)	صغير/ صغيره
little: a little	*showaya*	شويه
live: he/she lives	*ye^aeesh* (m)/ *te^aeesh* (f)	يعيش / تعيش
liver	*kibda* (f)	كبده
living-room	*antray* (m)	انتريه
loaf	*regheef* (m)	رغيف
local	*maHaeli* (m)/ *maHalaya* (f)	محلي / محليه
lock	*terbaes* (m)	ترباس
lock: he/she locks	*yetarbis* (m)/ *tetarbis* (f)	يتربس/ تتربس
London	*landan* (f)	لندن
lonely	*waHeed* (m)/ *waHeeda* (f)	وحيد/ وحيده
long	*Taweel* (m)/ *Taweela* (f)	طويل / طويله
long-distance call	*masafa* (f) *Taweela*	مسافه طويله
look: he/she looks (at)	*yeboS (^aala)* (m)/ *teboS (^aala)* (f)	يبص/ تبص
he/she looks after	*yakhod baeloo* (m)/ *takhod balha* (f)	بأخذ باله / تأخذ بالها
he/she looks for	*yedawar ^aala* (m)/ *tedawar ^aala* (f)	يدورعلي / تدورعلي

he/she looks like	*yeshbih* (m)/ *teshbih* (f)	يشبه / تشبه
loose (*clothes*)	*khafeef* (m)/ *khafeefa* (f)	خفيف / خفيفه
lorry	*looree* (m)	لورى
lorry-driver	*sawa' looree* (m)	سواق لورى
lose: he/she loses	*yafqod* (m)/*tafqod* (f)	يفقد / تفقد
...is lost (*see p. 155*)	... *Da^a*	ضاع
lost property (office)	(*maktaeb*) (m) *il mafqoodaet*	مكتب المفقودات
a lot (of)	*kiteer* (m)/*kiteera* (f)	كتير / كتيره
lotion	*kreem* (m)	كريم
lottery	*lotaraya* (f)	لوتاريه
loud	*Sowt ^aalee* (m & f)	صوت عالى
lounge (*airport*)	*Saala* (f)	صاله
(*hotel*)	*Salown* (m)	صالون
love	*Hob* (m)	حب
love: he/she loves	*yiHeb* (m)/*tiHeb* (f)	يحب / تحب
lovely	*Helw* (m)/*Helwa* (f)	حلو / حلوه
low	*waaTi* (m)/*waTya* (f)	واطى / واطيه
lower	*awTa*	أوطى
lozenge (*for throat*)	*basteel* (m) (*lil zowr*)	باستيل (للزور)
lucky	*maHZooZ* (m)/ *maHZooZa* (f)	محظوظ / محظوظه
luggage	*shonaaT* (pl)	شنط
luggage allowance	*ishonaaT il masmooH biha*	الشنط المسموح بها
lump	*kotla* (f)	كتله
(*swelling*)	*waram* (f)	ورم
lunch	*ghadda* (f)	غذاء

M

machine	*makanna* (f)	ماكينه
machinist	*mikaneekee* (m)/ *mikaneekaya* (f)	ميكانيكى / ميكانيكيه

mad	*magnoon* (m)/ *magnoona* (f)	مجنون/ مجنونه
madam	*madaem* (f)	مدام
magazine	*megalla* (f)	مجله
mail	*bareed* (m)	بريد
main	*asaesee* (m)/ *asasaya* (f)	أساسي/ أساسيه
make (car etc.)	*marka* (f)	ماركه
make: he/she makes	*ye^amil* (m)/*te^amil* (f)	يعمل/ تعمل
make-up	*makyaj* (m)	ماكياج
male	*zakar* (m)	ذكر
man	*ragil* (m)	راجل
manager	*modeer* (m)/*modeera* (f)	مدير/ مديره
managing director	*modeer ^aam* (m & f)	مديرعام
many	*kiteer*	كتير
not many	*mish kiteer*	مش كتير
map	*khareeTa* (f)	خريطه
marble	*rokhaem* (m)	رخام
margarine	*margareen* (m)	مارجرين
market	*sooq* (m)	سوق
married	*metgawiz* (m)/ *metgawiza* (f)	متجوز/ متجوزه
marry: he/she gets married	*yetgawiz* (m)/ *tetgawiz* (f)	يتجوز/ تتجوز
mascara	*maskara* (f)	مسكره
masculine	*zakar* (m)	ذكر
mask (for protection)	*qinae^a* (m)	قناع
mass (church)	*qodas* (m)	قداس
match (game)	*matsh* (m)	ماتش
matches	*kabreet* (pl)	كبريت
material (cloth)	*o'maesh* (pl)	قماش
mathematics	*riyaDa* (f)	رياضه
matter: it doesn't matter	*mish mohim*	مش مهم
what's the matter?	*fi ay*	في ايه؟
mattress	*martaba* (f)	مرتبه
air mattress	*martabit hawa*	مرتبة هواء

248

mature (*cheese etc.*)	*qadeem* (m)/ *qadeema* (f)	قديم / قديمه
mayonnaise	*mayonayz* (m)	مايونيز
me (*see Basic grammar, p. 161*)	*ana*	أنا
with me	*ma^aaya*	معايا
meadow	*mar^a* (m)	مرعى
meal	*akla* (f)	أكله
mean: what does this mean?	*ya^nee ay*	يعنى أيه؟
meanwhile	*baynama*	بينما
measles	*HaSba* (f)	حصبه
German measles	*HaSba almaeni*	حصبه ألمانى
measure: he/she measures	*ye'ees* (m)/*te'ees* (f)	يقيس / تقيس
measurement	*ma'aaes* (m)	مقاس
meat	*laHma* (f)	لحمه
cold meats	*laHm baerid* (pl)	لحم بارد
mechanic	*mikaneekee* (m)/ *mikaneekaya* (f)	ميكانيكى / ميكانيكيه
medical	*Tebbee* (m)/ *Tebbaya* (f)	طبى / طبيه
medicine	*dawa* (f)	دواء
Mediterranean sea	*ibaHr ilabyaD ilmitawassiT*	البحر الأبيض المتوسط
medium (*steak*)	*noS noS* *noSi siwa*	نص نص نصف سواء
medium dry (*wine*)	*medyam*	مديم
meet: he/she meets	*ye'abil* (m)/*te'abil* (f)	يقابل / تقابل
meeting (*accidental*)	*moqabla* (f)	مقابله
(*business*)	*igtimae^a* (m)	أجتماع
melon	*shamaema* (f)	شمامه
watermelon	*baTeekha* (f)	بطيخه
member	*^odw* (m & f)	عضو
men	*rigaela* (pl)	رجاله
mend: he/she mends	*yeSallaH* (m)/ *tiSallaH* (f)	بصلح / تصلح

menu	*menyoo* (m)	منيو
message	*risaela* (f)	رساله
metal	*ma^adan* (m)	معدن
meter	*^aadaed* (m)	عداد
metre	*metr* (m)	متر
microwave oven	*maikrowayv* (m)	مايكرو وايڤ
midday	*iDohraya* (f)	الظهريه
middle	*mitawassiT* (m)/	متوسط/ متوسطه
	mitawassiTa (f)	
middle-aged	*fi montaSaf*	فى منتصف العمر
	il ^aomr	
midnight	*fi noS ilayl*	فى نصف الليل
migraine	*meegrayn* (m)	ميجراين
mild	*khafeef* (m)/	خفيف/ خفيفه
	khafeefa (f)	
mile	*meel* (m)	ميل
milk	*laban* (m)	لبن
milkshake	*milkshayk* (m)	ملك شيك
mill	*TaHoona* (f)	طاحونه
mince	*laHma*	لحمه مفرومه
	mafrooma (m)	
mind: do you mind	*^aandak* (to m)/	عندك/ عندك
(if) . . .?	*^aandik* (to f)	مانع . . . ؟
	maeni^a . . .	
I don't mind	*ma^aandeesh maeni^a*	معنديش مانع
minibus	*minibas* (m)	مينى باس
minister	*wazeer* (m)/	وزير/ وزيره
	wazeera (f)	
minute (*time*)	*de'e'a* (f)/*da'ayi'* (pl)	دقيقه/ دقائق
mirror	*miraaya* (f)	مرءاه
Miss	*aenisa* (f)	أنسه
miss: he/she misses		
(*bus etc.*)	*faetoo* (m)/*fat-ha* (f)	فاته/ فاتها
(*nostalgia*)	*waHshoo* (m)/	واحشو/ واحشها
	waHesh-ha (f)	
mist	*Dabaab* (m)	ضباب

250

mistake	*ghalTa* (f)	غلطه
he/she is mistaken	*ghalTaan* (m)/	غلطان/ غلطانه
	ghalTaana (f)	
mixed	*khalaT* (m)/	خلط/ خلطت
	khalaTit (f)	
mixture	*makhlooT* (pl)	مخلوط
model	*modayl* (f)	موديل
modern	*modaern* (m & f)	مودرن
moisturiser	*kraym* (m) *moraTib*	كريم مرطب
monastery	*dayr* (m)	دير
money	*filoos* (pl)	فلوس
month	*shahr* (m)	شهر
monument	*naSb tizkaeri* (m)	نصب تزكارى
moon	*'amar* (m)	قمر
moped	*fesba* (f)	فسبه
more	*aktar*	اكثر
no more	*kifaeya*	كفايه
morning	*SabaH* (m)	صباح
mortgage	*rahn* (m)	رهن
mosque	*game^a* (m)	جامع
mosquitoes	*namoos* (pl)	ناموس
mosquito net	*namoosaya* (f)	ناموسيه
most (of)	*mo^aZam*	معظم
mother	*'om* (f)	أم
mother-in-law	*Hama* (f)	حماه
my mother-in-law	*Hamaeti* (f)	حماتى
motor	*maTowr* (m)	موتور
motorbike	*motosekl* (m)	موتوسيكل
motorboat	*lansh* (m)	لنش
motor racing	*saba'* (m) *saiyaraat*	سباق سيارات
motorway	*otostraad* (m)	أوتوستراد
mountain	*gabal* (m)	جبل
mountaineering	*tasaloq il gibael*	تسلق الجبال
mouse	*far* (m)	فأر
moustache	*shanab* (m)	شنب
mouth	*bo'* (m)	بق
move: he/she moves	*ye^aazil* (m)/*te^aazil* (f)	يعزل/ تعزل

Mr	*isayed*	السيد
Mrs	*isayeda*	السيده
much	*kiteer*	كثير
not much	*mish kiteer*	مش كثير
mug	*fingaen* (m)	فنجان
mullah (*Muslim religious leader*)	*shaykh* (m)	شيخ/إمام
murder	*qatl* (m)	قتل
museum	*matHaf* (m)	متحف
music	*mazeeka* (f)	مزيكه
musical	*mosiqi* (m)/ *mosiqaya* (f)	موسيقى/موسيقيه
musician	*molaHin* (m)/ *molaHina* (f)	ملحن/ملحنه
Muslim	*moslim* (m)/ *moslima* (f)	مسلم/مسلمه
must: you must . . .	*laezim* . . .	لازم . . .
mustard	*mostarda* (f)	مستارده
my (*see Basic grammar, p. 160*)		
mystery	*loghz* (m)	لغز

N

nail (*DIY*)	*mosmaar* (m)	مسمار
(*finger/toe*)	*Dofr* (m)	ظفر
nail clippers/scissors	*maqaS* (m) *Dawafir*	مقص أظافر
nail file	*mabraD* (m) *Dawafir*	مبرض أظافر
nail polish	*maniker* (m)	مانيكير
naked	*ᵃeryaen* (m)/ *ᵃeryaena* (f)	عريان/عريانه
name	*ism* (m)	أسم
my name is . . .	*ismi* . . .	أسمى . . .
what is your name?	*ismak ay* (to m)/ *ismik ay* (to f)	اسمَك ايه/ اسمِك ايه
napkin	*mandeel* (m)	منديل

English	Transliteration	Arabic
nappies	*gheyar* (pl) *lil baybee*	غيار للبابيى
narrow	*Daiya'* (m)/*Daiya'a* (f)	ضيق/ ضيقه
national	*qawmee* (m)/ *qawmaya* (f)	قومى/ قوميه
nationality	*ginsaya* (f)	جنسيه
natural	*Tabee^aee* (m)/ *Tabee^aaya* (f)	طبيعى/ طبيعيه
naturally	*Tabee^aee*	طبيعى
naughty	*sha'ee* (m)/*sha'aya* (f)	شقى/ شقيه
navy	*baHaraya* (f)	بحريه
navy blue	*azra'* (m)/*zar'a* (f)	أزرق/ زرقاء
near (to)	*orayyib* (min)	قريب (من)
nearby	*orayyib* (m)/ *orayyiba* (f)	قريب/ قريبه
nearest	*a'rab*	أقرب
nearly	*t'areeban*	تقريباً
necessary	*Darooree* (m)/ *Darooraya*	ضرورى/ ضروريه
it is necessary	*laezim*	لازم
necklace	*^aoqd* (m)	عقد
need: he/she needs	*meHtaeg* (m)/ *meHtaega* (f)	محتاج/ محتاجه
needle	*ebra* (f)	إبره
negative (*photo*)	*negateef* (m)	نيجاتيف
neighbour	*gaar* (m)/*gaara* (f)	جار/ جاره
neither . . . nor	*la . . . walla*	لا . . . ولا
nephew (*brother's son*)	*ibn akhooya*	إبن أخويا
(*sister's son*)	*ibn okhti* (m)	أبن أختى
nervous	*metnarviz* (m)/ *metnarviza* (f)	متنرفز/ متنرفزه
net	*shabaka* (f)	شبكه
never	*abadan*	أبداً
new	*gideed* (m)/*gideeda* (f)	جديد/ جديده
New Year	*^aam gideed*	عام جديد
news	*akhbaar* (pl)	أخبار

253

newspaper	*gornaal* (m)	جرنال
newspaper kiosk	*koshk* (m) *igaraiyid*	كشك الجرائد
next	*ba^ad* (m & f)	بعد
next to	*ganb*	جنب
nice (*person*)	*Zareef* (m)/*Zareefa* (f)	ظريف/ ظريفه
(*thing*)	*Helw* (m)/*Helwa* (f)	حلو/ حلوه
niece (*brother's daughter*)	*bint akhooya*	بنت أخويا
(*sister's daughter*)	*bint okhti*	بنت أختى
night	*layl* (m)	ليل
nightclub	*nayt klab* (m)	نايت كلوب
nightdress	*'ameeS* (m) *nowm*	قميص نوم
no	*la'a*	لأ
nobody	*mafeesh Had*	مفيش أحد
noise	*dawsha* (f)	دوشه
noisy (*person*)	*dawshagi* (m)/ *dawshagaya* (f)	دوشجى/ دوشجيه
(*place, thing*)	*dawsha* (m & f)	دوشه
non-alcoholic	*bidoon khamra*	بدون خمر
non-smoking	*mafeesh tadkheen*	مفيش تدخين
none	*wala waHid* (m)/ *wala waHda* (f)	ولا واحد/ ولا واحده
normal	*^aedee* (m)/ *^aedaya* (f)	عادى/ عاديه
normally	*^adatan*	عادة
north	*shamael*	شمال
nose	*manakheer* (f)	مناخير
nosebleed	*nazeef aenfi* (m)	نزيف انفى
nostril	*fatHit* (m) *il aenf*	فتحة الأنف
not	*la*	لا
note (*bank*)	*bankenowt* (m)	بنكنوت
notepad	*daftar* (m)	دفتر
nothing (else)	*wala Haga (tanya)*	ولا حاجه (تانيه)
now	*delwa'ti*	دلوقتى
nowhere	*wala makaen*	ولا مكان
nuclear	*Zarree* (m)/*Zarraya* (f)	ذرى/ ذريه
nuclear power	*il Taqa* (f) *iZarraya*	الطاقه الذريه

254

number	*nemra* (f)	نمره
nurse	*momarriD* (m)/	ممرض/ ممرضه
	momariDa (f)	
nut (*DIY*)	*Samoola* (f)	صاموله
nuts	*mikassaraat* (pl)	مكسرات
nylon	*naylon* (m & f)	نايلون

O

oasis	*waeHa* (f)	واحه
oar	*migdaef* (m)	مجداف
object	*shay'* (m)	شيء
obvious	*waaDiH* (m)/	واضح/ واضحه
	waDHa (f)	
occasionally	*aHyaenan*	أحياناً
occupied (*toilet*)	*mashghool* (m)/	مشغول/ مشغوله
	mashghoola (f)	
odd (*strange*)	*ghareeb* (m)/	غريب/ غريبه
	ghareeba (f)	
(*not even*)	*fardi* (m)/*fardaya* (f)	فردي/ فرديه
of course	*Tab^aan*	طبعاً
off (*power*)	*maTfi* (m)	مطفأ
offended	*it-haen* (m)/*it-haenit* (f)	إتهان/ اتهانت
offer	*^aarD* (m)	عرض
special offer	*^aarD khaaS*	عرض خاص
office	*maktaeb* (m)	مكتب
officer (*police etc.*)	*zaabit* (m)/*zabta* (f)	ضابط/ ضابطه
official	*rasmi* (m)/*rasmaya* (f)	رسمي/ رسميه
often	*ghaliban*	غالياً
how often?	*kaem marra*	كم مره؟
oil	*zayt* (m)	زيت
OK	*owkay*	اوكي
old (*people*)	*^aagooz* (m)/*^aagooza* (f)	عجوز/ عجوزه
(*places, things*)	*qadeem* (m)/	قديم/ قديمه
	qadeema (f)	

English	Transliteration	Arabic
(places, things)	qadeem (m)/ qadeema (f)	قديم / قديمه
how old are you?	*andak kaem sana (to m)/ *andik kaem sana (to f)	عندك كام سنه؟/ عندِك كام سنه؟
how old is he/ she/it?	*andoo (m)/ *andaha (f) kaem sana	عنده/ عندها كام سنه؟
I am . . . years old	ana *andi . . . sana	انا عندى . . . سنه
old-fashioned	da'a qadeema	دقه قديمه
olive	zatoon (pl)	زيتون
olive oil	zayt (m) zatoon	زيت زيتون
on	*ala	على
(light etc.)	miwalla* (m)/ miwalla*a (f)	مولع/ مولعه
once	marra	مره
onion	baSala (f)/baSal (pl)	بصله/ بصل
only	bas	بس
open	maftooH (m)/ maftooHa (f)	مفتوح/ مفتوحه
open: he/she opens	yeftaH (m)/teftaH (f)	يفتح/ تفتح
opera	obra (f)	اوبرا
operation	*amalaya (f)	عمليه
opinion: in my opinion	fi ra'yi	فى رأى
opposite	Ded	ضد
opposite the house	oddaem ilbayt	امام البيت
optician	naddaraati (m)	نظاراتى
optional	ikhtiyaeri (m)/ ikhtiyaeraya (f)	أختيارى/ أختياريه
or	aw	أو
orange (fruit)	borto'an	برتقال
(colour)	borto'aeni	برتقالى
order: he/she orders	yoTlob (m)/toTlob (f)	يطلب/ تطلب
ordinary	*aedi (m)/*aedaya (f)	عادى/ عاديه
organise: he/she organises	yenaZam (m)/ tenaZam (f)	ينظم/ تنظم

original	*gideed* (m)/*gideeda* (f)	جديد/ جديده
other	*akhar* (m)/*okhra* (f)	اخر/ اخرى
others	*il akhareen*	الأخرين
our (*see* Basic grammar, p. 160)		
out (of . . .)	*khaerig (il . . .)*	خارج (ال . . .)
outdoor	*barra*	بره
over	*fow'*	فوق
overcast (*weather*)	*ma'loob*	مقلوب
overcoat	*balToo* (m)	بالطو
overtake: he/she overtakes	*yesba'* (m)/*tesba'* (f)	يسبق/ تسبق
owe: he/she owes	*mitdayin* (m)/ *mitdayna* (f)	متداين/ متداينه
I owe you . . .	*ana mitdayin . . .*	انا متداين . . .
own: he/she owns	*yemlik* (m)/*temlik* (f)	يملك/ تملك
owner (of . . .)	*SaHib (il . . .)*	صاحب (ال . . .)

P

package tour	*reHla* (f) *shamila*	رحله شامله
packet	*bako* (m)	باكو
paddle (*canoeing*)	*migdaef* (m)	مجداف
padlock	*terbaes* (m)	ترباس
page	*SafHa* (f)	صفحه
pain	*waga*^a (m)	وجع
painful	*biyewga*^a (m)/ *bitewga*^a (f)	بيوجع/ بتوجع
painkiller	*DeD ilalam* (m)	ضدالألم
paint	*booya* (f)	بويه
paint: he/she paints		
(*pictures*)	*yersim* (m)/*tersim* (f)	يرسم/ ترسم
(*walls*)	*yebayaD* (m)/ *tebayaD* (f)	يبيض/ تبيض
painter (*artist*)	*rassaem* (m)/ *rassaema* (f)	رسام/ رسامه
(*artisan*)	*bohyagi* (m)/ *bohyagaya* (f)	بوهيجى/ بوهيجيه

painting (*art*)	*rasm* (m)	رسم
pair	*gowz*	جوز
palace	*'asr* (m)	قصر
pale	*shaHib* (m)/	شاحب/ شاحبه
	shaHba (f)	
palm tree	*nakhla* (f)	نخله
pants (*men's underwear*)	*libaes* (m)	لباس
paper	*wara'a* (f)	ورقه
paper clip	*dabboos* (m)	دبوس
paraffin	*gaez* (m)	جاز
paralysed	*mashlool* (m)/	مشلول/ مشلوله
	mashloola (f)	
parcel	*Tard* (m)	طرد
pardon?	*ªan iznak* (to m) /	عن إذنك؟/ عن إذنك؟
	ªan iznik (to f)	
parents	*ahl* (pl)	أهل
park	*ginayna* (f)	جنينه
park: he/she parks	*yerkin* (m)/*terkin* (f)	يركن/ تركن
parking	*raekn* (m)	ركن
car park	*maw'aef* (m) *saiyaraat*	موقف سيارات
no parking	*mamnooª il intiZaar*	ممنوع الأنتظار
parking meter	*ªadaed il intiZaar*	عدادالأنتظار
parliament	*barlamaen* (m)	برلمان
part	*goz'* (m)	جزء
parting (*hair*)	*far'* (m)	فرق
(*farewell*)	*wadaeª* (m)	وداع
partly	*goz'ayan*	جزئيا
partner	*shereek* (m)/	شريك/ شريكه
	shereeka (f)	
party	*Hafla* (f)	حفله
pass (*permit*)	*izn* (m)	إذن
pass (*on road*): he/she passes	*yeªadi* (m)/*teªadi* (f)	يعدى/ تعدى
passenger	*raekib* (m)/*raekiba* (f)	راكب/ راكبه

English	Transliteration	Arabic
passion	*ᵃaTifa* (f)	عاطفه
passport	*basbor* (m)	باسبور
passport control	*gawazaet* (pl)	جوازات
past	*maaDee*	ماضى
in the past	*fil maaDee*	فى الماضى
pasta	*makarowna* (f)	مكرونه
pastille	*bastilla* (f)	باستله
pastry	*ᵃageena* (f)	عجينه
path	*Taree'* (m)	طريق
patient (hospital)	*mareeD* (m)/ *mareeDa* (f)	مريض/ مريضه
pattern (template)	*batrown* (m)	باترون
pavement	*raSeef* (m)	رصيف
pay: he/she pays	*yedfaᵃ* (m)/*tedfaᵃ* (f)	يدفع/ تدفع
peas	*bisella* (pl)	بسله
peace	*salaem* (m)	سلام
peach	*khowkh* (m)	خوخ
peanut	*sodaeni* (m)	سودانى
pear	*kommitra* (f)	كمثرى
pedal	*gadown* (m)	جدون
pedal-boat	*'aerib* (m) *bi gadown*	قارب بالجادون
pedestrian	*moshaeh* (pl)	مشاه
pedestrian crossing	*ᵃoboor* (m) *ilmoshaeh*	عبورالمشاه
peel: he/she peels	*ye'ashar* (m)/ *te'ashar* (f)	يقشر/ تقشر
peg	*mashbak* (m)	مشبك
pen	*'alam* (m)	قلم
pencil	*'alam roSaaS* (m)	قلم رصاص
pencil sharpener	*barraya* (f)	برايه
penfriend	*moraasil* (m)/ *morasla* (f)	مراسل/ مراسله
penicillin	*bansileen* (m)	بنسلين
penknife	*maTwa* (f)	مطوه
pension	*maᵃaesh* (m)	معاش
pensioner	*ᵃala il maᵃaesh*	على المعاش
people	*naes* (pl)	ناس

English	Transliteration	Arabic
pepper	*filfil* (m)	فلفل
green pepper	*filfil akhDar*	فلفل أخضر
red pepper	*filfil aHmar*	فلفل أحمر
peppermint	*ne^ana^a* (m)	نعناع
per	*fi*	في
per hour	*fi sa^a*	في ساعه
per week	*filizboo^a*	في الأسبوع
perfect	*tamaem* (m & f)	تمام
performance	*^arD* (m)	عرض
perfume	*barfaen* (m)	برفان
perhaps	*yemkin*	يمكن
period (*menstrual*)	*^aeda* (f) *shahraya*	عاده شهريه
period pains	*alaem* (pl) *il ^aeda* *ishahraya*	الام العاده الشهريه
perm	*barmanant* (m)	برماننت
permit	*izn* (m)	إذن
work permit	*izn ^amal*	إذن عمل
permit: he/she permits	*yesmaH* (m)/ *tesmaH* (f)	يسمح / تسمح
person	*shakhS* (m)	شخص
personal	*shakhSee* (m)/ *shakhSaya* (f)	شخصي / شخصيه
personal stereo	*wokman* (m)	واكمان
petrol	*banzeen* (m)	بنزين
petrol can	*^elbit* (f) *banzeen*	علبة بنزين
petrol station	*maHaTit* (f) *banzeen*	محطة بنزين
petticoat	*'ameeS* (m) *Hareemi*	قميص حريمي
pharaoh	*far^own* (m)	فرعون
philosophy	*falsafa* (f)	فلسفه
photocopy	*Soora* (f)	صوره
photocopy: he/she photocopies	*yeSawar* (m)/ *tiSawar* (f)	يصور / تصور
photo(graph)	*Soora* (f)	صوره
photographer	*miSawaraati* (m)/ *miSawarataya* (f)	مصوراتي / مصوراتيه
photography	*taSweer* (m)	تصوير
phrase book	*kitaeb* (m) *^ibaraat*	كتاب عبارات

English	Transliteration	Arabic
physics	*Tabee^aa* (f)	طبيعه
piano	*biano* (m)	بيانو
pick: he/she picks (*chooses*)	*yekhtar* (m)/ *tekhtar* (f)	يختار/ تختار
(*flowers etc.*)	*yo'tof* (m)/ *to'tof* (f)	يقطف/ تقطف
pick up (*fetch*): he/she picks up	*yegeeb* (m)/*tegeeb* (f)	يجيب/ تجيب
picnic	*nozha* (f)	نزهه
picture	*Soora* (f)	صوره
piece	*goz'* (m)	جزء
pier	*raSeef* (m)	رصيف
pierced	*makhroom* (m)/ *makhrooma* (f)	مخروم/ مخرومه
pig	*khanzeer* (m)	خنزير
pigeon	*Hamaem* (m)	حمام
pills	*Hoboob* (pl)	حبوب
(*contraceptive*)	*Hoboob man^a ilHaml*	حبوب منع الحمل
pillow	*makhadda* (f)	مخده
pillowcase	*kees* (m) *makhadda*	كيس مخده
pilot	*Taiyaar* (m)	طيار
pilot light	*^aayn* (f)	عين
pin	*daboos* (m)	دبوس
pineapple	*ananaes* (m)	اناناس
pink	*bamba* (f)	بمبه
pipe (*smoking*)	*beeba* (f)	بيبه
(*drain*)	*masoora* (f)	ماسوره
place	*makaen* (m)	مكان
plain	*saeda*	ساده
plan (*of town etc.*)	*khareeTa* (f)	خريطه
plane	*Taiyaara* (f)	طياره
plant	*nabaet* (pl)	نبات
plaster (*sticking*)	*blaster* (m)	بلستر
plastic	*blastik* (m)	بلاستيك
plastic bag	*shanTa* (f) *blastik*	شنطه بلاستيك
plate	*Taba'* (m)	طبق
platform	*raSeef* (m)	رصيف

play (*theatre*)	masraHaya (f)	مسرحيه
play: he/she plays		
(*instrument, sport*)	yel^aab (m)/tel^aab (f)	يلعب / تلعب
(*record/tape/CD*)	yedawar (m)/ tidawar (f)	يدور / تدور
pleasant	Zareef (m)/Zareefa (f)	ظريف / ظريفه
please	min faDlak (to m)/ min faDlik (to f)	من فضلك / من فضلك
pleased	sa^aeed (m)/ sa^aeeda (f)	سعيد / سعيده
plenty (of)	kiteer (m)/kiteera (f)	كثير / كثيره
pliers	kammaesha (f)	كماشه
plimsolls	gazma (f) kawetch	جزمه كاوتش
plug (*bath*)	sadaeda (f)	سداده
(*electrical*)	kobs (m)	كبس
plumber	sabaek (m)	سباك
pneumonia	iltihaeb (m) re'awi	إلتهاب رئوى
pocket	gayb (m)	جيب
point	no'ta (f)	نقطه
poison	sem (m)	سم
poisonous	masmoom (m)/ masmooma (f)	مسموم / مسمومه
pole	qotb (m)	قطب
police	bolees (pl)	بوليس
police car	^aarabayit (f) ibolees	عربيه البوليس
police station	maHaTit (f) ibolees	محطة البوليس
polish (*for shoes etc.*)	dahaen (m)	دهان
polite	mo'addab (m)/ mo'addaba (f)	مؤدب / مؤدبه
political, politician	siyaesi (m)/siyasaya (f)	سياسى / سياسيه
politics	siyaesa (f)	سياسه
polluted	molawas (m)/ molawasa (f)	ملوث / ملوثه
pollution	talawos (m)	تلوث
pool (*swimming*)	Hammaem SibaHa (m)	حمام سباحه
poor	fa'eer (m)/fa'eera (f)	فقير / فقيره
pop (*music*)	bob (m)	بوب

Pope	*il baaba* (m)	البابا
popular	*sha^abi* (m)/	شعبى / شعبيه
	sha^abaya (f)	
pork	*khanzeer* (m)	خنزير
port	*meena* (f)	ميناء
porter	*shayael* (m)	شيال
porthole	*shibbaek* (m) *fil 'aerib*	شباك فى القارب
portion	*goz'* (m)	جزء
portrait	*Soora* (f)	صوره
positive (*sure*)	*mo'akad* (m)/	مؤكد / مؤكده
	mo'akada (f)	
(*photo*)	*positeef* (m)	بوزيتيف
possible	*momkin*	ممكن
as soon as possible	*fawran*	فوراً
possibly	*gayiz*	جائز
post (*mail*)	*bareed* (m)	صندوق بريد
post: he/she posts	*yeb^aat* (m)/*teb^aat* (f)	يبعث / تبعث
postbox	*Sandoo'* (m) *bareed*	صندوق بريد
postcard	*kart* (m)	كارت
poster	*Soora* (f)	صوره
postman	*bosTagi* (m)	بوسطجى
post office	*bosTa* (f)	بوسطه
postpone: he/she	*ye'agil* (m)/*te'agil* (f)	يؤجل / تؤجل
postpones		
pot (*for cooking*)	*Halla* (f)	حله
potato	*baTaTis* (pl)	بطاطس
pottery	*khazaf* (m)	خزف
potty (*child's*)	*asraya* (f)	قصريه
pound (*money*)	*ginay* (m)	جنيه
(*sterling*)	*isterleenee*	أسترلينى
pour: he/she pours	*yedlo'* (m)/*tedlo'* (f)	يدلق / تدلق
powder	*bodra* (f)	بودره
talcum powder	*bodrit* (f) *talg*	بودرة تلج
powdered milk	*bodrit* (f) *laban*	بودرة لبن
power (*electricity*)	*kahraba* (f)	كهرباء
power cut	*'aT^a* (m) *ikahraba*	قطع الكهرباء
pram	*^aarabayit* (f) *aTfaal*	عربية أطفال

263

prefer: he/she prefers	*yefaDal* (m)/ *tefaDal* (f)	يفضل / تفضل
pregnant	*Haemil* (f)	حامل
prepare: he/she prepares	*yegahiz* (m)/ *tegahiz* (f)	يجهز / تجهز
prescription	*roshetta* (f)	روشته
present (*gift*)	*hidaya* (f)	هديه
president	*raiyyis* (m)/ *raiyissa* (f)	رئيس / رئيسه
press (*newspapers*)	*SaHaefa* (f)	صحيفه
press office	*il maktaeb* (m) *iSaHafi*	المكتب الصحفى
pretty	*gameel* (m)/ *gameela* (f)	جميل / جميله
price	*taman* (m)	ثمن
priest	*'asees* (m)	قسيس
prime minister	*ra'ees* (m) *il wizaara*	رئيس الوزراء
primus stove	*baboor* (m) *gaez*	بابورجاز
prince	*'ameer* (m)	أمير
princess	*'ameera* (f)	أميره
print (*photo*)	*Soora* (f)	صوره
print: he/she prints	*yeTba^a* (m)/*teTba^a* (f)	يطبع / تطبع
prison	*segn* (m)	سجن
private	*shakhSee* (m)/ *shakhSaya* (f)	شخصى / شخصيه
prize	*gayza* (f)	جائزه
probably	*gayiz*	جائز
problem	*moshkila* (f)	مشكله
producer (*TV, theatre etc.*)	*montig* (m)/ *montiga* (f)	منتج / منتجه
profession	*mehna* (f)	مهنه
professor	*ostaez* (m)/*ostaeza* (f)	أستاذ/ أستاذه
profit	*maksab* (m)	مكسب
programme	*birnaemig* (m)	برنامج
prohibited	*mamnoo^a* (m)/ *mamnoo^{a}a* (f)	ممنوع / ممنوعه
promise: he/she promises	*yew^{a}id* (m)/*tew^{a}id* (f)	يوعد / توعد

264

pronounce: he/she pronounces	*yestahagga* (m)/ *tistahagga* (f)	يستهجئ/ تستهجئ
how do you pronounce this?	*istahagga di*	استهجئ دى؟
proper	*maZbooT* (m)/ *maZbooTa* (f)	مظبوط/ مظبوطه
property *(land)*	*melk* (m)	ملك
prophet	*rasool* (m)	رسول
Protestant	*brotostant* (m)/ *brotostantaya* (f)	بروتسنت/ بروتسنتيه
public *(n)*	*isha*ᵃ*b* (pl)	الشعب
(adj)	*ᵃaem* (m)/*ᵃaema* (f)	عام/ عامه
public holiday	*'agaeza* (f) *rasmaya*	اجازه رسميه
public relations	*ᵃilaqat ᵃaema*	علاقات عامه
pull: he/she pulls	*yished* (m)/*tished* (f)	يشد/ تشد
pulses *(food)*	*boqool* (pl)	بقول
pump up: he/she pumps up	*yenfokh* (m)/ *tenfokh* (f)	ينفخ/ تنفخ
puncture	*khorm* (m)	خرم
pure	*na'ee* (m)/*na'aya* (f)	نقى/ نقيه
purple	*orgwaeni* (m)/ *orgwanaya* (f)	اورجوانى/ اورجوانيه
purse	*kees* (m)	كيس
push: he/she pushes	*yezo'* (m)/*tezo'* (f)	يزق/ تزق
push-chair	*ᵃarabayit* (f) *aTfaal*	عربية أطفال
put: he/she puts	*yeHoT* (m)/*teHoT* (f)	يحط/ تحط
pyjamas	*bijaema* (f)	بيجاما
pyramid	*haram* (m)/*ahraam* (pl)	هرم/ أهرام

265

Q

quality	*qeema* (f)	قيمه
quantity	*kemayya* (f)	كميه
quarter	*robᵃ* (m)	ربع
quay	*raSeef* (m)	رصيف
queen	*malika* (f)	ملكه
question	*soo'ael* (m)	سؤال

queue	*Taboor* (m)	طابور
quick	*saree^a* (m)/*saree^aa* (f)	سريع / سريعه
quickly	*bisor^aa*	بسرعه
quiet	*haedi* (m)/*hadya* (f)	هادئ / هادئه
quite	*'awi*	قوى
Qu'ran (Koran)	*qor'an* (m)	قرآن

R

rabbi	*Hakhaem* (m)	حاخام
rabbit	*arnab* (m)	أرنب
rabies	*maraD* (m) *ikalb*	مرض الكلب
racecourse	*saba'* (m)	سباق
racing (*horse*)	*saba'* (m) *il khayl*	سباق الخيل
(*motor*)	*saba'* (m) *saiyaraat*	سباق سيارات
racket (*tennis etc.*)	*maDrab* (m)	مضرب
radiator	*radyater* (m)	رادياتير
radio	*radyo* (m)	راديو
radioactive	*ish^aae^ai* (m)	إشعاعى
radio station	*maHaTit* (f) *radyo*	محطة راديو
railway	*sekka* (f) *Hadeed*	سكه حديد
railway station	*maHaTit* (f) *sekka* *Hadeed*	محطة سكه حديد
rain	*maTara* (f)	مطر
rain: it's raining	*bitmaTar*	تمطر
raincoat	*balToo* (m) *maTar*	بالطو مطر
rape	*ightiSaab* (m)	إغتصاب
rare	*naedir* (m)/*nadra* (f)	نادر / نادره
(*steak*)	*nay fi nay*	نئ فى نئ
rash (*on skin*)	*TafH* (m) *geldi*	طفح جلدى
raspberries	*toot* (pl)	توت
rat	*far* (m)	فأر
rate (*speed*)	*nesbit* (f) *isor^aa*	نسبة السرعه
(*tariff*)	*nesbit* (f) *itaman*	نسبة الثمن
raw	*nay* (m)/*naya* (f)	نئ / نئه
razor (*blade*)	*moos* (m)	موس

266

English	Transliteration	Arabic
reach: he/she reaches	*yewSal* (m)/*tewSal* (f)	يصل/ تصل
read: he/she reads	*ye'ra* (m)/*te'ra* (f)	يقرأ/ تقرأ
reading	*'iraya* (f)	قراءه
ready	*gaehiz* (m)/*gahza* (f)	جاهز/ جاهزه
real (*authentic*)	*aSlee* (m)/*aSlaya* (f)	أصل/ أصليه
really	*Ha'ee'ee*	حقيقى
rear	*khalfi* (m)/ *khalfaya* (f)	خلفي/ خلفيه
reason (*cause*)	*sabab* (m)	سبب
(*rationality*)	*ªa'lee* (m)	عقلي
receipt	*waSl* (m)	وصل
receiver (*telephone*)	*samaeªa* (f)	سماعه
reception	*istikbael* (m)	إستقبال
receptionist	*mowaZafit (f) ilistikbael*	موظفة أستقبال
recipe	*Taree'a* (f)	طريقة
recognise: he/she recognises	*yataªarraf* (m)/ *tataªarraf* (f)	يتعرف/ تتعرف
recommend: he/she recommends	*yewaSee* (m)/ *tewaSee* (f)	يوصى/ توصى
record	*segil* (m)	سجل
record: he/she records	*yesagil* (m)/*tesagil* (f)	يسجل/ تسجل
record-player	*steryo* (m)	ستريو
recover: he/she recovers	*yekhif* (m)/*tekhif* (f)	يخف/ تخف
red	*aHmar* (m)/*Hamra* (f)	أحمر/ حمراء
Red Crescent	*il hilael laHmar* (m)	الهلال الأحمر
Red Cross	*iSaaleeb laHmar*	الصليب الأحمر
Red Sea	*ibaHr ilaHmar*	البحر الأحمر
reduction	*tawfeer* (m)	توفير
refill (*gas*)	*amboobit* (f) *botagaez*	انبوبة بوتاجاز
refrigerator	*talaega* (f)	ثلاجه
refugee	*laegi'* (m)/*laegi'a* (f)	لاجئ/ لاجئه
refund	*istirdaed* (m)	استرداد
refund: he/she refunds	*yesterid* (m)/ *testerid* (f)	يسترد/ تسترد
region	*manTi'a* (f)	منطقه

register: he/she registers	*yesagil* (m)/*tesagil* (f)	يسجل / تسجل
registration	*tasgeel* (m)	تسجيل
registration number	*raqam* (m) *itasgeel*	رقم التسجيل
relation	*'areebee* (m)/*'aribti* (f)	قريبى / قريبتى
religion	*deen* (m)	دين
remain: he/she remains	*yestana* (m)/ *testana* (f)	يستنى / تستنى
remember: he/she remembers	*yeftekir* (m)/ *teftekir* (f)	يفتكر / تفتكر
remove: he/she removes	*yen'il* (m)/*ten'il* (f)	ينقل / تنقل
rent	*iygaar* (m)	إيجار
rent: he/she rents	*ye'aggar* (m)/*te'aggar* (f)	يأجر / تأجر
repair: he/she repairs	*yeSalaH* (m)/ *teSalaH* (f)	يصلح / تصلح
repeat: he/she repeats	*yekarar* (m)/ *tekarar* (f)	يكرر / تكرر
reply	*rad* (m)	رد
reply: he/she replies	*yerod* (m)/*terod* (f)	يرد / ترد
report	*taqreer* (m)	تقرير
report: he/she reports	*yokhbir* (m)/ *tokhbir* (f)	يخبر / تخبر
rescue: he/she rescues	*yenqiz* (m)/*tenqiz* (f)	ينقذ / تنقذ
reservation	*Hagz* (m)	حجز
reserve: he/she reserves	*yeHgiz* (m)/*teHgiz* (f)	يحجز / تحجز
reserved	*maHgooz* (m)/ *maHgooza* (f)	محجوز / محجوزه
responsible	*mas'ool* (m)/ *mas'oola* (f)	مسؤول / مسؤوله
rest: he/she rests	*yerayaH* (m)/ *terayaH* (f)	يريح / تريح
restaurant	*maT^{a}am* (m)	مطعم
restaurant-car	*^{a}arabayit* (f) *il 'akl*	عربة الأكل
result	*nateega* (f)	نتيجه

English	Transliteration	Arabic
retired	alal maaesh (m & f)	على المعاش
return (*ticket*)	raiyiH gay	رايح جاي
return: he/she returns	yerga (m)/terga (f)	يرجع/ ترجع
reverse: he/she reverses	yakis (m)/takis (f)	يعكس/ تعكس
rheumatism	romatizm (m)	روماتيزم
ribbon	shereeT (m)	شريط
rice	roz (m)	ارز
rich	ghanni (m)/ ghannaya (f)	غني/ غنيه
ride (*horse, bicycle etc.*): he/she rides	yerkab (m)/terkab (f)	يركب/ تركب
right	SaHeeH (m)/ SaHeeHa (f)	صحيح/ صحيحه
right (*place*)	yemeen	يمين
on the right	alal yemeen	على اليمين
ring (*jewellery*)	khaetim (m)	خاتم
ripe	reTib (m)/reTba (f)	رطب/ رطبه
river	nahr (m)	نهر
River Nile	nahr ineel	نهر النيل
road	Taree' (m)	طريق
roadworks	ashghael (pl) Toro'	اشغال طرق
roast	fil forn	في الفرن
rob: he/she robs	yesra' (m)/tesra' (f)	يسرق/ تسرق
robbery	ser'a (f)	سرقه
roof	SoT-H (m)	سطح
room	'owda (f)	حجره
(*space*)	makaen (m)	مكان
rope	Habl (m)	حبل
rose	zahra (f)	زهره
rotten	bayiZ (m)/bayZa (f)	بايظ/ بايظه
rough (*surface*)	kheshin (m)/ kheshna (f)	خشن/ خشنه
(*sea*)	baHr (m) hayig	بحر هائج
round	midawar (m)/ midawara (f)	مدور/ مدوره
roundabout (*road*)	dawaraan (m)	دوران

English	Transliteration	Arabic
row (*theatre etc.*)	*Saf* (m)	صف
row: he/she rows (*boat*)	*ye'adif* (m)/*te'adif* (f)	يقذف/ تقذف
rowing boat	*'aerib ta'deef* (m)	قارب تجديف
royal	*malaki* (m)/ *malakaya* (f)	ملكى/ملكيه
rubber	*kawetch* (m)	كاوتش
rubber band	*astik* (m)	استك
rubbish	*zibaela* (f)	زباله
rucksack	*shanTit* (f) *Dahr*	شنطه
rude	*'aleel il'adab* (m)/ *'aleelit il'adab* (f)	قليل الأدب قليلة الأدب
ruins	*aTlal* (pl)	أطلال
ruler (*for measuring*)	*masTara* (f)	مسطره
rum	*rom* (m)	روم
run: he/she runs	*yegree* (m)/*tegree* (f)	يجرى/ تجرى
rush hour	*sa*ⁱ*it* (f) *ilziHaem*	ساعة الزحام
rusty	*meSadi* (m)/ *meSadaya* (f)	مصدئ/ مصدئه

S

English	Transliteration	Arabic
sad	*Hazeen* (m)/ *Hazeena* (f)	حزين/ حزينه
safe (*strongbox*)	*khazna* (f)	خزنه
safe (*adj*)	*'amaen* (m)/ *'amaena* (f)	أمان/ أمانه
safety pin	*daboos mashbak* (m)	دبوس مشبك
sail	*shira*ⁱ (m)	شراع
sail: he/she sails	*yibHar* (m)/*tibHar* (f)	يبحر/ تبحر
sailing	*ibHaar* (m)	إبحار
sailing boat	*markib* (f) *shira*ⁱ*aya*	مركب شراعيه
sailor	*baHaar* (m)	بحار
saint	*qedees* (m)	قديس
salad	*salaTa* (m)	سلطه
salami	*salaemi* (m)	سلامى
sale	*okasyown* (m)	اوكازيون

English	Transliteration	Arabic
sales representative	*baya^a* (m)/*baya^a a* (f)	بياع/ بياعه
salmon	*salamon* (m)	سلمون
salt	*malH* (m)	ملح
salty	*maeliH* (m)/*malHa* (f)	مالح/ مالحه
same	*shaba*	شبه
sample	*^ayenna* (f)	عينه
sand	*raml* (m)	رمل
sandals	*Sandal* (m)	صندل
sandwich	*sandawich* (m)	سندونش
toasted sandwich	*towst* (m)	توست
sandy	*ramli* (m)/*ramlaya* (f)	رملي/ رمليه
sanitary towels	*fowaT SiHaya* (pl)	فوط صحيه
sauce	*SawS* (m)	صوص
saucepan	*kasarolla* (f)	كسروله
saucer	*Taba'* (m)	طبق
sauna	*sowna* (f)	سونا
sausage	*sego'* (m)	سجق
save: he/she saves		
(*money etc.*)	*yeHawish* (m)/	يحوش/ تحوش
	teHawish (f)	
(*rescue*)	*yenqiZ* (m)/	ينقذ/ تنقذ
	tenqiZ (f)	
say: he/she says	*ye'ool* (m)/*te'ool* (f)	يقول/ تقول
scald	*yeHra'* (m)/*teHra'* (f)	يحرق/ تحرق
scales	*meeZaen* (pl)	ميزان
scarf (*ladies'*)	*isharb* (f)	إيشارب
(*woolly*)	*kofaya* (m)	كوفيه
scene	*manZar* (m)	منظر
scenery	*mashaehid* (pl)	مشاهد
scent	*reeHa* (f)	ريحه
school	*madrasa* (f)	مدرسه
science	*^iloom* (pl)	علوم
scientist	*^aelim* (m)/*^aelma* (f)	عالم/ عالمه
scissors	*ma'aS* (m)	مقص
scooter	*skootar* (f)	سكوتر
score	*nateega* (f)	نتيجه
what's the score?	*ayhil nateega*	ايه النتيجه؟
Scotland	*skotlanda* (f)	سكوتلندا

English	Transliteration	Arabic
Scottish	*skotlandi* (m)/ *skotlandaya* (f)	إسكوتلندى/ إسكوتلنديه
scratch	*khadsh* (m)	خدش
scratch: he/she scratches	*yehrosh* (m)/ *tehrosh* (f)	يهرش/ تهرش
screen (*partition*) (*cinema, TV etc.*)	*sitara* (f) *shaesha* (f)	ستاره شاشه
screw	*mosmar alawowz* (m)	مسمار قلاووز
screwdriver	*mifak* (m)	مفك
scuba-diving	*ghaTs* (m) *^aameeq*	غطس عميق
sculpture	*naHt* (m)	نحت
sea	*baHr* (m)	بحر
seasick	*dawar* (m) *ibaHr*	دوارالبحر
season	*moosim* (m)	موسم
season ticket	*karnay* (m)	كارنيه
seat	*korsi* (m)	كرسى
seatbelt	*Hizaem* (m) *ikorsi*	حزام الكرسى
second	*taeni*	تانى
second (*time period*)	*sanya* (f)	ثانيه
secret (*n*)	*ser* (m)	سر
(*adj*)	*serri* (m)/*seraya* (f)	سرى/ سريه
secretary	*sekerter* (m)/ *sekertera* (f)	سكرتير/ سكرتيره
section	*qesm* (m)	قسم
see: he/she sees	*yeshoof* (m)/ *teshoof* (f)	يشوف/ تشوف
seem: he/she seems	*yabdoo* (m)/ *tabdoo* (f)	يبدو/ تبدو
it seems to me . . .	*yabdoo li* . . .	يبدو لى . . .
self-service	*ikhdim nafsak* (for m)/*ikhdimi nafsik* (for f)	أخدم نفسك/ اخدم نفسك
sell: he/she sells	*yebee^a* (m)/*tebee^a* (f)	يبيع/ تبيع
send: he/she sends	*yeb^aat* (m)/*teb^aat* (f)	يبعث/ تبعث
senior citizen	*kibeer fissaen* (m)/ *kibeera fissaen* (f)	كبير فى السن/ كبيره فى السن
sensible	*^aa'il* (m)/*^aa'la* (f)	عاقل/ عاقله
sentence	*gomla* (f)	جمله

272

English	Transliteration	Arabic
separate(d)	*monfaSil* (m)/ *monfaSila* (f)	منفصل / منفصله
septic tank	*tank* (m) *il magaeri*	تنك مجارى
serious	*razeen* (m)/*razeena* (f)	رزين / رزينه
serve: he/she serves	*yekhdim* (m)/ *tekhdim* (f)	يخدم / تخدم
service (church)	*qidaes* (m)	قداس
service charge	*Dareebit* (f) *khedma*	ضريبة خدمه
set (collection)	*Ta'm* (m)	طقم
several	*ªedat*	عدة
sew: he/she sews	*yekhaiyaT* (m)/ *tekhaiyaT* (f)	يخيط / تخيط
sewing	*khiyaaTa* (f)	خياطه
sex	*gens* (m)	جنس
shade (not sun)	*Zel* (m)	ظل
shampoo	*shamboo* (m)	شامبو
sharp	*Haed* (m)/*Haeda* (f)	حاد / حاده
(pain)	*shideed* (m)/ *shideeda* (f)	شديد / شديده
shave: he/she shaves	*yeHla'* (m)/*teHla'* (f)	يحلق / تحلق
shaving cream/foam	*kraym Hila'a* (m)	كريم حلاقه
she (see p. 158)	*haya* (f)	هى
sheep	*kharoof* (m)	خروف
sheet (bed)	*milaya* (f)	ملاءه
(paper)	*wara'a* (f)	ورقه
sheikh	*shaykh* (m)/ *shaykha* (f)	شيخ / شيخه
shelf	*raf* (m)	رف
shell (egg)	*ishr* (f) *bayDa*	قشر بيض
(nut)	*ishr* (f) *sodaeni*	قشر سودانى
(sea)	*Sadafa* (f)	صدفه
shellfish	*Haiyawanaet Sadafaya* (pl)	حيوانات صدفيه
shelter	*malga'* (m)	ملجأ
sherry	*sheri* (m)	شرى
shiny	*laemiª* (m)/*lamªa* (f)	لامع / لامعه
ship	*markib* (f)	مركب
shirt	*'ameeS* (m)	قميص

shock (*electric*)	**Sadma** (f) *kahrobae'aya*	صدمه كهربائيه
(*emotional*)	**Sadma** (f) *ªatifaya*	صدمه عاطفيه
shocked	**maSdoom** (m)/ **maSdooma** (f)	مصدوم/ مصدومه
shoe	**gazma** (f)	جزمه
shoelace	**robaaT** (f) *il gazma*	رباط الجزمه
shoe polish	**warneesh** (m) *il gezam*	ورنيش الجزم
shoe repairer's	**gazmagi** (m)	جزمجى
shoe shop	**maHal** (m) *aHzaya*	محل احذيه
shop	**maHal** (m)	محل
shop assistant	**bayaª** (m)/**bayaªa** (f)	بياع/ بياعه
shopping: he/she goes shopping	**yeroH** (m)/ **teroH** (f) *isoo'*	يروح/ تروح السوق
shopping centre	**markaz** (m) *togaeri*	مركز تجارى
short	**osaiyar** (m)/ **osaiyara** (f)	قصير/ قصيره
shorts	**short** (m)	شورت
shout: he/she shouts	**yezaªa'** (m)/ **tezaªa'** (f)	يزعق/ تزعق
show	**ªarD** (m)	عرض
show: he/she shows	**yeªriD** (m)/**teªriD** (f)	يعرض/ تعرض
shower	**dosh** (m)	دوش
shrink: he/she shrinks	**yekesh** (m)/**tekesh** (f)	يكش/ تكش
shrunk	**kash** (m)/**kashit** (f)	كش/ كشت
shut	**ma'fool** (m)/ **ma'foola** (f)	مقفول/ مقفوله
shutter	**sheesh** (m)	شيش
sick (*ill*)	**ªayaen** (m)/ **ªayaena** (f)	عيان/ عيانه
I feel sick	**ªayiz** (m)/**ªayza** (f) *astafragh*	عايز/ عايزه استفرغ
side	**ganb** (m)	جنب
sieve	**mankhol** (m)	منخل
sight	**naZar** (m)	نظر

English	Transliteration	Arabic
sightseeing: he/she goes sightseeing	*yetfarag* (m)/*titfarag* (f) *ala il ma**aelim*	يتفرج/ تتفرج على المعالم
sign	*loHit* (f) *i**laenaet*	لوحة إعلانات
sign: he/she signs	*yemDi* (m)/*temDi* (f)	يمضى/ تمضى
signal	*ishaara* (f)	إشاره
signature	*imDa* (f)	إمضاء
silent	*saekit* (m)/*sakta* (f)	ساكت/ ساكته
silk	*Hareer* (m)	حرير
silver	*faDDa* (f)	فضه
similar	*shebh*	شبه
simple	*baseeT* (m)/ *baseeTa* (f)	بسيط/ بسيطه
since	*min*	من
sing: he/she sings	*yeghanni* (m)/ *teghanni* (f)	يغنى/ تغنى
single (*room*)	*mofrad* (m)	مفرد
(*ticket*)	*raiyiH*	رايح
(*unmarried*)	*aezib* (m)/*mish metgawiza* (f)	عازب/ مش متجوزه
sink	*Howd* (m)	حوض
sir	*sayed* (m)	سيد
sister	*okht* (f)	أخت
sister-in-law: my sister-in-law	*nisebti* (f)	نسيبتى
sit (down): he/she sits	*yo'**od* (m)/*to'**od* (f)	يقعد/ تقعد
sitting (down)	*a**id* (m)/*'a**da* (f)	قاعد/ قاعده
site (*tourist*)	*ma**alim* (pl)	معالم
size	*ma'aaes* (m)	مقاس
skate: he/she skates	*yitzaHlaq* (m)/ *titzaHlaq* (f)	يتزحلق/ تتزحلق
skates (*roller*)	*agal tazaHloq* (pl)	عجل تزحلق
skating	*tazaHloq* (m)	تزحلق
skimmed milk	*laban* (m) *makshooT*	لبن مقشوط
skin	*geld* (m)	جلد
skirt	*gonella* (f)	جونله
sky	*sama* (f)	سماء
sleep: he/she sleeps	*yinaem* (m)/*tinaem* (f)	ينام/ تنام
sleeper/sleeping-car	*arabayit* (f) *inowm*	عربية النوم

sleeping bag	*sleebing bag* (f)	بسليبنج باج
sleeve	*kom* (m)	كم
slice	*kharTa* (f)	خرطه
sliced	*makhrooT* (m)/ *makhrooTa* (f)	مخروط / مخروطه
slide (*film*)	*slaiyd* (m)	سلايد
slim	*rofaiya* (m)/ *rofaiya*a (f)	رفيع / رفيعه
slip (*petticoat*)	*'ameeS* (m) *Hareemi*	قميص حريمى
slippery	*mezaHla'* (m)/ *mezaHla'a* (f)	مزحلق / مزحلقه
slow	*baTee'* (m)/ *baTee'a* (f)	بطئ / بطيئه
slowly	*biboT'*	ببطئ
small	*Soghayar* (m)/ *Soghayara* (f)	صغير / صغيره
smell	*reeHa* (f)	ريحه
smell: it smells of . . .	*reeHit . . .*	ريحة . . .
smile	*ibtisaema* (f)	إبتسامه
smile: he/she smiles	*yebtesim* (m)/ *tebtesim* (f)	يبتسم / تبتسم
smoke	*dokhaen* (m)	دخان
smoke: he/she smokes	*yedakhan* (m)/ *tedakhan* (f)	يدخن / تدخن
smoked	*midakhan* (m)/ *midakhana* (f)	مدخن / مدخنه
smooth	*na*a*im* (m)/*na*a*ma* (f)	ناعم / ناعمه
sneeze: he/she sneezes	*ye*a*Tas* (m)/*te*a*Tas* (f)	يعطس / تعطس
snorkelling	*ghaTs* (m)	غطس
snow	*talg* (m)	ثلج
so (*thus*) (*therefore*)	*keda* *wi* a*ashan keda*	كده و علشان كده
soap	*Saboon* (m)	صابون
sober	*razeen* (m)/ *razeena* (f)	رزين / رزينه
socialism	*ishtirakaya* (f)	اشتراكيه

English	Transliteration	Arabic
socialist	*ishtiraki* (m)/ *ishtirakaya* (f)	اشتراكى/ اشتراكيه
social worker	*mowazaf* (m)/ *mowazafa* (f) *she'oon igtima*ª*iya*	موظف/ موظفه شؤون اجتماعيه
sociology	ª*ilm* (m) *igtimae*ª	علم اجتماع
socket	*bareeza* (f)	بريزه
socks	*shorabaat* (pl)	شرابات
soda (water)	*(maiyit) Sowda* (f)	(مياه) صودا
soft	*na*ª*im* (m)/*na*ª*ma* (f)	ناعم/ ناعمه
soft drink	*mashroob* (m) *khafeef*	مشروب خفيف
soldier	ª*askari* (m)	عسكرى
solicitor	*moHaemi* (m)/ *moHamaya* (f)	محامى/ محاميه
solid	*Salb* (m)/*Salba* (f)	صلب/ صلبه
some	*showaya*	شويه
somehow	*biTaree'a aw biokhra*	بطريقه او بأخرى
someone	*shakhSin mae*	شخص ما
something	*shay'*	شئ
sometimes	*sa*ª*aet*	ساعات
somewhere	*fi makaenin mae*	فى مكان ما
son	*ibn* (m)	إبن
song	*oghnaya* (f)	أغنيه
son-in-law	*gowz* (m) *binti*	جوز بنتى
soon	*qareeban*	قريباً
as soon as possible	*fowran*	فوراً
sore	*moltahib* (m)/ *moltahiba* (f)	ملتهب/ ملتهبه
sorry: I'm sorry	*aesif* (m)/*asfa* (f)	أسف/ أسفه
(regret)	*nadmaen* (m)/ *nadmaena* (f)	ندمان/ ندمانه
sort	*now*ª (m)	نوع
sound	*Sowt* (m)	صوت
soup	*shorba* (f)	شوربه
sour	*HaemiD* (m)/ *Haemda* (f)	حامض/ حامضه
south	*ganoob* (m)	جنوب

277

English	Transliteration	Arabic
souvenir	*tizkar* (m)	تزکار
space	*faraagh* (m)	فراغ
(*universe*)	*faDaa'* (m)	فضاء
spade	*garoof* (m)	جاروف
spanner	*moftaeH* (m) *Sawameel*	مفتاح صواميل
spare	*iDaafi* (m)/ *iDafaya* (f)	إضافي/ إضافية
spare time	*waqt* (m) *iDaafi*	وقت إضافي
spare tyre	*kawetch* (m) *istibn*	کاوتش استبن
sparkling (*wine, water*)	*fawaar* (m) *fawaara* (f)	فوار/ فواره
speak: he/she speaks	*yetkalim* (m)/ *tetkalim* (f)	يتكلم/ تتكلم
special	*khaaS* (m)/ *khaaSa* (f)	خاص/ خاصه
special offer	*ᵃarD* (m) *khaaS*	عرض خاص
specialist	*motakhaSiS* (m)/ *motakhaSiSa* (f)	متخصص/ متخصصه
speciality	*takhaSoS* (m)	تخصص
spectacles	*naDara* (f)	نظاره
speed	*sorᵃa* (f)	سرعه
speed limit	*Hodood* (pl) *isorᵃa*	حدود السرعه
spend: he/she spends		
(*money*)	*yeSrif* (m)/*teSrif* (f)	يصرف/ تصرف
(*time*)	*ye'aDi* (m)/ *te'aDi* (f)	يقضي/ تقضى
Sphinx	*abool howl* (m)	ابوالهول
spices	*ᵃoToor* (pl)	عطور
spicy	*miᵃaTar* (m)/ *miᵃaTarra* (f)	معطر/ معطره
spinach	*sabaenikh* (pl)	سبانح
spirits (*drinks*)	*mashroobaet rawHaya* (pl)	مشروبات روحيه
splinter	*shaZya* (f)	شاظيه
spoil: he/she spoils	*yetlif* (m)/*tetlif* (f)	يلف/ تلف
sponge (*bath*)	*safinga* (f)	سفنجه
spoon	*maᵃla'a* (f)	معلقه

sport	*riyaaDa* (f)	رياضه
spot	*bo'ªa* (f)	بقعه
(*place*)	*makaen* (m)	مكان
sprained	*malwi* (m)/*malwaya* (f)	ملوى/ ملويه
spray	*rash* (m)	رش
spring (*season*)	*rabeeª* (m)	ربيع
square (*in town*)	*midaen* (m)	ميدان
(*shape*)	*morabaª* (m)	مربع
stadium	*istaed* (m)	استاد
stain	*bo'ªa* (f)	بقعه
stainless steel	*solb* (m) *naqi*	صلب نقى
stairs	*sellim* (m)	سلم
stalls (*theatre*)	*daraga 'oola*	درجه أولى
stamp (*postage*)	*Taabiª* (m)/	طابع/ طوابع
	Tawaabiª (pl)	
stand (*stadium*)	*minaSa* (f)	منصه
stand (up): he/she	*wae'if* (m)/*wa'fa* (f)	واقف/ واقفه
stands		
stapler	*dabaesa* (f)	دباسه
star (*in sky; film*)	*negm* (m)/*negma* (f)	نجم/ نجمه
start	*bidaya* (f)	بدايه
start: he/she starts	*yebda'* (m)/*tebda'* (f)	يبدأ/ تبدأ
starter (*food*)	*faetiH* (m) *ishahaya*	فاتح الشهيه
state	*Haela* (f)	حاله
station	*maHaTa* (f)	محطه
station master	*naZir* (m) *il maHaTa*	ناظر المحطه
stationer's	*maktaba* (f)	مكتبه
statue	*timsael* (m)	تمثال
stay: he/she stays	*yestana* (m)/*testana* (f)	يستنى/ تستنى
(*in a hotel*)	*yeskon* (m)/*teskon* (f)	يسكن/ تسكن
steak	*boftayk* (m)	بوفتيك
steal: he/she steals	*yesra'* (m)/*tesra'* (f)	يسرق/ تسرق
steam	*bokhaar* (m)	بخار
steamer	*baekhira* (f)	باخره
steel	*Solb* (m)	صلب
steep	*monHadir* (m)/	منحدر/ منحدره
	monHadira (f)	
step	*sellema* (f)	سلمه

279

step-brother	'akh (m) mish she'ee'ee	أخ مش شقيقى
step-children		
(husband's children)	ªayael (pl) gowz	عيال جوز
(wife's children)	ªayael (pl) miraat	عيال مرات
step-daughter		
(husband's child)	bint (f) gowz	بنت جوز
(wife's child)	bint (f) miraat	بنت مرات
step-father	zowg il 'om (m)	زوج الأم
step-mother	zowgit il 'ab (f)	زوجة الأب
step-sister	okht (f) mish she'e'ti	أخت مش شقيقى
step-son		
(husband's child)	ibn (m) gowz	ابن جوز
(wife's child)	ibn (m) miraat	ابن مرات
stereo	steryo (m)	ستريو
sterling: pound sterling	isterleenee (m)	إسترلينى
steward (air)	moDeef (m)	مضيف
stewardess (air)	moDeefa (f)	مضيفه
stick	laz' (m)	لازق
sticking plaster	blaster (m)	بلاستر
sticky	milaza' (m & f)	ملزق
sticky tape	lazae' (m)	لزاق
stiff	gaemid (m)/gamda (f)	جامد/ جامده
still	saekin (m)/sakna (f)	ساكن/ ساكنه
(non-fizzy)	ªada	عاده
sting	lasªa (f)	لسعه
sting: it stings	lasaª (m)/lasaªit (f)	لسع/ لسعت
stock exchange	borSa (f)	برصه
stockings	shorab (m) Hareemee	شراب حريمى
stolen	masroo' (m)/ masroo'a (f)	مسروق/ مسروقه
stomach	meªda (f)	معده
stomach-ache	wagaª (m) fil meªda	وجع فى المعده
stone	Tooba (f)	طوبه
stop (bus etc.)	maHaTa (f)	محطه

English	Transliteration	Arabic
stop: he/she stops	*wa'af* (m)/*wa'afit* (f)	وقف/وقفت
stop!	*qof*	قف!
stopcock	*maHbas* (m)	محبس
storey	*dowr* (m)	دور
story	*Hikaya* (f)	حكايه
stove	*forn* (m)	فرن
straight	*mostaqeem* (m)/ *mostaqeema* (f)	مستقيم/مستقيمه
straight on	*ªala Tool*	على طول
strange, stranger	*ghareeb* (m)/ *ghareeba* (f)	غريب/غريبه
strap	*Tow'* (m)	طوق
straw (*drinking*)	*shalimo* (f)	شاليمو
strawberries	*firawla* (pl)	فراوله
stream	*gadwal* (m)	جدول
street	*shaeriª* (m)	شارع
street light	*noor* (m) *ishaeriª*	نورالشارع
stretcher	*na'aela* (f)	نقاله
strike	*iDrab* (m)	إضراب
string	*khayT* (m)	خيط
stripe	*shereeT* (m)	شريط
striped	*mi'alim* (m)/ *mi'alima* (f)	مقلم/مقلمه
strong	*qawee* (m)/ *qawaya* (f)	قوى/قويه
stuck	*malzoo'* (m)/ *malzoo'a* (f)	ملزوق/ملزوقه
student	*Taalib* (m)/ *Taaliba* (f)	طالب/طالبه
studio (*radio/TV*)	*stodyo* (m)	ستوديو
study: he/she studies	*yedris* (m)/*tedris* (f)	يدرس/تدرس
stupid	*ªabeeT* (m)/ *ªabeeTa* (f)	عبيط/عبيطه
style	*isloob* (m)	إسلوب
subtitled	*motargam* (m)	مترجم
suburb	*DaHaya* (f)	ضاحيه
succeed: he/she succeeds	*yengaH* (m)/ *tengaH* (f)	ينجح/تنجح

English	Transliteration	Arabic
success	*nagaeH* (m)	نجاح
suddenly	*fag'a*	فجأة
sugar	*sokkar* (m)	سكر
suit	*badla* (f)	بدله
suitable	*monaesib* (m)/ *monasba* (f)	مناسب/ مناسبه
suitcase	*shanTa* (f)	شنطه
summer	*Sayf* (m)	صيف
sun	*shams* (f)	شمس
sunburn	*Darba* (f) *shamsaya*	ضربه شمسيه
sunglasses	*naDara* (f) *shamsaya*	نظاره شمسيه
sunny	*shamsi* (m)	شمسى
sunshade	*shamsaya* (f)	شمسيه
sunstroke	*Darbit* (f) *shams*	ضربه شمس
suntan oil	*zayt* (m) *ilismirar*	زيت الأسمرار
supermarket	*soobar markit* (m)	سوبر ماركت
supper	*ᵃasha* (m)	عشاء
supplement	*ogra* (f) *iDafaya*	أجرة إضافيه
suppose: I suppose so	*ᵃala ma a ᵃtaqid*	على ما اعتقد
suppository	*liboos* (m)	لبوس
sure	*akeed*	اكيد
surface	*SaT-H* (m)	سطح
surname	*ism* (m) *il ᵃela*	اسم العائله
surprise	*mofag'a* (f)	مفاجأه
surprised	*indahash* (m)/ *indahashit* (f)	اندهش/ اندهشت
surrounded by	*moHaaT bi*	محاط ب
sweat: he/she sweats	*yeᵃra'* (m)/*teᵃra'* (f)	يعرق/ تعرق
sweater	*bolowvar* (m)	بولوفر
sweatshirt	*fanela* (f)	فانله
sweep: he/she sweeps	*yeknos* (m)/*teknos* (f)	يكنس/ تكنس
sweet	*Helw* (m)/*Helwa* (f)	حلو/ حلوه
sweetener	*miHali* (m)	محلي
sweets	*Halawayaet* (pl)	حلويات
swelling	*waram* (m)	ورم
swim: he/she swims	*yeᵃoom* (m)/ *teᵃoom* (f)	يعوم/ تعوم

swimming	*ªowm* (m)	عوم
swimming pool	*Hammaem SibaHa* (m)	حمام سباحه
swimming trunks	*mayo* (m)	مايوه
swimsuit	*mayo* (m)	مايوه
switch	*moftaeH* (m)	مفتاح
switch off: he/she switches off	*yeTfi* (m)/*teTfi* (f)	يطفى/ تطفى
switched off	*maTfi* (m)/ *maTfaya* (f)	مطفى/ مطفيه
switch on: he/she switches on	*yewalaª* (m)/ *tiwalaª* (f)	يولع/ تولع
switched on	*mowalaª* (m)/ *mowalaªa* (f)	مولع/ مولعه
swollen	*waerim* (m)/*warma* (f)	وارم/ وارمه
symptoms	*aªraad* (pl)	أعراض
synagogue	*maªbad* (m) *yahoodi*	معبد يهودى
synthetic	*morakab* (m & f)	مركب
system	*gihaez* (m)	جهاز

T

table	*tarabayza* (f)	ترابيزه
tablet	*Habaya* (f)	حبابه
table tennis	*bing bong* (m)	بنج بونج
tailor	*tarzi* (m)	ترزى
take: he/she takes		
(*bus etc.*)	*yerkab* (m)/*terkab* (f)	يركب/ تركب
(*carry*)	*yaekhod* (m)/ *taekhod* (f)	يأخذ/ تأخذ
(*exam, test*)	*yemteHin* (m)/ *temteHin* (f)	يمتحن/ تمتحن
(*photo*)	*yeSawar* (m)/ *tiSawar* (f)	يصور/ تصور
it takes an hour	*yestaghraq saªa*	يستغرق ساعه
taken (*seat*)	*maHgooz* (m)/ *maHgooza* (f)	محجوز/ محجوزه

English	Transliteration	Arabic
take off: he/she takes off (*clothes*)	*ye'la^a* (m)/*te'la^a* (f)	يقلع / تقلع
it is taking off (*plane*)	*iqlaa^a*	إقلاع
talcum powder	*bodrit* (f) *talg*	بودرة ثلج
talk: he/she talks	*yetkalim* (m)/ *tetkalim* (f)	يتكلم / تتكلم
tall	*Taweel* (m)/*Taweela* (f)	طويل / طويله
tame	*aleef* (m)/*aleefa* (f)	اليف / اليفه
tampon	*tambon Tibbi* (m)	تمبون طبى
tap	*Hanafaya* (f)	حنفيه
tape (*adhesive*)	*shereeT laza'* (m)	شريط لزاق
(*cassette*)	*shereeT tasgeel* (m)	شريط تسجيل
tape measure	*il metr* (m)	المتر
tape recorder	*gihaez tasgeel* (m)	جهاز تسجيل
taste	*Ta^am* (m)	طعم
taste: it tastes good	*Ta^amo* (m) *Helw*/ *Ta^amaha* (f) *Helw*	طعمه حلو/ طعمها حلو
tax	*Dareeba* (f)/ *Dara^ayib* (pl)	ضريبه / ضرائب
taxi	*taksi* (m)	تاكسى
taxi rank	*maw'af* (m) *taksi*	موقف تاكسى
tea	*shay* (m)	شاى
teach: he/she teaches	*yeddaris* (m)/ *teddaris* (f)	يدرس / تدرس
teacher	*moddarris* (m)/ *moddarissa* (f)	مدرس / مدرسه
team	*faree'* (m)	فريق
teapot	*baraad* (m)	براد
tear: he/she tears	*ye'aTa^a* (m)/*te'aTa^a* (f)	يقطع / تقطع
teaspoon	*ma^ala'it* (f) *shay*	معلقة شاى
teat (*for baby's bottle*)	*bazaeza* (f)	بزازه
tea-towel	*fooTa* (f)	فوطه
technical	*fanni* (m)/*fannaya* (f)	فنى / فنيه
technology	*teknolojya* (f)	تكنولوجيه
teenager	*morahiq* (m)/ *morahiqa* (f)	مراهق / مراهقه

telegram	*teleghraaf* (m)	تلغراف
telephone: he/she telephones	*yoTlob* (m)/ *toTlob* (f)	يطلب / تطلب
telephone	*tilifown* (m)	تليفون
telephone box	*koshk* (m) *tilifown*	كوشك تليفون
telephone card	*kart* (m) *tilifown*	كارت تليفون
telephone directory	*daleel* (m) *tilifownaet*	دليل تليفونات
television	*televisyown* (m)	تلفزيون
telex	*teleks* (m)	تلكس
tell: he/she tells	*ye'ool* (m)/*te'ool* (f)	يقول / تقول
temperature	*daragit il Harara* (f)	درجة الحراره
he/she has a temperature	*ªando* (m)/ *ªandaha* (f) *Harara*	عنده / عندها حراره
temple	*maªbad* (m)	معبد
temporary	*mo'aqat* (m & f)	مؤقت
tender (*meat*)	*Tari* (m)/*Taraya* (f)	طرى / طريه
tennis	*tenis*	تنس
tennis ball	*korit* (f) *tenis*	كرة تنس
tennis court	*malªab* (m) *tenis*	ملعب تنس
tennis shoes	*gazmit* (f) *tenis*	جزمة تنس
tent	*khayma* (f)	خيمه
tent peg	*watad* (m) *il khayma*	وتد الخيمه
tent pole	*ªamood* (m) *il khayma*	عمود الخيمه
terminal (*airport*)	*maHaTa* (f)	محطه
terminus	*maw'af* (m)	موقف
terrace	*tiraas* (m)	تراس
terrible	*raheeb* (m)/*raheeba* (f)	رهيب / رهيبه
terrorist	*fidae'ee* (m)/ *fida'aya* (f)	فدائي / فدائيه
thank you (very much)	*shokran (gazeelan)*	شكراً (جزيلاً)
that (one)	*da*	ده
the	*il*	ال
theatre	*masraH* (m)	مسرح
their (*see* Basic grammar, p. 158)		
them (*see* Basic grammar, p. 158)		
(*direct obj*)	*homma*	هم
(*indirect obj*)	*lohom*	لهم

then	ba^adayn		بعدين
there	hinaek		هناك
there is/are	fi		فى
therefore	^aashan keda		علشان كده
thermometer	termometr (m)		ترمومتر
these	dowl		دول
they	homma		هما
thick	sameek (m)/ sameeka (f)		سميك/ سميكه
thief	Harami (m)/ Haramaya (f)		حرامى/ حراميه
thin	rofaiya^a (m)/ rofaiya^aa (f)		رفيع/ رفيعه
thing	shay' (m)		شئ
think: he/she thinks	yefakar (m)/tifakar (f)		يفكر/ تفكر
(believe)	ya^ataqid (m)/ ta^ataqid (f)		يعتقد/ تعتقد
I don't think so	ma^ataqidsh		مأعتقدش
third	taelit		ثالث
thirsty: I'm thirsty	^aaTshaen (m)/ ^aaTshaana (f)		عطشان/ عطشانه
this	da (m)/di (f)		ده/ دي
those	dowl		دول
thread	khayT (m)		خيط
throat	zowr (m)		زور
throat lozenges/ pastilles	basteel (pl) lil zowr		باستيل للزور
through	khilael		خلال
throw: he/she throws	yermi (m)/termi (f)		يرمى/ ترمى
throw away: he/she throws away	yeDaiya^a (m)/ teDaiya^a (f)		يضيع/ تضيع
thumb	ibhaem (m)		إبهام
thunder	ra^ad (m)		رعد
ticket	tazkara (f)/ tazakir (pl)		تزكره/ تزاكر
ticket office	shibaek (m) il Hagz		شباك الحجز
tide	il mad wil gazr (m)		المدوالجزر

tidy	*monaZam* (m)/ *monaZama* (f)	منظم / منظمه
tie	*karafaTa* (f)	كرافته
tie: he/she ties	*yorboT* (m)/ *torboT* (f)	يربط / تربط
tight	*daya'* (m)/*daya'a* (f)	ديق / ديقه
tights	*shoraab* (m) *Hareemee*	شراب حريمى
till (*until*)	*lighayit*	لغاية
time (*once, twice etc.*)	*marra* (f)	مره
time (*see p. 172*)	*zaman* (m)	زمان
timetable	*gadwal* (m)	جدول
tin	*ᵃelba* (f) *SafeeH*	علبه صفيح
tin foil	*wara'* (m) *alamonyom*	ورق الومنيوم
tinned	*maHfooZ* (m)/ *maHfooZa* (f)	محفوظ / محفوظه
tin opener	*fataeHa* (f)	فتاحه
tip (*in restaurant etc.*)	*ba'sheesh* (m)	بقشيش
tired	*taᵃbaen* (m)/ *taᵃbaena* (f)	تعبان / تعبانه

tissues	*wara' naᵃim* (pl)	ورق ناعم
to	*ila*	إلى
toast	*towst* (m)	توست
tobacco	*Tonbaq* (m)	طنباق
tobacconist's	*bitaᵃ isagayir* (m)	بتاع السجاير
today	*inaharda* (f)	النهارده
together	*sawa*	سواء
toiletries	*adawaet izzeena* (pl)	أدوات الزينه
toilet(s)	*towalit* (m)	تواليت
toilet paper	*wara' towalit* (pl)	ورق تواليت
toilet water	*maiyit towalit* (f)	ماية تواليت
toll	*Dareebit moroor* (f)	ضريبة مرور
tomato	*TamaTim* (m)	طماطم
tomb	*ma'bara* (f)	مقبره
tomorrow	*bokra* (m)	بكره
tongue	*lisaen* (m)	لسان
tonic water	*maiyit tonik* (f)	مياه تونيك
tonight	*ilayla* (f)	الليله

too	kamaen	كمان
tool	adae (f)	اداه
tooth	sinna (f)	سنه
toothache	waga* (m) sinaen	وجع سنان
toothbrush	forshit (f) sinaen	فرشة سنان
toothpaste	ma*goon (m) sinaen	معجون سينان
top (*summit*)	qemma (f)	قمه
on top of	fow' il qemma	فوق القمه
torch	baTarayyit (f) noor	بطارية نور
torn	ma'Too*a (m)/	مقطوع/ مقطوعه
	ma'Too*a (f)	
total	magmoo*a (m)	مجموع
touch: he/she	yelmis (m)/telmis (f)	يلمس/ تلمس
touches		
tough (*meat*)	qasi (m)/qasya (f)	قاسى/ قاسيه
tour	gawla (f)	جوله
tour: he/she tours	yelif (m)/telif (f)	يلف/ تلف
tourism	siyaHa (f)	سياحه
tourist	sayiH (m)/sayHa (f)	سايح/ سايحه
tourist office	maktaeb (m) siyaHa	مكتب سياحه
tow: he/she tows	yegor (m)/tegor (f)	يجر/ تجر
towards	fitigae	فى اتجاه
towel	fooTa (f)	فوطه
tower	borg (m)	برج
town	madeena (f)	مدينه
town centre	wesT il balaed (f)	وسط البلد
town hall	il baladya (f)	البلديه
tow rope	Habl gar (m)	حبل جر
toy	le*ba (f)	لعبه
track (*path*)	Taree' (m)	طريق
(*rail*)	sekka (f) Hadeed	سكه حديد
tracksuit	traksoot (m)	تراك سوت
trade union	itiHaed *omael (m)	اتحاد عمال
traditional	taqleedi (m)/	تقليدى/ تقليديه
	taqleedaya (f)	
traffic	moroor (m)	مرور
traffic jam	takados (m) il moroor	تكدس المرور

traffic lights	*isharaat* (pl) *il moroor*	اشارات المرور
trailer	*maqtoora* (f)	مقطوره
train	*'atr* (m)	قطار
by train	*bil 'atr*	بالقطار
training shoes (*trainers*)	*gazma kawetch*	جزمه كاوتش
tram	*tromaiy* (f)	ترام
tranquilliser	*mohadi'* (m)	مهدئ
translate: he/she translates	*yetargim* (m)/ *tetargim* (f)	يترجم/ تترجم
translation	*targamma* (f)	ترجمه
travel	*saffar* (m)	سفر
travel: he/she travels	*yisaefir* (m)/ *tisaefir* (f)	يسافر/ تسافر
travel agency	*wikaelit saffar* (f)	وكاله سفر
travellers' cheques	*shikaet siyaHaya* (pl)	شيكات سياحيه
travel sickness	*dowar* (m) *saffar*	دوار سفر
tray	*Sanaya* (f)	صينيه
treatment	*ᵃilaeg* (m)	علاج
tree	*shaggara* (f)	شجره
trip	*reHla* (f)	رحله
trousers	*bantalown* (m)	بنطلون
trout	*samak il aTrooT* (m)	سمك الأطروت
truck	*looree* (m)	لورى
true	*saHeeH* (m)/ *saHeeHa* (f)	صحيح/ صحيحه
that's true	*saH*	صح
try (*attempt*): he/she tries	*yeHawil* (m)/ *tiHawil* (f)	يحاول/ تحاول
try on: he/she tries on	*ye'ees* (m)/*te'ees* (f)	يقيس/ تقيس
T-shirt	*tishert* (m)	تشيرت
tube (*underground*)	*anbooba* (f) *metro il anfa'* (m)	انبوبه مترو الانفاق
tuna	*toona* (f)	تونه
tunnel	*nafa'* (m)	نفق
turn: he/she turns	*yeHawid* (m)/ *teHawid* (f)	يحود/ تحود

English	Transliteration	Arabic
turn off: he/she turns off (*light*)	*yeTfi* (m)/*teTfi* (f)	يطفئ / تطفئ
twice	*maritayn*	مرتين
twin beds	*sereerayn* (pl)	سريرين
twins	*taw'am* (pl)	توأم
twisted	*mabroom* (m)/ *mabrooma* (f)	مبروم / مبرومه
type (*sort*)	*now*ᵃ (m)	نوع
type: he/she types	*yeTba*ᵃ (m)/ *teTba*ᵃ (f)	يطبع / تطبع
typewriter	*'aela katba* (f)	أله كاتبه
typical	*namoozagi* (m)/ *namoozagaya* (f)	نموزجي / نموزجيه

U

English	Transliteration	Arabic
ugly	*qabeeH* (m)/ *qabeeHa* (f)	قبيح / قبيحه
ulcer	*qorHa* (f)	قرحه
umbrella	*shamsaya* (f)	شمسيه
uncle	*ankil* (m)	انكل
uncomfortable	*mish moreeH* (m)/ *mish moreeHa* (f)	مش مريح / مش مريحه
underground (*tube*)	*metro il anfa'* (m)	مترو الأنفاق
under(neath)	*taHt*	تحت
underpants	*libaes* (m)	لباس
underpass	*mamar* (m)	ممر
understand: he/she understands	*faehim* (m)/*fahma* (f)	فاهم / فاهمه
I don't understand	*mish faehim* (m)/ *mish fahma* (f)	مش فاهم / مش فاهمه
understood	*mafhoom* (m)/ *mafhooma* (f)	مفهوم / مفهومه
underwater	*taHt il maiya* (f)	تحت المياه
underwear	*malaebis dakhilaya* (pl)	ملابس داخليه
undress: he/she undresses	*ye'la*ᵃ (m)/*te'la*ᵃ (f)	يقلع / تقلع

unemployed	*aaTil* (m)/ *aaTla* (f)	عاطل/ عاطله
unfortunately	*lil 'asaf*	للأسف
unhappy	*za^alaen* (m)/ *za^alaena* (f)	زعلان/ زعلانه
uniform	*yooniform* (m)	يونيفورم
university	*gam^aa* (f)	جامعه
unleaded petrol	*banzeen* (m) *min ghayr roSaaS*	بنزين من غير رصاص
unless	*ila iza*	إلا إذا
unpleasant	*ghayr mostaHab*	غير مستحب
unscrew: he/she unscrews	*yeftaH* (m)/ *teftaH* (f)	يفتح/ تفتح
until	*Hatta*	حتى
unusual	*mish ^aadi* (m)/ *mish ^aadaya* (f)	مش عادى/ مش عاديه
unwell	*moreeD* (m)/ *moreeDa* (f)	مريض/ مريضه
up	*fow'*	فوق
upper	*a^ala* (m & f)	أعلى
upstairs	*fow'*	فوق
urgent	*mista^agil* (m)/ *mista^agila* (f)	مستعجل/ مستعجله
urine	*bowl* (m)	بول
us	*iHna*	إحنا
use	*isti^amael*	استعمال
use: he/she uses	*yista^amil* (m)/ *tista^amil* (f)	يستعمل/ تستعمل
useful	*mofeed* (m)/ *mofeeda* (f)	مفيد/ مفيده
useless	*mish mofeed* (m)/ *mish mofeeda* (f)	مش مفيد/ مش مفيده
usually	*^aadatan*	عادة

V

| vacant | *faaDi* (m)/ *faDya* (f) | فاضى/ فاضيه |
| vacuum cleaner | *hoover* (m) | هوڤر |

vacuum flask	*tormos* (m)	ترمس
valid	*saaliH* (m)/*salHa* (f)	صالح/ صالحه
valley	*waedi* (m)	وادى
valuable	*qayim* (m)/ *qayima* (f)	قيم/ قيمه
valuables	*ashya' qayima* (pl)	أشياء قيمه
van	*ªarabaya* (f) *na'l*	عربة نقل
vase	*vaasa* (f)	فازة
veal	*bitello* (f)	بتللو
vegetables	*khoDar* (pl)	خضار
vegetarian	*nabaeti* (m)/ *nabaetaya* (f)	نباتى/ نباتيه
vehicle	*ªarabaya* (f)	عربيه
vermouth	*vermoot* (m)	ثرموت
very	*'awi*	قوى
vest	*fanella* (f)	فانله
vet	*biTari* (m)/ *biTaraya* (f)	بيطري/ بطريه
via	*ªan Taree'*	عن طريق
video cassette	*shereeT vidyo kassett* (m)	شريط فيديو كاسيت
video recorder	*tasgeel* (m) *vidyo*	تسجيل فيديو
view	*manZar* (m)	منظر
villa	*villa* (f)	فيلا
village	*qarya* (f)	قريه
vinegar	*khal* (m)	خل
vineyard	*mazaeriª koroom* (pl)	مزارع كروم
virgin	*ªazra'* (f)	عزراء
Virgin Mary	*maryam il ªazra'*	مريم العزراء
visa	*visa* (f)	ثيزا
visit	*ziyaara* (f)	زياره
visit: he/she visits	*yezoor* (m)/*tezoor* (f)	يزور/ تزور
visitor	*Dayf* (m)/*Dayfa* (f)	ضيف/ ضيفه
vitamin	*vitameen* (m)	ثيتامين
vodka	*vodka* (m)	ثودكا
voice	*Sowt* (m)	صوت
volleyball	*volleebowl* (f)	ثولى بول

voltage	*volt* (m) *il kahraba*	فولت الكهرباء
vote: he/she votes	*yintaekhib* (m)/ *tintaekhib* (f)	ينتخب/ تنتخب

W

wage	*ogra* (f)	أجره
waist	*wesT* (m)	وسط
waistcoat	*Sidayri* (m)	صديري
wait (for): he/she waits	*yestana* (m)/*testana* (f)	يستنى/ تستنى
waiter	*garsown* (m)	جرسون
waitress	*garsowna* (f)	جرسونه
waiting room	*Hogrit* (f) *ilintizaar*	حجرةالأنتظار
Wales	*waylz* (f)	وايلذ
walk: he/she walks	*yemshi* (m)/*temshi* (f)	يمشى/ تمشى
he/she goes for a walk	*yetmasha* (m)/ *tetmasha* (f)	يتمشى/ تتمشى
walking stick	*ªaSaiya* (f)	عصاه
wall	*HayTa* (f)	حائط
wallet	*maHfaza* (f)	محفظه
walnut	*ªayn* (f) *gamal*	عين جمل
want: I want, would like	*ªayiz* (m)/*ªayza* (f)	عايز/ عايزه
war	*Harb* (f)	حرب
First/Second World War	*il Harb* (f) *il ªalamaya il 'oola/tanya*	الحرب العالميه الأولى/ الثانيه
Six Day War	*Harb yonyo*	حرب يونيو
warm	*daefi* (m)/*daefya* (f)	دافئ/ دافئه
wash: he/she washes	*yeghsil* (m)/*teghsil* (f)	يغسل/ تغسل
he washes up	*yeghsil il mawaªeen*	يغسل المواعين
washable	*qabil* (m)/*qabila* (f) *lil ghaseel*	قابل/ للغسيل
wash-basin	*HowD* (m)	حوض
washing	*ghaseel* (m)	غسيل
washing machine	*ghassaela* (f)	غساله
washing powder	*Saboon* (m) *ghaseel*	صابون غسيل

293

English	Transliteration	Arabic
washing-up liquid	Saboon (m) mawa^aeen	صابون مواعين
wasp	Daboor (m)	ضبور
wastepaper basket	sabat (m) zibaela	سبت زباله
watch	sa^aa (f)	ساعه
watch: he/she watches	yetfarag (m)/ titfarag (f)	يتفرج / تتفرج
watchstrap	ostayk (m)	أستيك
water	maiya (f)	مياه
mineral water	maiya ma^adanaya	مياه معدنيه
distilled water	maiya m'aTara	مياه مقطره
water heater	sakhaen (m)	سخان
watermelon	baTeekha (f)	بطيخه
waterfall	shallael (m)	شلال
waterproof	watarproof (m & f)	ووتر بروف
water-skiing	watarskee (m)	تزحلق مائى
wave (sea)	mowga (f)	موجه
wave: he/she waves	yeshaewir (m)/ teshaewir (f)	يشاور / تشاور
wax	sham^a (m)	شمع
way (manner)	Taree'a (f)	طريقه
(route)	Taree' (m)	طريق
this way, that way (direction)	il Taree' da	الطريق ده
way in	dekhool (m)	دخول
way out	khoroog (m)	خروج
we	iHna	إحنا
weather	gaw (m)	جو
weather forecast	inashra (f) il gawaya	النشره الجويه
wedding	zifaef (m)	زفاف
week	izboo^a (m)	اسبوع
weekend	weekend (m)	ويك اند
weekly	izboo^aee (m)/ izboo^aaya (f)	اسبوعى / اسبوعيه
weigh: he/she weighs	yewzin (m)/tewzin (f)	يوزن / توزن
weight	wazn (m)	وزن
well	kwayyis (m)/ kwayissa (f)	كويس / كويسه
as well	kamaen	كمان

well done (*steak*)	*maZbooT*	مظبوط
(*congratulations*)	*mabrook*	مبروك
Welsh	*min waylz*	من وايلز
west	*gharb* (m)	غرب
western	*gharbee* (m)/	غربى/ غربيه
	gharbaya (f)	
wet	*mablool* (m)/	مبلول/ مبلوله
	mabloola (f)	
wetsuit	*badlit* (f) *ghaTs*	بدلة غطس
what (is)?	*ay*	ايه؟
wheel	*ᵃagala* (f)	عجله
wheelchair	*korsi* (m) *lil*	كرسى للمقعدين
	moqᵃadeen	
when?	*imta*	متى؟
where (is/are)?	*fayn*	فين؟
which?	*ay*	أى؟
while	*baynama*	بينما
whisky	*wiski* (m)	ويسكى
whisky and soda	*wiski bil sowda*	ويسكى بالصودا
white	*abyaD* (m)/*bayDa* (f)	أبيض/ بيضه
(*with milk*)	*bilaban*	باللبن
white coffee	*'ahwa bilaban*	قهوه باللبن
who?	*meen*	من؟
who is it?	*meen howa* (m)/	من هو؟
	meen haya (f)	من هى؟
whole	*kaemil* (m)/*kamla* (f)	كامل/ كامله
why?	*lay*	ليه؟
why not?	*lay la'*	ليه لأ؟
wide	*waeseᵃ* (m)/*wasᵃa* (f)	واسع/ واسعه
widow	*armala* (f)	أرمله
widower	*armal* (m)	أرمل
wife	*zowga* (f)	زوجه
my wife	*miraati* (f)	مراتى
wild	*motawaHish* (m)/	متوحش/ متوحشه
	motawaHisha (f)	

win: he/she wins	*yeksaeb* (m)/ *teksaeb* (f)	يكسب / تكسب
who won?	*meen kesib*	مين كسب؟
wind	*reeH* (m)	ريح
windmill	*TaHoonit* (f) *hawa*	طاحونة هواء
window	*shibaek* (m)	شباك
(shop)	*vatreena* (f)	فترينه
windsurfing	*TazaHloq* (m) *shira*ⁱ	تزحلق شراعى
windy: it's windy	*hawa* (m) *gaemid*	هواء جامد
wine	*nebeet* (m)	نبيت
wine merchant	*baya*ᵃ (m) *nebeet*	بياع نبيت
wing	*ginaH* (m)	جناح
winter	*isheta* (m)	شتاء
with	*ma*ᵃ*a*	مع
without	*min ghayr*	من غير
woman	*sit* (f)	ست
wonderful	*hayil* (m)/*hayla* (f)	هائل / هائله
wood	*khashab* (m)	خشب
(forest)	*ghaeba* (f)	غابه
wool	*Soof* (m)	صوف
word	*kilma* (f)	كلمه
work	*shoghl* (m)	شغل
(job)	*shoghlaena* (f)	شغلانه
(task)	*ma'mooraya* (f)	مأموريه
work: he/she/it works	*yishtaghal* (m)/ *tishtaghal* (f)	يشتغل / تشتغل
world (n)	*idonya* (f)	الدنيا
(adj)	*ᵃalami* (m)/ *ᵃalamaya* (f)	عالمى / عالميه
worried	*'al'aen* (m)/ *'al'aena* (f)	قلقان / قلقانه
worse	*awHash*	أوحش
worth: it's worth . . .	*'eemto* (m)/ *'eemet-ha* (f) . . .	قيمته / قيمتها . . .
it's not worth it	*mayestahilsh* (m)/ *matistahilsh* (f)	مايستهلش / ماتستهلش

296

wound (*hurt*)	*garH* (m)	جرح
wrap (up): he/she wraps	*yelef* (m)/*telef* (f)	يلف/ تلف
write: he/she writes	*yektib* (m)/*tektib* (f)	يكتب/ تكتب
writer	*kaetib* (m)/*katba* (f)	كاتب/ كاتبه
writing paper	*wara' kitaeba* (m)	ورق كتابه
wrong (*incorrect*)	*ghalaT* (m & f)	غلط

X

X-ray	*ishae^aa* (f)	إشاعه

Y

yacht	*yakht* (m)	يخت
yawn: he/she yawns	*yetaewib* (m)/ *tetaewib* (f)	يتشائب/ تتشائب
year	*sana* (f)/*sineen* (pl)	سنه/ سنين
leap year	*sana kabeesa* (f)	سنه كبيسه
yellow	*aSfar* (m)/*Safra* (f)	أسفر/ سفره
yes	*aywa*	أيوه
yesterday	*imbariH* (m)	إمبارح
yet	*Hata il'aen*	حتى الآن
yoghurt	*zabaedi* (m)	زبادى
you (*see* Basic grammar, *p. 158*)	*inta* (m)/*inti* (f)	أنتَ/ أنتِ
young	*soghayar* (m)/ *soghayara* (f)	صغير/ صغيره
your(s) (*see* Basic grammar, *p. 158*)		
youth	*shabaeb* (pl)	شباب
youth hostel	*bayt* (m) *ishabaeb*	بيت الشباب

Z

English	Transliteration	Arabic
zebra crossing	*ᵃoboor* (m) *ilmoshaeh*	عبور المشاه
zip	*sosta* (f)	سوسته
zoo	*Hadeeqit il Haiyawaenaet* (f)	حديقة الحيوانات
zoology	*ᵃilm il Haiyawaen* (m)	علم الحيوان

NOTES

EMERGENCIES

(*see also* Problems and complaints, *page 151*)

You may want to say

Phoning the emergency services

The police, please
il bolees min faDlak/faDlik

The fire brigade
il maTafi

An ambulance
*il is*aef*

There's been a robbery
HaSal Ser'a

There's been an accident
HaSal Hadsa

There's a fire
fi Haree'a

I've been attacked/mugged
*Had i*tada *alaya*

I've been raped
Had ightaSabni

There's someone ill
*fi waHid *ayaen* (m)/
*fi waHda *ayaena* (f)

There's someone injured
fi waHid itgaraH (m)/
fi waHda itgaraHit (f)

It's my husband
gowzi

It's my wife
miraati

It's my son
ibni

It's my daughter
binti

It's my friend
SaHbi (m)/*SaHbiti* (f)

Please come immediately
*ta*aloo fowran*

The address is . . .
*il *enwaen* . . .

My name is . . .
ismi . . .

My telephone number is . . .
nemreti . . .

Where is the hospital?
fayn imostashfa

Where is the police station?
fayn maHatit ibolees

At the police station/hospital

Is there anybody here who
  speaks English?
*fi Had hena biyetkalim
  ingleezi*

May I speak to the British
  Embassy?
*momkin akalim isifara
  ilingleezaya*

I want to speak to a woman
ªayza akalim waHda sit

I want a lawyer
ªayiz/ªayza moHaemi

You may hear

fi ay
What is the matter?

HaSal ay
What has happened?

*ismak wi ªenwaenak/
  ismik wi ªenwaenik*
Your name and your address

Hanibªat ªarabayit bolees
We will send a police car

Hanibªat ªarabayit maTafi
We will send the fire brigade

Habªat ªarabayit isªaef
I am sending an ambulance

The police

ismak/ismik ay
What is your name?

ªenwaenak/ªenwaenik ay
What is your address?

HaSal ay
What happened?

HaSal fayn
Where did it happen?

momkin towSif li . . .
Can you describe . . .?

*ta^aala/ta^aali ma^aana li ism
    ibolees*
Come with us to the police
    station

*inta ma'booD ^aalayk/inti
    ma'booD ^aalayki*
You're under arrest

The doctor

(*see* Health, page 140)

biyewga^a fayn
Where does it hurt?

ba^aalak/ba^aalik 'ad ay keda
How long have you been
    like this?

ba'alo 'ad ay keda
How long has he been like
    this?

ba'alha 'ad ay keda
How long has she been like
    this?

laezim tiroH imostashfa
You will have to go to
    hospital

Emergency shouts

Help (me)!
ilHa'ooni

Police!
bolees

Stop!
qof

Stop thief!
imsik Harami

Fire!
Haree'a

Look out!
khod baelak (to m)/
  khodi baelik (to f)

Danger! Gas!
khaTar gaez

Get out of the way!
ifsaH iseka (to m)/
  ifsaHi iseka (to f)

Call the police
oTlob/oTlobi ibolees

Call the fire brigade
oTlob/oTlobi imaTafi

Call an ambulance
oTlob/oTlobi il isªaef

Call a doctor
oTlob/oTlobi doktowr

Get help quickly
*oTlob/oTlobi mosaªda
  bisorªa*

It's an emergency
Halit Tawari'

ALL-PURPOSE PHRASES

Hello
ahlan wa sahlan

Goodbye
ma ᵃassalaema

Good morning
SabaH il kheer

Good evening
misa' il kheer

Good night
tisbaH ᵃala kheer (to m)/
   tisbaHi ᵃala kheer (to f)

Yes
aywa

No
la'a

Please
min faDlak (to m)/
   min faDlik (to f)

Thank you (very much)
shokran (gazeelan)

Don't mention it
il ᵃafw

I don't understand
mish faehim (m)/*fahma* (f)

I speak very little Arabic
batkalim ᵃarabi baseeT

I don't know
mish ᵃarif (m)/*ᵃarfa* (f)

Pardon?
la mo'akhza

Would you repeat that,
   please?
*kamaen marra min faDlak/
   faDlik*

More slowly
bishwaysh

Again, please
taeni min faDlak/faDlik

Can you show me in the
   book?
*momkin tiwareenee fil
   kitaeb*

Can you write it down
   (here)?
momkim tiktibha (hena)

Do you speak English?
inta bititkalim ingleezi (to m)
inti bititkalimi ingleezi (to f)